a history of children's play
NEW ZEALAND, 1840–1950

a history of

 The University of Pennsylvania Press · Philadelphia · 1981

Brian Sutton-Smith

children's play

New Zealand 1840-1950

First published in the United States by
the University of Pennsylvania Press

First published in New Zealand by New Zealand
Council of Educational Research

Designed by Adrianne Onderdonk Dudden

Photos on pp. 33, 48, 138, 194, and 297 are reproduced
courtesy of Alexander Turnbull Library, Wellington,
New Zealand.

Frontispiece and line drawings on pp. ii, 1, 149,
and 281 are reproduced courtesy of Richard Kennedy.

Library of Congress Cataloging in Publication Data

Sutton-Smith, Brian.
   A history of children's play.

Bibliography: p.
   Includes index.
   1. Play—New Zealand—History.   I. Title.
GV149.S87   790.1'922'09931   81–51140
ISBN 0–8122–7808–9   AACR2

contents

3 A PERSONAL EPILOGUE

I want to pay special tribute to the many folklorists of games and play who have preceded me, particularly to Dorothy Howard, whom I came to know personally. In my relative isolation in New Zealand, I found that their work supported my belief that this kind of study was worthwhile. In some ways my own work parallels theirs, but it has a different orientation.

We have all been interested in history. In early folk-game studies, it was thought that history could be arrested before it slipped away (Strutt 1903; Newell 1883), even that the origins of current civilization could be traced through historical folk-game materials (Tylor 1888; Gomme 1894; Bett 1929; Spence 1947). More recently, Peter Opie (1963) has presented the view that the collected games of children reveal the continuity of human nature. He says, "Man himself, as the study of folklore shows, alters little, certainly less than do his surroundings; and

I sometimes wonder if the total quantity of traditional lore does not remain fairly constant."

The present work deals, by contrast, with the assumption that the historical record is more remarkable for the changes that it exhibits than for its constancies. The apparent difference may lie in Opie's study of a traditional country, England, and in my study of a pioneering one, New Zealand, with little history of European settlement. There is, of course, a longer history of Maori settlement in New Zealand, but that story must be told elsewhere, and my part of it has already been documented (1951:317–30). If one looks to the game and play histories of the United States for some ruling on this contrast between play as a record of continuity and as a record of change, there is both the kind of record that documents tradition (Newell 1883; Brewster 1953) and the kind that emphasizes modernity and change (Knapp and Knapp 1976). It seems probable, however, that comparative ratios of continuity and discontinuity across historical time cannot be assessed without more systematic records of play and games than those presently available. In contrast to the work of the Opies, however, it is the aim of the present work to provide evidence that in the New Zealand setting the general character of child play and games and leisure habits has changed drastically since the 1840s. Furthermore, this documentation is meant to challenge that kind of adult thinking which assumes that the answers to present dilemmas can be found or ignored with homilies on the idylls of a playful yesterday.

My own interest in children's play was prompted in 1948 by the children of standard three at Brooklyn School in Wellington.* I had been reading to them from *The Book of Wiremu* by Stella Morice and discovered their interest in "realistic" details of the New Zealand scene. This led to my own children's stories, *Our Street* (Wellington: Reed, 1950), *Smitty Does a Bunk* (Wellington: Price-Milburn, 1961), and *The Cobbers* (Wellington: Price-Milburn, 1976). More important, having had my own imagination for childhood aroused by this process of

---

*Standards correspond approximately to grades. Grades 1–6 equals standards 1–6.

storytelling, I became intensely interested in the imaginative world of childhood other than my own. In the years from 1949 to 1951, facilitated by a New Zealand University doctoral fellowship, I traveled around New Zealand, interviewing many aged informants and observing in many schools. The names of those who contributed information during these peregrinations are contained in Appendix 1, along with further information on the sources of information used throughout this work. I interviewed over 250 persons, some of them quite elderly, and received reports from 650 Teachers College and University students; their comments are introduced into the text with the date and place to which they refer. In addition, I visited 32 schools and received reports from 19 others. While oral reports could take me back only until around 1870, I relied for earlier material on school jubilee magazines and other written sources, such as the school logbooks kept by the teachers in those days. As a result, there emerged a historical picture of the changes that had occurred in children's play between 1840 and 1950, and this book is the record of those changes.

Formal descriptions of the games have been published in *The Folkgames of Children* (1972) and will not be repeated here. At that time the concern was more with games as texts than with the contexts in which games were played. My earlier book, therefore, was about the games as texts. This one, however, is about the larger context of children's play in New Zealand history. Although the present work was written at the same time as those other records (1950–52), the increased theoretical interest in context makes its publication now possible.

If there is a bias in the sources used in this work it is clearly on behalf of the South Island and the southern part of the North Island, which are overrepresented in the data presented here. This means that Scottish and English influences are maximized and the impact of the Maoris upon the pakeha (non-Maoris) is minimized. In the early days the Maoris lived almost entirely in the northern part of the North Island. Furthermore, they were largely confined to rural areas and had little influence on most pakeha children. In 1951, about the time this work was completed, only 30 percent of Maoris lived in urban centers. By 1980 that figure was 80 percent, so the effect of the

Maoris on the play of pakeha children from 1950 to 1980 is quite another story, yet untold. Unexamined also is the impact of the influx of other Polynesians, Samoans, and Tongans, as well as the lesser impact of the many postwar Europeans, Yugoslavs, Greeks, and Dutch on the play of New Zealand children.

I am particularly indebted to my mother, Nita Katherine Sutton, who first typed this manuscript in 1952; to my father Ernest James Smith born 1890 and still chipper in this year 1980; and to my wife, Shirley Lucille Hicks, who retyped a more recent version. At the time of first writing I also received much encouragement from those outstanding New Zealand educationists Ray Chapman-Taylor, F. L. Combs, and H. C. D. Somerset. More recently, Alistair Campbell and Elaine Marland have been helping me at long distance with the references.

Looking back at this work twenty-five years after its first draft, I take wry pleasure in reading again about my attempts to extricate the school picnic from the church picnic and the church picnic from the community picnic. This all seems to be fully in accord with my children's novels and my subsequent monographic social scientific accumulation of insight into the game of noughts and crosses (tic-tac-toe) (1972) and more recently my breaking the code in Ring a Ring a Roses (1978). All these, and the others—the hoops and shanghais, the Fly the Garter and Spang Weazling—have in common that in them life is lived more vividly than in most other places. This work is a toast to that vivification and to those moments of childhood immortality that I have here shared in a vicarious way.

BRIAN SUTTON-SMITH
Philadelphia
May 1981.

NORTH ISLAND

NOTE ON NEW ZEALAND

New Zealand is a small country of about three million people, situated 1,200 miles to the southeast of Australia. It is composed of two large, thin islands (100–200 miles wide), covering some 1,000 miles between latitudes 34 and 47 degrees south. The climate is temperate, the backbones of both islands are mountainous, and agriculture is extensive. Some 1,000 years ago it was inhabited by a Polynesian group called the Maoris. It became a British colony in 1842 and self-governing in 1867. Over 90 percent of the settlers were originally of British origin, though in recent years there has been an infusion of other European and Polynesian peoples. The major cities in the North Island are Auckland and Wellington (the capital), and in the South Island,

Golden Bay
Takaka
Motueka
Karamea Havelock
Nelson Picton
Blenheim
Westport Murchison
Reefton MARLBOROUGH
Greymouth NELSON
Hokitika Kaikoura

WESTLAND CANTERBURY Woodend
Christchurch

Ashburton

Timaru

OTAGO
Wanaka
Queenstown Cromwell Oamaru
Alexandra
Palmerston

SOUTHLAND Dunedin
Balclutha

Invercargill
Bluff

SOUTH ISLAND

Christchurch and Dunedin. Auckland is the most populous, but none of the cities had more than several hundred thousand people in the period covered by this work, 1840–1950.

NOTE ON MAPS

The maps show all the large towns as well as the provinces of New Zealand. The location of the smaller districts or schools can be discovered by consulting Appendix 3, where they are listed along with their provincial locations or the towns in which they are to be found. City suburbs are not listed in the index but are accompanied by the town of which they are a part within the main text.

This book gives a child's-eye view of the progress of New Zealand from British colonization in 1840 until 1950. While the children themselves can know little of the political and economic backdrop to the stage on which they will produce their playful account for us, they are nevertheless mightily affected by it. At our beginning point, 1840, the nineteenth-century Western world is in the throes of its centuries-long transition from an agrarian to an industrial society. Masses of people have been cut loose from the tribal and parochial ties that had previously ordered their lives. The growing cities of the world are afloat with immigrants from farms or foreign places.

In *Oliver Twist* of the late 1830s, Charles Dickens comments bitterly on the British poor law of 1834, which he depicts as treating pauperism as a crime and driving even more persons to criminality and vice. At about the same time, 1837, a

New Zealand Company has been founded and is advocating "planned settlement" overseas, where for a sufficient price people can both purchase land and provide passage for the laborers who will work the farms. The company suggests that large numbers of migrants will be welcomed in the new countries, thus offering its own solution to the problems portrayed by Dickens.

But in New Zealand the new settlements are not economically productive, and the condition of the workers in this new and unkempt wilderness is not much better than it was in the country from which they had come. Before there is export prosperity through refrigeration fifty years later, there will be much hardship as well as isolated wars with the Polynesian inhabitants over the possession of land. Furthermore, the educated who settle the country will bring with them the dominant Western response to the sight of large groups of ungoverned and ungovernable children wandering the streets, namely, that they should be brought under social control by universal education. This education, it is said, will take the "larrikins" or "urchins" or "ragamuffins" off the streets. It will remove them from the "contagion of bad company." They will cease to be "pests of society" and victims of "low-bred idleness." Education will be "a process of mass instruction and rigid discipline designed to produce at the minimum cost a working population that is literate, orderly and not inconveniently critical of its lot" (Campbell 1941:75). At first there will be attempts to render this social control through private, class, church, and dame schools. In the course of the century, however, these will all prove inadequate to the task, and the attempt will be taken over by the central public authority just as it was so taken over in most Western countries. Despite bitter conflicts between sectarians of various kinds, nearly all will ultimately combine in the view that at least at the elementary level the children of the masses must be brought under public control. The fear of urchins seems to have been greater than the fear of God in most of Western society! After elementary school there is apprenticeship and work. The secondary-school systems at this time will be left largely to the privileged, or occasionally to provide an avenue for those of special talent. But they will remain under private or sectarian control until the twentieth century.

In New Zealand a newly agrarian people were caught by the educational philosophies being thus devised for the urban industrial masses, the lower classes and immigrants of the world. In Part One of this book, covering the years 1840–90, we see how the children commented in their own way on this process of settlement and education. The opinion could be ventured that the unusual mixture of agrarian existence in everyday life and an industrial social philosophy in the schools shaped the lower and yeoman classes of New Zealand immigrants in peculiar ways. They became on the one hand avowedly self-reliant and egalitarian as a result of their new and pioneering kind of existence. But perhaps as a result of their schooling and the continued dominance of a British upper-class tradition of mores and manners, they were also somewhat shamefaced in social character. What still impresses one about New Zealand children, even today, is their vigorous, outdoor, assertive healthiness, as contrasted with their relative uneasiness of social habit. It seems as if the official education system, at least in the first one hundred years, was aimed at keeping the children "in their place." Children were taught to "mind their place" and not to "show off" or "act better than they should be," even though the realistic representatives of those class attitudes (aristocrats and servants) were nowhere in sight. The prestige of the mother country and of upper-class British life was so omnipresent that it became difficult to develop social manners appropriate to the very real accomplishments of the people themselves. Instead there continued a self-deprecatory imitation of a lower middle-class British code of manners.

In Part Two, covering the years 1890–1950, we witness the second great shift in population control brought about in industrialized societies of the modern world. The schools had clearly proven insufficient for the task. Leisure time must also be provided for and organized. In this period there is a new emphasis on the control of children by means of playgrounds, organized sports, and physical education lessons. The family, however, is still its own arbiter of family leisure and private play life.

In the Personal Epilogue we take up briefly the third great shift in social control now going on. In a television and computer society, informational and symbolic modes of control become central to education and leisure. These modes contrast strongly with the types of clerical and manual preparation required of schools in the earlier period, when routine skills as well as physical endurance were sufficient. The new modes of control that are currently with us highlight the fact that the story told in these pages is now largely history. It is an era that is over. In these pages children shift from playing hoops on the way to school along muddy roads to playing rugby in interschool competition in well-kept parks. In our epilogue there is noted an even greater shift toward playing with toys and watching television many hours a day. The family is no longer a private asylum.

1 the control of children at school
1840-1890

1 *pioneer children*

The first children played their way to New Zealand by imitating the sailors, climbing on the rigging, wading in the deck water, snowballing one another, fishing off the side, running races, and on some occasions even playing round games. But our glimpse—like their experience—is a fleeting one.

There are several important points to note about the play and games of children in New Zealand in the early years. First, in a pioneering settlement children were an economic asset. They were often left with little spare time to play. Second, when they did have spare time the boys especially tended to use it exploring and experimenting with the wildlife and adventures offered by the natural environment, not playing traditional games. Third, as there was no tradition of play, no established hamlet "greens" or village sports, children had to learn their play habits where they could. Older children, who would have been their natural teachers, were largely occupied with work. And where they were not thus occupied, neither they nor adults could tell the younger children what tradition said they should and must do, for these younger children were the first white children to play in the new land. In these circumstances children had to make their own approach to play, although there were many traditional ways that they found were relevant to the new environment. And some of their play arose from their imitation of the adult life going on around them. Since adult activities were often of a crude nature, the children's play activities naturally mirrored that fact. Fourth, the Maori wars (1860–70) placed an additional restriction on the freedom of children and their play in the North Island provinces. Given all these conditions, there was no great opportunity for the development of traditional games in the colony's earliest years. Whether or not the settlers knew many games, they would have had little opportunity to put their knowledge into practice.

The necessity for children to work was not only a well-established principle in the religious philosophies of the time, it was also the inevitable and often crushing burden of the pioneer state. In the very earliest days nothing was provided. Everything had to be done by the settlers themselves: washing, making bread, making clothes, making soap, and making lights. Children could help with these tasks.

The Poneke boys of the very early days (1840–1850) had no easy times. Many of them were sent to work at a very tender age; some assisted their parents at house building, and brick making, and shell burning and tree felling; while those not actually set to do a day's work had to help at home to make both ends meet. The younger members of the family had to provide the necessary firewood for the household, and although in the earlier years the fuel was convenient yet the labour of wood chopping was considerable for the hardy youths of eight and nine, upon whom devolved the duty. (1900; Wellington)

In some cases children may have made a game out of these activities, but it is doubtful if any but the very first days were as exhilarating or more or less a picnic for the children, as some have suggested. Further, in the early days large numbers of settlers had more to deal with than the natural difficulties of pioneering. From the very beginning they had to contend with an economic arrangement that bred poverty, and their natural difficulties were augmented by the insecurity of unemployment. Of course the conditions children faced differed from home to home. It is perhaps a step nearer reality to deal with rural and town children separately, always remembering that in the earliest years the life of a town child differed very little from that of his rural counterpart.

Consider first the rural children. The position of some rural children appears to have been similar to that of children who lived in an earlier condition of English village life before the commons were enclosed. In Lark Rise, for example, we get a glimpse of "Old Sally," who spent her childhood in this condition at the beginning of the nineteenth century. "Everybody worked; the father and mother from daybreak till dark. Sally's job was to mind the cow and drive the geese to the best green patches" (F. Thompson 1945:69). Lady Barker's description of the New Zealand "Cockatoo" children in the early days is similar. These "Cockatoos" were laborers who had earned, or brought to New Zealand, sufficient money to buy a little land, generally not very good land, in the back country.

They have an abundance of excellent food. Each cottager has one or two cows, and the little ones take these out to pasture on the hills, so they are in the open air nearly all the day: but their ignorance is appalling! Many of them have never even been christened; there was no school or church within thirty miles or more. . . . The father and elder sons work hard all day; the mother has to do everything, even to making the candles, for the family; there is not time or possibility of teaching children. (Barker 1870:iii)

Although the conditions children lived with were not everywhere as rigorous as this, there can be no doubt that work came first, both in principle and practice, in most rural areas until the end of the century. The school holidays, for example, were adapted to the seasonal demands of the farmer's year. The Christmas and summer holidays lasted only ten days. Children went back for a fortnight, and then there was a long harvest holiday. This holiday, which was held at the end of January and continued into February, was in fact no holiday at all for the older children. Even after 1877, when school attendance became compulsory, the recurrent demands for the labor of rural children continued to assert themselves, as is well recorded in various Wairarapa country school logbooks:

A big falling off in attendance is due to the heavy work at home the children are obliged to do in the morning before coming to school. (Horoeka Logbook, November 30, 1900)

Shearing is now in full swing and the attendance of the boys has fallen in consequence, M—— and J—— will be absent for some time. (Ngaturi Logbook, October 23, 1898)

Two eldest C—— away looking after cows. (Ngaturi Logbook, August 3, 1898)

Even today in rural areas heavy demands are often made upon the time of children.

In towns, once the first few years of pioneering were over and notwithstanding the notorious "sweated" child labor of the 1880s, there appear to have been fewer demands made upon the time of children. Speaking of the late 1840s in Wellington, an elderly informant interviewed by the *Evening Post* in 1912 said, "Those were long and happy days for the children. Very few household tasks, and very little schooling" (Best 1912). In the towns there were a variety of interesting and novel occurrences to attract the children when they were free from work or school. For example, the arrival of boats was always a time of activity. In Dunedin of the 1840s there were "the chubby faced children romping on the newly landed goods, the robust boys ever doing something—here rowing a boat, there pulling a rope—doing more mischief than good." In Wellington, "red letter days in the schoolboy's calendar were those on which a cattle ship arrived from Sydney." Often the cattle overran the town and the ubiquitous schoolboy was there during school hours—for which, of course, he received a whacking the next day. "Then there were the wild, attractive scenes sometimes when whalers came ashore after a successful season to knock down their cheque." They had rowing and swimming contests, and there would be fights in Upper Sydney Street, Wellington, when "often, unseen by those below, there crouched among the ti tree sundry youths who might have been better employed elsewhere." There were also a variety of exciting visitors: the Toms, Guards, Worsers, Barretts, and Rauparaha.

Easily imagine the dread fascination the savage chief exercised upon the youth of Petone. . . . There was life and colour and movement when the redcoats landed. I shall never forget the 14th Regiment—"the Fighting Fourteenth". The cry would go down the beach: "Up with your shutters and put out your light, the 14th are coming down." And all the lights were out in a moment, for come they did, smashing windows and everything else which came in their way. One summer morning, between three and four o'clock, we heard the strains of martial music— tramp, tramp, tramp, they went marching by. We jumped out of bed to see them pass. The band struck up, I remember—"Oh Susannah, don't you cry for me, I'm going to Alabama, my true love for to see." The men took up the chorus and it swelled through the air, something fine to hear. Men of the fighting fourteenth—they were shot down like pigeons by Rauparaha and his men. (1840s; Wellington)*

---

*In 1843 Te Rauparaha and warriors forced survey parties to stop their activity in Nelson province and subsequently slaughtered an armed party sent to prevent this interference.

The practice of keeping a pig, an English village custom, was tried in most of the early settlements. Pigs were always escaping, much to everyone's consternation.

We had strange pets, too. My father bought a little white pig from a Maori woman for sixpence. Adolphus we called him. He was bathed each day, and slept in a little box at the foot of the cubby-house till he grew too big. He followed us everywhere. Adolphus, however, put on weight, and a sad though usual fate befell him. . . . All the children in Wellington gathered to see the milking of the first cow. To my mind it was a pretty sight, the boys in their nondescript garments, the girls in their prints and sunbonnets. . . . One of the first warehouses on the Quay was surmounted by a lion, and the children were told that when the lion heard the cannon roar (daily at 12) it would open its mouth. Many a time I've seen them waiting and watching. . . . The hill behind Lambton Quay was a favourite haunt of growing lads; there, ensconced amongst the ti tree, they overlooked the scattered township, speculated on the shipping, on the future as boys understand it. . . . [After the earthquake of 1848] when the morning dawned the sea had re-treated, leaving behind a harvest of fish and oysters, and all sorts of queer things. We children had a fine time, but the mothers were left lamenting.

Once settled, and with little guidance from adults, children soon established for themselves a pattern of play appropriate to the environment in which they found themselves. It was a pattern of play chiefly of the kind that would be labeled "hunting skills." Thus in Wellington, (1840s)

---

the freedom of the settlement was consoling, the fine white sandy beach, from Pipitea to Oriental Bay, was a precious possession; and as yet there were few bathing restrictions and fewer vigilant police-men bent on curtailing the enjoyment of young Wellington. Then besides sea-fishing there were numerous streams, with the Te Aro Swamp available where inungas and eels could with little skill and very homely fishing outfit, be easily captured. The stem of the

toe-toe was rod enough, while the flax fibre provided a line sufficiently tough to pull the eel from his slimy haunts. Why, on Te Aro
flat boys could get conveniently lost for a day, be unseen and almost
undiscoverable, amongst the flax bushes, and yet enjoy themselves
to their heart's content. There sometimes a pair of rascals would
betake themselves provided, one with tobacco and the other with
a pipe and suffer initiation to the fragrant (or nauseous) weed.

In Christchurch it can be assumed that Hagley Park, which is
said to have been a wilderness of four hundred acres of fern,
flax, tutu, toetoe, and low scrub, provided a similar refuge for
boyhood. In Dunedin,

Pioneering appealed to children. All reminiscences of childhood in
the early days breathe that excitement and joy that come from
carefree living in the open air. The hills enticed youngsters to
scramble and explore and the bush made a natural playground with
supplejacks to swing on and trees to climb and sometimes a valley
to call across while the woods on the otherside "tossed back out
voices."

Even the children at school had their share. Running past
Wellington's first school was the Kumutoto Stream,

long since covered in, running down what is now Woodward Street,
where the boys at dinner time caught eels and bullies, while on its
banks where now stands the Wellington Club was the Kumutoto Pa
with its dusky inmates peering through the palisades at the strange-
ness of pakeha ways. Further back was the hilly ground covered
with manuka scrub, and in the gullies heavier bush ripe for bird-
nesting.

As the years passed, large numbers of working-class children continued to be effectively banned from school attend-

ance because their parents could not afford the fees. Presumably in urban areas some of these children worked (practically all would do so in rural areas). Some are likely to have indulged in hunting pursuits, and others in some of the games to be set out in later chapters. By the 1860s in the towns their numbers were becoming too great to pass unnoticed. In Dunedin there were "idle, loitering groups of boys who spent their days in the public streets" (Butchers 1929:225) and in 1867 a commissioner's report called attention "to the number of uneducated children in the city and suburbs of Auckland. In the Pensioner settlement, and in the more recently established military immigrant settlements their condition is most deplorable (ibid.:228). And at Tua Marina, Marlborough, there is record of a letter written to the *Marlborough Express,* December 23, 1867, protesting along the same lines. "For the past two years we have been promised a school at Tua Marina. It is not commenced yet, and I wonder if it is ever to be. Crime is on the increase." The writer adds, "You may even see men, and boys too, breaking the Sabbath like so many pagans," but whether this is an illustration of the crime that is going on, or just an additional emphasis, is hard to say. The chances are that these "loitering" children imitated some of the rougher sides of the life going on about them. Speaking of 1870, Reeves says, "Education was not universal, and the want of recreation and human society was so great as to lead notoriously to drunkenness and coarse debauchery (1934:244). Indeed, drunkenness and assault were the most frequent offenses before the lower courts of the day. In these circumstances we cannot expect too much from the "loitering" children. Some of them appear to have formed gangs. In Wellington we read:

The Thorndon and Te Aro ends of the town were declared rivals to each other. . . . Clay Point, the corner of Willis Street and Lambton Quay, was the boundary line, and woe-betide any boy caught trespassing out of business hours. . . . Occasionally youthful bands of Te Aro "flats" and Thorndon "sharps" met by arrangement, armed with branches of Ti-tree, or other weapon, and for the time being settled the question of superiority. There was very little friendly intercourse between the boys of the two ends of the town. (MacMorran 1900:7)

The boys of Thorndon Flat would go out on the warpath, stripped to the waist, dubbed with whale oil (stolen) and red ochre, and armed with sticks. Their great ambition was to catch the Te Aro flat boys unawares, which was seldom. A great encounter would take place and there would be a regular fight. This was a favourite game and borrowed from the Maoris. The ring leaders would be threatened parentally with the stocks. Yes, we actually had stocks. They stood on Thorndon Flat, at once a menace to evil doers and an object of derision. I never saw them used.

These gangs of nineteenth-century children were expressing the hostility that existed between neighboring districts throughout and for many years after the Provincial Era. Later, when rugby football became a national criterion of "maleness," these same district rivalries usually came to a head on the day of the annual football match. Football came to serve the purposes of interdistrict hostility in New Zealand, just as it had served those purposes in England for hundreds of years. One informant, for example, claims there was seldom a rugby match in the 1890s between Waikouaiti and Palmerston South that did not involve fights among the players and/or the spectators, and in some cases among both together. This example could be multiplied many times. Even today (1940s) intense and often unpleasant feelings crop up in football matches between rival districts.

There are many other examples of the way in which pioneer children relatively untutored in the ways of the past developed in their own spare time. A. E. Campbell (1941:8) cites an inspector's report in the 1880s on the nature of many of the children. The inspector complains of "the marked want of common politeness. . . . They are sure to disregard your civil salutation, and probably laugh rudely in your face and stare you out of countenance. There are even villages in which I account it an honour not to have my name called out as I pass along the street." And Lady Barker (1870:58) states:

I cannot say that I think colonial children prepossessing in either manners or appearance in spite of their ruddy cheeks and sturdy limbs. Even quite little things are pert and independent, and give the idea of being very much spoiled. When you reflect on the utter absence of anyone who can really be called a nurse, this is not to be wondered at. The mothers are thoroughly domestic and devoted to their home duties, far more so than the generality of the same class at home. . . . [the] colonial sister is very hard worked. . . . The poor mother has [the children] with her all day long; if she goes out to pay visits (the only recognized social duty here) she has to take the elder children with her, but this early introduction into society does not appear to polish the young visitors manners in the least.

One of the "young visitors" recalled:

We were carefree children run rather wild, with little clothes and no boots except on Sunday and inclined to laugh at anything and everyone. While very young we went shooting, rode horses and were pitched off on our heads, and played in small canoes. Good taste was not studied in our ideas of humour. When we were kindly entertained we sometimes returned home pretending the food had disagreed with us. On one occasion the sickness was so well acted that one of the family lost his tea. (Brereton 1947:6)

Two informants recollected:

We never played formal games much. We were forced to play them at an occasional tea party, but we were surly and antagonistic to that sort of thing. We preferred to be where we were most of the time—in the bush with shanghais or chasing. (1890; Takaka)*

We were at the best gauche in the company of adults or the opposite sex. (1895; Gisborne)

Before the advent of universal education, there was some concern about the children loitering in the streets. The answer to why they were so assertively independent may elude us, but their excessive independence must have been due in part to the fact that they were untutored in the ways of the past and had no traditional avenues through which to direct their energies. This condition must have depended to a great extent upon the fact—implicit in Lady Barker's statement—that neither their mothers nor other adults had the time to inculcate in them the traditional customs and manners of English society or to develop new ones appropriate to the place and time. Indeed, preoccupied with an immense number of household tasks, mothers must have encouraged independence in their infants from the earliest years—an independence which was unmollified by training in the social graces.**

From the early missionary days, New Zealand children had known the excitement and dangers of Maoris threatening in the vicinity. The restricting effect of this "threat" upon their play is seen in the following reports, which concern Wellington in 1843, just after the Wairau massacre, when twenty-two whites attempting a land survey in Nelson were killed:

---

*Appendix 1 contains the informants and dates listed under each of the towns used in these citations throughout this work. The sources of information are thus traceable to a personal interview, a written report, a school visit, a logbook, or a school jubilee record. When the place name is undated, this is because the informant failed to provide the date, as is typical in school jubilee magazines.

**Although these remarks may apply to most working-class pioneer children, they need not apply to children reared in homes of a more elevated class status, in which servants were employed.

These were days of great peril, days when mothers charged their children not to stray into the scrub or brush, when boys in the twilight scarcely dare to run out for the necessary firewood lest the dusky foe should dart out, when the report of a gun, used in pigeon shooting, was construed into the threatened attack of the Maori. (MacMorran 1900:6)

For nearly thirty years the wonderful Maori warriors kept the North Island colonists in a perpetual state of anxiety. (Butchers 1929:93)

Further evidence to this effect is provided in the following account, which I took from an eighty-six-year-old woman who spent her childhood at Tuakau in the Waikato during the late 1860s and early 1870s:

I was born in Birmingham in 1864 and came out to New Zealand with my parents in 1865. On the voyage out, thirty of some hundred children died of whooping cough. Three days before we arrived in Auckland a young brother was born. From Auckland we went to Tuakau, where my grandfather had set up a bakery business. He sold most of his bread up the Waikato River at Mercer. And it was not a long stop from here to Rangariri, where one of the most important battles with the Maoris had been fought by General Cameron in 1864. Tuakau was a small settlement with only a scattering of families, most of whom were Roman Catholics. In 1868 the birth of another brother made my mother seriously ill. I remember them shifting her away from the district because they feared attacks from the Maoris. [Pronounced "Moorees" by this elderly woman.] But she received little attention and died shortly afterwards. As there was no cow in the district at that time, the baby boy was brought up by my grandmother on the suck of a muslin bag containing bread and sugar. He lived to eighty years.
   At Tuakau in the danger periods of the early seventies it was our job as children to go up on an island in the middle of the

Waikato River and watch for Maoris coming downstream. While we were there we spent most of our time talking or chopping down cabbage trees. That was our favorite occupation—to see how many cabbage trees we could chop down. We ate some berries too. We called them "cat's tails" and fetched them down with a forked manuka stick. These berries were bead-shaped and, when the corner was stripped off, tasted like jelly. At home we stole cream to have with them. The pheasants were very fond of these berries.

At other times we were expected to watch for the Maoris all day from the top of a hill down by the beach, because my grandfather had his bakehouse down by the landing. If we saw a lot of Maoris coming down the river, we would run and give the warning, and everybody would fly off to the blockhouse. At one stage my father was called with the militia to Mercer, and in an engagement there had the top of one of his fingers bitten off in a fight with a Maori. We washed his finger with bluestone as it went septic. Most of the "Moorees" who accumulated by landing were "tame Moorees" not "savage Moorees." They would cook "punga" there in a stone oven in a hollow by the landing place. Sometimes two tribes would meet there and do war dances until the earth trembled. We were so frightened we would run off and hide under our beds.

When I was eight years old I went to the first school. It was just a shed with beams across the top. I remember one Maori boy coming dressed only in a shirt which hung down to his ankles. There was another boy, an Irish boy, who always wore his father's red uniform. The master beat him so frequently that the boy finally "took to" the master, jumped out of the window, and never came back. At that school we had only one song. It was called "Ring the Bell, Watchman." Most of our lunch hour we spent in the bush around about the school. But we did have one game. It was called Sides. There were two sides, and they had turns at rushing across the space by the school. The side that got the most over without being stopped by the other side would win the game. In the bush there were peach and cherry trees, and we hunted for the fruit when it was in season.

Out of school we also spent most of our time in the bush. Some of the children stole corn from a Maori's plantation, and the owner came to school and demanded retribution. When in season we would fish for whitebait at the beach. Usually we would take my grandfather's fishing net instead of using our own scrim. We would get a hiding for doing this. If possible we would get it dry again afterwards so that he wouldn't know we'd had it. We also fished for mullet and *kawai* and of course swam in the river in the summer. Some of the older boys shot pheasants. In the summer, too, we sledged down the grassy slopes on sacks, pulling each other in turns. At home, we had no toys. I never saw marbles, tops, or dolls, and regarded it as a special treat to be allowed to look into my grandmother's boxes of clothes and to play with my mother's crinoline.

Then there was always work to do. When my father took the bread to Mercer in the canoe, it was my job to go with him in the boat and bail the water out. The river was our best means of transport. In winter the roads were up to the horses' knees in mud. Cattle and stores had to be swum across the river at times. Another job we sometimes got was to fetch a woman's cows for her. She would give us a penny for doing this. The cows had bells around the necks and would wander off for miles in the bush. When they were brought back, they were milked into a round tin. Another job was to fetch water from the river for an old lady. The children next door made harness and cart and put their dog into it. They used the cart to bring tins of water up from the river and to have rides in. For a while also there was money to be made from a Scotsman who made flax into rope. He gave us sixpence an afternoon for turning the rope wheel while he walked backwards with the tow 'round his middle. When one strand was done, another would be done the same way—us turning the wheel and him walking backwards. At this time the rope-maker worked on the beach and he would pay anybody, man, woman or child, to turn his wheel. Later he built a water mill to do the job.

At twelve I went to Newmarket, Auckland, and saw my first train and my first banana [1876]. Our only recreation there was at the Sunday school, where we had sing-songs, and at Sunday school picnics. There was nothing else. I was too young to go to the "plays," although I did once see a circus.

The value of the above account is that it shows clearly the way the Maori wars affected the play of children. It shows also that their play was without many formal games because it took place in a relatively unpeopled environment, an environment without tradition and in which the adults were too hard at work to spend time on children's recreation. Further, it was an environment in which the children themselves were often too hard at work to have time to play. In this account there is mention of only one traditional game.

2 on the way to school

After the first decades of colonization, children were increasingly brought into schools, and by 1877, elementary schooling was made universal and compulsory for all children. For the first time the children in every district had a definite place for games. Before that there was seldom a community center where all could—and did—play regularly. Now, because of compulsory school attendance, children were forced to attend five times a week on a common ground, and games proliferated. As a result, the period between 1870 and 1905 was the heyday of unorganized games in New Zealand. During that time, all children were brought by the accident of universal education to a free, secular, and compulsory village green. Herded together, and with little direct adult guidance, they carried on the games and the sports acquired at picnic, parlor, and sports meetings from older children and from the homeland memories of their parents and grandparents.

The initiation of universal schooling created also a number of byways of play. The "pathways to school," often walks or rides of many miles and of hours in length, became tributary playgrounds pouring in upon the central point. Children living far off or who worked nearby did not arrive at school until nine o'clock (and often later) and they left the school precisely at closing time in order to cover the long distance back home or to help with household chores. They played along the way to and from school, especially on the way home, when they could all set out together. Perhaps it would be more accurate to say that on the way to and from school they played when they could, for the conditions of the roads along which they traveled were not always suitable to any kind of play:

The children had to travel long distances to school by various means, on sledges, on ponies, on horses, and in horse-drawn conveyances of all kinds; but by far the commonest method was on foot over rough and muddy roads and tracks or across country through grass and tussocks. When they reached the school there were no asphalt playgrounds, and in wintertime the mud of the roads challenged the mire of the playground. (1890; Tokomairiro)

There is in one school logbook a report of a letter sent to a certain gentleman, "asking that eighteen chains of road from the bridge over the Waianiwa creek be gravelled, for the pupils are wading to the knees in mud and water." One elderly informant describes his plight as a child:

As a boy of about six years, with heavy boots, I trudged to school a distance of about two and three quarter miles on roads, partly unformed through mud and tussocks, and in the winter months it was almost impossible to arrive at school dry; there would always be a ring of children around the school fire having their clothes dried and others sitting in their desks with brown paper round their legs.

It is little wonder, then, that one informant said, "We had plenty of exercise walking to school, let alone playing" (1880; Hampden). These conditions meant that footwear had to be solid—not the kind that lent itself to rapid or supple movements. The New Zealand Physical Training Syllabus of 1920, digressing on footwear, remarks, "Even if boots and shoes are of good quality, they are often stiff and unyielding." No wonder, considering the state of the roads throughout the preceding fifty years. In the North bare feet were often possible, but in settlements with no eye for such things, not on Sundays. Clothing was seldom more suited to free play than the boots, although it could be argued that it was quite suited to some of the turbulent types of play that characterized the times. Informants describe the clothing of the period:

For boys there were galatea jackets, moleskin, velveteen, or corduroy trousers, long thick woollen stockings, caps of all shapes and sizes, hobnailed boots dubbined or oiled. For girls, woollen dresses in winter, print in summer, long woollen stockings, pinafores, sunbonnets, and leather boots. (1870; Invercargill)

Many of the lads wore long trousers kept up by a wonderful belt fastened in some cases by venomous-looking brass snakes. (1870; Waianiwa)

When the boys' moleskin trousers were wet, presumably owing to external causes, they would give off a rather unpleasant, damp smell. It is reported that in some places boys insisted on having these trousers patched with square patches. If they were patched with circular patches, the boy who owned them would be jeered at and fondly called "Cat's Eye" by his associates, an appellation that could be silenced only with fists (1870; Dunedin). In some areas the children's clothing was almost as rough as the playgrounds themselves. "When it was wet we would wear just a sack to keep the rain off us. That's all we had" (1880; Hampden). Nevertheless, neither rain nor mud would stop children from playing permanently.

Given these conditions, what did children play on their way to and from school? Flora Thompson (1945:157) sets the stage: "It has been said that every child is born a little savage and has to be civilized. The process of civilization had not gone very far with some . . . children; although one civilization had them in hand at home and another at school, they were able to throw off both on the road between the two places and revert to a state of nature." Here is a typical boyhood account of play on the way home from school:

The journey home from school often had its little incidents. We would get as far as Kennard's gravel pit. That would be our first stop. Kennards used that wide water hole for their duck pond. Of course, there would come a day when someone would be sure to kill one of their ducks. . . . Our next stop . . . would be the spring by McPherson's. We would play 'round there getting a drink. Someone would get his head ducked in the water, and that generally would start a fight. Before we left we would dirty up the water so that girls did not get a drink. . . . I remember one time there was a swarm of bees settled in a hollow post by the side of the road. Every night we would throw stones at the post. Soon there were no bees left. . . . As we travelled we began to get hungry. Just over the fence was McDermid's turnip patch. "Let's have a turnip." About a dozen of us would go and get a turnip. We would have to pull two or three before we found one that suited us. We would keep this up every night. (1870–80; Waianiwa)

And here is an account of a girl going to the same school:

By 8:30 many children had collected at the store. We divided into groups, each choosing to walk with his or her particular chum. The Hall section was alive with insect life, crickets, and locusts chirruping gleefully. Fred Kennedy was an expert at finding a green one; he was sure to have one in his pocket. When looking for crickets and playing among the big tussocks, we often found clusters of potato berries that were good to eat. Nearing Willow Bank Farm we would see Mr. McDermid; if it was wintertime he would perhaps be helping Peter to get ready for a ploughing match. . . . Mr. McDermid had not much faith in our Southland weather; he would say to us, with a withering look to the South, "Girls, go home for your ulsters; this sunshine can't last, it will not be long dry." Not wanting any advice, we went on our way. . . . Next we would come to Annfield Farm, a home at which we feared to call. They had a dog called Jack which frightened Nicholas McNaughton and me one morning. In my bag I was then carrying a crochet needle which pierced my leg. We thought it very serious and called on the kindly assistance of Mr. McPherson, who removed the needle with all the tenderness of an expert surgeon. Passing on we came to an old homestead nestling beside delightful native bush. I remember this place by the beautiful raspberries growing in the garden. . . . Sometimes a child would have a message to give Johnnie Crawford, whose little home and garden were in from the main road. We have vivid recollections of luscious gooseberries grown in his garden and of his mother, a typical highland woman, who wore a beautiful white mutch [linen cap] with lace and frills, a wonder to us all. She was wont to remind us that we could never be as clever as the scotch lassies. But we retained our unspoken doubts on that point. . . . We would always see Mr. Kennard dressed for work in beautiful white moleskins, tied below the knee with "bow-yangs." He thought it wise to be on the road when the school children were near, for he had a fine flock of ducks swimming in the gravel pit beside his home. . . . Very often Mr. Robertson would be sitting on the edge of the bush just opposite the school. We children all enjoyed listening to the stories he had to tell of the very early pioneering days. . . . Very often we would get a ride to school. . . . The two seniors . . . would take us on horseback. It was a glorious sensation to canter along the road. Katie Wallace very often had her milk cart filled with children. (1870–80; Waianiwa)

Some games were particularly appropriate to the pathways to school and thus thrived. Games of movement had ample scope. What better place to gallop horses, drive hoops, whip tops, drive "cats" in Tipcat, walk on stilts, run races, leap the frog, follow the leader, play Follows in marbles, and skip.

Hoops were a world in themselves—a story of eager hours spent at the blacksmith's forge and of tightly held distinctions about the types of hoops used.

How we loved to watch the blacksmith and his assistant at work on the anvil, or making and fitting shoes to the never-ending line of horses. Best of all, when we had saved up sufficient to have a hoop made and watch him fashion and join it. (1890; Mangatainoka)

Sometimes the blacksmith would let us make our own. He would give us the piece of iron, and we would weld the seam. When the iron had been bent and the ends heated, we held the iron with a cloth and beat the ends together on the anvil. (1910; Takaka)

The blacksmith made them at ninepence each, and also a "cleak" to bowl them with, although it was far smarter just to have a stick. (1890; Waikouaiti)

They ranged in size from two feet six inches to six feet six inches, their size and thickness depending upon the size of the boy. (1880; Waimate)

Among the types of hoop was a thin iron one with a handle attached by a hook. These were made by blacksmiths expressly for the purpose, as distinct from other types, which were adaptations of things meant for other purposes. Such hoops were not accepted by boys as being "quite the thing" unless they were as high or higher than the owner, and even then the loop was detached before use. It was permissible but not favoured to use the open loop as a crook, but it was thought more masculine to strike the hoop repeatedly with a strong stick. (1903; Petone)

Wooden hoops that were commercially made were often used by girls and young children: "In the winter quarter we all had hoops, the girls with wooden ones and the boys with iron ones. I remember earlier than my school days seeing the street full of college girls all beating their hoops along" (1885; Nelson). Unfortunately these wooden hoops were inclined to warp and twist, but there were other types that could be had "free." Some were made of twisted fence wire, some from hoops off barrels, but these were of inferior quality.

Great favourites which for a time ousted all others were heavy iron rings which came off the big pipes used to bring water from dams to cities and which were used to protect the end of the pipes until these were fitted into place in the ground. There was no trouble in disposing of this scrap, for enough boys to absorb them all were always standing by waiting. Such hoops were dangerous to the public when bowled down sloping footpaths, as they often were. (1903; Petone)

Of less danger but used only by the very small children were the miniature hoops made out of tin lids. These were either attached to the end of a stick or swung along the road held by a piece of string fastened through their centers.

For hoop games there were racing, follow-the-leader, "just bowling around," and hoop-flicking, in which the hoop was spun forward and backward in the same way a napkin ring is often spun on the breakfast table. Winter was the main "season" for hoop games. "They were good things in winter to keep warm" (1875; Nelson). The team games that were played with hoops are evidence of the manner in which the older children of the day developed these unsophisticated plays to levels of complexity that made them not only tolerable but even a challenge to older children.

There were evenings when the hoops were out and races or long rambles took place, a dozen or more boys participating. Even stunts were not barred, for hurdles, tournament clashes, and bowling in and out among bottles often varied the programme. Every second

Saturday a hoop race was held a distance of about three miles. Of course, the juniors got a good start with their small hoops, but it was heartbreaking just when you thought you were doing well to see one of these six-foot hoops coming up in the rear; more heartbreaking still it was when one thought he would receive a prize and his hoop broke at the welded joint. (1880; Waimate)

In the team hoop dance there were about a half a dozen on each side. They lined up opposite each other in two rows. A hoop was bowled down the two rows by a side A person; then a side B person tried to run his hoop through the other at right angles. Turns were taken alternately, and the side won that ran the most hoops through without knocking the other hoops over. (1890; Takaka)

There they were—every day large numbers of children running their hoops to school. "I never remember going to school without a hoop," says one informant. "No message was a trouble if a boy could take his hoop; it removed the danger of tiredness," says another. But the roads could not remain like that forever. Hoops had to go. There are several reports of accidents around about the turn of the century. "Anyway, they were dirty contraptions," says one person (1890; Waikouaiti). Not that they completely disappeared. By the 1940s there was still an occasional report of iron hoops being used and even made. "The engineer makes them in the fitting shop" (1949; Denniston). And bicycle rims and automobile tires still play a small part in children's play. Tires can be used for all sorts of acrobatics in a way that the old, inflexible hoop could not be. They can be stood on, turned over in a handstand, or used as a conveyance. "Curled up inside we were rolled over by someone else. It was important to keep your hands inside the rim, otherwise they would be crushed" (1934; Carterton). However, these latter-day hoops have not taken the others' place and are a sporadic rather than seasonal childhood play. Perhaps one of their greatest weaknesses is that they do not allow you to tell another boy to go and "bowl his hoop" when you want him to make himself scarce.

Another game that disappeared as traffic thickened on the roads and the flax disappeared into the hinterland was Whip Top, the most highly esteemed of the early top games.

The whip top was a piece of wood about an inch and a half to two inches long worked to a point into which an iron peg was inserted and driven flush with the wood, not projecting as with the peg top. It was usually varnished, and the top surface was painted in target circles, though often we used to decorate them in designs to satisfy ourselves. They were started by being spun with the hands and then whipped along with a whip. There was a special point at which the top had to be hit to get the maximum result in speed and distance. Undercutting often resulted in a sudden spurt, but the second or third hit tangled the tops, resulting in a stop to sort them out. Races, of course, were the main issue with tops, and in season they were great rivals with the hoops. It was nothing uncommon to see dozens of youngsters whipping their tops to school, perhaps a mile or more away. Hurdles or targets, usually of kerosene tins, were often called on to vary the game. One unfortunate danger with tops was that they sometimes went through windows, particularly when they were undercut, and as the top usually carried the name of the owner somewhere on it, it was useless making a run for it. (1880; Taranaki)

The whip Top was a relatively slow means of progress compared with the racing whip top. These were mushroom-shaped tops about 1½ inches across the top and 2½ to 3 inches long.

They were capable of being hit fifteen yards or more and retaining their spin on good roads until the owner caught up to them once more. Races ranged up to a quarter of a mile in length. The tops could be started as in plain Whip Top, though the best start for a race was made by binding two soft fine strands of special whip round the stem of the top, laying the top carefully on the road so as not to loosen the strands, pointing the top towards the winning post, and then on the word "go" giving the top a sharp flick forward with the whip. The rule was that a top "going down," must be restarted from the point of failure. There was "no creeping up" allowed. The top whips were made from flax strips and had handles from two and a half to three feet long. The "know-alls" always chose the "black-edged" flax, and the racing experts always used the "skinned" flax, that is, white, fine fibers prepared Maori fashion with a pocketknife. Whips often had extra strands wound 'round the handle as a reserve because the whip might not retain its maximum effectiveness to the end of the game. (1880; Taranaki)

The season for Whip Top was winter, beginning in the autumn when the flax was in the best condition for the game. It is still (1950) played occasionally, although mainly in isolated rural areas, particularly by Maoris in North Auckland settlements.

Another way to diversify—and perhaps even delay—the approach to school was to travel by stilts. These were of several types. There were the small, innocuous variety, which were like shoes and were strapped to the feet. Sometimes these clog-like stilts were just a block of wood or tin; in other cases they had two sides like an inverted U. The proper stilts were made of long sticks 5 to 10 feet long with blocks of wood attached to the sticks at any distance from 1 to 5 feet above the ground. These blocks sometimes had straps in which the feet could fit. "We reckoned the leather straps were dangerous because you couldn't get your foot out quickly enough if you fell" (1910; Raikaia). A variety of games were played with stilts. Apart from walking on them, children waded through puddles and in streams. They played with them mainly in winter, when there was some incentive to get off the ground. They had races with them, competed to see who could walk on the highest stilts, played a crude soccer with a tin or soft ball between two sticks or two caps for a goal, and had "cockfights" in which great groups of boys jostled each other in a struggle on sticks. The seasons for stilts were short. It was not a game that normally lent itself to longevity. At Palmerston North between 1915 and 1920, however, one of the local drapers offered a pair of stilts free with every new suit of clothes purchased. This led to an extended season of play in which the drapery stilts, one foot off the ground, competed cockfighting fashion with one another and with other homemade stilts often stilted at a higher level above the ground.

Skipping was another way of moving along the road to school:

On a winter afternoon on the way home we would select two long smooth willow sticks of last year's growth and bind together securely with flax about a foot or eighteen inches of the swishy ends. Taking the stiffer ends, one in each hand we would skip along the road, turning the rope either forwards or backwards over our heads and varying it by crossing hands. After a good deal of practice at this we would count our steps in any pattern that took our fancy, for instance, right hand over left, left hand over right, open and repeat indefinitely. Or it might be three times right over left, one step open, three times over right, one step open, and so on. By this method we would finally arrive at home. (1900; Lower Moutere)

Other methods of transport were of equal interest:

Even to make flax reins and turn ourselves into a spanking team of horses and their driver was better than trudging along like tired swaggers [bums] hanging on to traps and milk carts. Any vehicle passing along was eagerly availed of, and often we would take a lot of whip before we would let go. . . . There were sometimes as many as eight riders covering that staunch, good-natured horse from his ears to his tail. They faced backwards. The boys would hit the horse and stir him to trot, and then the girls would slide to the ground one at a time over his tail. (1870; Waianiwa)

We would select a stone and kick it before us for miles, but this was frowned on by parents and teachers as too destructive of shoe leather. (1900; Moutere)

We followed the leader everywhere: along the rails on the side of the road, up the banks and through the mud. (1875; Dunedin)

Taking three steps forward and two back all the way. Walking only on shadows or only on damp places. (1911; Blenheim)

But there were other types of games, besides games of movement, which the children played to and from school. For example, there were games of hunting and accurate shooting which children played with shanghai, bow and arrow, peashooters, clay shooters, slings, and pop, elastic, and spring guns. These are dealt with fully in Chapter 8. There were also plays that involved an interest in nature: the collection of flowers and ferns, the tasting of natural foods, berries, and fruit. These are also dealt with in Chapter 8.

In addition, the pathways to school were a place for pranks and tricks, for antisocial plays, for raiding orchards, throwing stones, lighting fires, and staging fights. As one teacher of the time said, "I don't know why it is, but the children quarrel very much on the way to and from school." Here beyond the civilizations of home and school a variety of group antagonisms displayed themselves.

No history of the school would be complete without some reference to the collective and individual fights that took place. There always existed a certain amount of enmity between Waianiwa and Wright's bush, expressed in showers of stones, clods, sticks, and abusive language. Individual fights were almost a daily experience. (1870; Waianiwa)

It was a case of those going up the road versus those going down it, and we fought whenever we could. (1900; Takaka)

The boys in this valley challenged the ones from the church valley. Dozens on each side challenged each other to fight. All lined up and picked opponents one after the other and set to, one fight at a time. This did not happen very often. (1890; Wakefield)

Feuds between schools also occurred. Boys from the Braigh School were often afraid to walk past the Central School alone. They either quickly passed the danger zone or formed a party strong enough to resist the enemy. Boys from Central School took similar precautions when passing the Braigh School, but they rarely had occasion to travel in that direction. (1900; Waipu)

It was the home gully versus the wet gully. Occasionally we united to fight the town. (1900; Naseby)

Religious differences, especially those between Protestants and Catholics, were always regarded as legitimate grounds for conflict. Innumerable jingles center around this particular dispute. As Davin says, "Most of the kids were Protestants. They'd very likely go to Hell when they died for singing: 'Catholic dogs/Jump like frogs/Don't eat meat on Friday.' Then when Mick and his friends sang: 'Protestant dogs/Jump like frogs/Do eat meat on Friday,' both sides would pick up stones out of the gravelly road and begin to fight. But, of course, that was only in the evening on the way home from school" (Davin 1947:10). More often the rhymes were briefer and more biting: "Catholic dogs stink like frogs" or "Catholic, Catholic ring the bell, Proddy dog, Proddy dog, go to hell."

In an age when most transport was on foot or by horse it was perhaps not surprising that the first common children's playground was created by these modes of locomotion to school. Though the journey was often arduous games appropriate to roadways soon made their appearance. Games of movement: hoops, whip tops, stilts and skipping were evoked by the character of the journey while pilfering and fighting were made possible by the lack of adult supervision in this no man's land between home and school.

3 inside the schoolhouse

After their journey, sometimes through mush and mire, and sometimes with stilts, hoops, or whip tops, and perhaps even against the opposition of rival factions, the children finally arrived at the school. Unfortunately, when they arrived there they sometimes found that the roadway was the lesser of the two evils, that the conditions within the school were even more harsh than they had been on the way to school, that the schoolhouse was not a haven of rest and peace at the end of their journey. This fact had important effects upon their playground play and the "plays" they attempted to get away with inside the schoolhouse.

The Syllabus of 1877 was narrow and formal, and teaching methods in accord with it were often boring and rigid. "The months immediately preceding the examination were apt to degenerate into an orgy of cram, involving much 'keeping-in,' long hours of home-work, and unremitting punishment for 'carelessness' or 'laziness' (A. E. Campbell 1941:85). For children used to an open-air life and the hard work mentioned in Chapter 1, this type of routine was oppressive. Consider, for example, the following account of a boy's life in the 1880s at Queenstown, and then consider how this boy would have taken to the above routine.

As a boy playing games and generally finding amusement in the eighties, one of my outstanding recollections is that practically *nothing* was provided for us to help us in our play. From our own initiative, labour and pence (hard-earned), we had to achieve our play in the hard way. This rule applied to the making of such things as shanghais (from forked manuka sticks), stilts, kites, sledges, skates, hoops (from the blacksmith), building huts and forts, and last but not least, excavating and levelling off a piece of sloping ground in the school ground on which the older boys could play cricket. For bathing, swimming, and boating, Lake Wakatipu provided the water. For climbing and mountaineering, the hills surrounding Queenstown (not forgetting the well-known Remarkable, 7,688 feet, which I scaled on two occasions) gave us full scope for our energies. On the same hills we engaged in rabbiting with traps, ferrets, dogs, and guns, also the shooting of wild goats. Bird-nesting was tame, but it found its place. Gymnastics on the horizontal bar came into the picture. Horse-riding was a daily event at which the writer became so expert as to emulate the circus rider standing erect on the horse's back whilst it was in active motion!

Little wonder that "often enough . . . there existed a state of open warfare between teachers and pupils, with rebellion from below breaking out at periodic intervals and being put down from above by merciless flogging (A. E. Campbell 1947: 87). Many informants have spoken of the occasion when a big boy who had been beaten and strapped for a long period finally came into open conflict with the teacher, broke his cane, or did some other rebellious act and left the school forever! For example:

At ten years old I consistently got sums right that the bigger boys in their early teens could not, for which they received a tongue-lashing and were held to shame. Finally once, when the teacher's back was turned, one of the older boys turned to me and hissed, "You little black bitch!" I began to cry. The teacher wanted to know why. And the boy concerned was caned, but in the midst of the whacking he suddenly seized that cane, broke it, and walked out of the school for life. (1879; Karamea)

The number of tales about flagellating teachers is legion. One of the causes contributing to this friction was the age of the boys. Many of them did not start school until age eight, nine, or ten and were well into their teens by the time they reached or neared standard four (in New Zealand "standards" correspond approximately to "grades"). On behalf of a teacher appropriately nicknamed "the thrashing machine," it is said, "It should be remembered in his favour that many of his pupils,

Children in class, 1919.

fresh from farms and runs, were approaching manhood, and were husky youths at that, tough customers in a rough and tumble. Some of them, I believe, wore kilts" (1880; Invercargill).

The roughness of community life has already been mentioned. This, and the surly attitude of some children toward authority, would contribute to the stern atmosphere on the school scene. One can readily believe that in some cases thrashing was a form of pedagogic self-defense, in others that the thrasher was merely doing what many adults of the day deemed appropriate to do with unruly children. In the Takaka district there is a story that around the turn of the century a teacher strapped a four-year-old boy 144 times and killed him. It may not be a fact, but fact or no, it is a significant legend. Another story of the early days in Dunedin claims that between 1870 and 1880 the education board issued "punishment books" in order to put a stop to the immense amount of punishment going on. Instances of punishment were to be listed in the books during the year, and the books were to be returned at its end. The story goes that the books were filled before the first term ended and that the board ran out of its supply. Such examples of heavy punishment and turbulent conditions are numerous. Children, however, seemed to be able to make a game out of almost any situation, and there is a report of a grim game in which the boys competed to see who could get the most supplejacks to take back to the teacher as canes (1880; Takaka). More often, however, the children were simply sent out by the teacher to the bush to cut a "nice bit of supplejack" to be used on themselves. There is a report of another teacher who had the outside edges of his strap hand-stitched with copper wire to prevent the boys from cutting it up.

There are reports of schoolboy strikes in these years. A report from Hampden (1885) speaks of a teacher who was a former military man: "Boys who broke his law would be put into 'coventry,' and any other children who spoke to them would be tanned." One morning, by conspiracy, and sick of the long-endured suffering, the boys "went for him." The teacher rushed for the door and they after him. At the door he stopped, locked it, turned around and rolled up his sleeves and "beat up those kids till twelve o'clock." And there are other stories of rebellion:

Influenced by press reports of the maritime strike, between twenty or thirty of us declared a "strike," and one morning, instead of marching into school, we marched off to Seaward bush and stayed there until hunger drove us home. (1890; Invercargill)

Between 1895 and 1900 the standard four to six children of George Street School, Dunedin, struck for less homework. We waylaid a boy who was sent to our homes with letters for our parents and prevented him from carrying out the mission. At two o'clock we sent a note by a small boy, outlining our demands for less homework. At three o'clock we turned up in force at school to see if our demands had been acceded to. We were thereupon forcibly seized and strapped.

There was a riot at Mount Cook School shortly after he went there. . . . The master of standard six, a Mr. Reeves, had his arm broken in the fracas, and rioting schoolboys took the cane from the headmaster, a Mr. Hardy, and used it on him in the course of this historic rebellion against authority. Inkwells were thrown through windows and the constabulary were called in the restore order. (1875–85; Wellington)

A sole-charge female teacher was chased 'round and 'round the building by the older pupils. Fortunately for her, the school committee chairman happened to be riding along the road past the school. He went in and restored order. (1910; Hawkes Bay)

I was an observer of a riot about 1906. It began with the morning whacking for spelling. The headmaster was pelted with inkwells and slates and then rushed and "downed." About six advanced adolescents were expelled. (1906; Christchurch)

The struggle between teacher and children usually went on in less overtly rebellious terms. Some examples of typical classroom "play" expressions of this rebellious motif are found in an account of the years 1899–1905 in Waitara:

Once a flounder was nailed to the underside of the master's table. He could not see it, but after a day or so he could smell it, and very plainly at that. He kept pulling the drawer out and hunting around the table, but not examining it from underneath.

Boys who were required to touch their toes to receive corporal punishment sometimes donned an extra pair of trousers to soften the blow. Once, the inner pair of trousers being longer in the leg than the outer pair by that reason revealed their presence. The insertion of cardboard or leather in the seat of the trousers was a useful precaution, if its presence was not revealed in one way or another, which was frequently and unhappily the case.

Another trick was to chew paper into soft wads and place it at the end of a flat ruler, through springiness of which the paper was shot through the air with great speed. When it hit the ceiling it remained stuck. The school ceiling consequently was well spotted over most of its surface with these, to us, delightful splodges. But the master was not amused, as, owing to the height of the ceiling, their removal was difficult.

On Fridays we used to have singing, and one of the boys was deputed to drape the tonic sol-fa table (which consisted of a long canvas scroll and rolled up like a window blind) over the blackboard for exhibition to the class. By constant wear and tear the scroll developed a split in the middle, and to the great delight of the class of both sexes, and the annoyance of the master, the boys used to so arrange it that one of the wooden pegs on which the blackboard rested used to protrude through the split and look like nobody's business. The master with his wand used always to adjust the scroll so that the peg would remain hidden.

One song we used to sing had these lines: "Far away, far away, over the hills and meadow gay, etc." The first "far away" was sung full voice, and the second quite softly. Some of the very rude boys would add a letter to the word "far," and while everyone sang the first "far away" lustily (with embellishments) the master could not detect anything wrong, but on one occasion they forgetfully sang the second "far away" as loudly as the first, while the rest of the class sang it softly. And then of course there was trouble.

The use of singing as a "vent" is reported elsewhere, and any teacher of experience knows that it is readily used by children for this purpose even today. Referring to their first school in 1877, held in a church for lack of other accommodation, one writer says, "At the close of each day we sang hymns, and the favourite hymn was 'There are angels hovering 'round.' The teacher had no need to ask us to sing louder" (Ravensbourne, Dunedin).

Other accounts of schoolroom mischief abound:

When our sentry at the peephole in the frosting of the window reported "all clear," Charles R., who knew more about the playing of a Jew's harp than he did of history, entertained us with jigs and reels to the time beat of many feet, until the lookout gave the warning, whereupon everybody was busy at lessons again. (1870; Waianiwa)

While the teacher was absent the class usually held an animated conversation on the doings of the Kelly Gang.* (1890; Invercargill)

We put sugar and aniseed in the ink. This wasn't noticeable when the ink was being used, but when the books were piled up on the teacher's desk it glued the lot together. (1890; Takaka)

One day, when Mr. McLeod was teaching two classes, Fred tacked the legend "Mac is an ass" on his coattails. The girls gave him away and Fred was expelled. (1890; Takaka)

Mr. G. had a habit when addressing scholars of standing on a form, a work of supererogation, considering he was over six feet. His pedal extremities, being proportioned to his height, were naturally

*A group of bandits from Australia.

of interest to those of us occupying the seat on which he stood. So while his head was in the air one day, we were busy with a foot rule recording sundry interesting dimensions when a titter from the rest of the class disturbed our operations and we looked up to find that his apparent absorption in the lesson he was giving was simply camouflage—that he was regarding with relish the whole proceedings. Our confusion on being discovered must have entertained him greatly. (1880; Albany Street School, Dunedin)

There are so many other examples that it must suffice to enumerate a few more in summary form: hiding the logbook in the ventilator; cutting the master's strap to pieces; drawing faces on the back of the celluloid collar of the boy in front; poking a ruler through a hole in the floor; sliding down the banisters both inside and outside school buildings; eating green apples in school; sticking darts into the roof; putting pins into other children; sticking a penholder to one's tongue and up one's nose; overloading the coal cart which the master was to push; chewing kauri gum and passing it around from mouth to mouth; chewing whole wheat in winter months; chewing coffee buns; passing conversation lollies; overflowing newly filled inkwells with lumps of carbide; stealing teachers' bicycle tires; stealing the school bell tongue; wearing out the desk footrail by rubbing at it continually with feet (competition to see who could get through first); exploding gunpowder in the classroom (for example, "Guy Fawkes Day occurred a day too soon in Manakau School, for Willie Hiwi exploded a detonator during lessons! Old pupils still recount how the marks of poor Willie's fingers lingered on the ceiling for years"). (1880; Manakau)

Considering the harsh conditions in the schools, it is natural that one of the most important informal plays of this period was "playing the wag." Other factors contributed to this "play" too. We have already mentioned the fact that even toward the end of the century children were still regarded as an economic asset in many rural areas, and New Zealand was dominantly a rural country until the end of the century. Labor was thought of as their lot, and little love was lost by many of the settlers for the children's new and compulsory tutor-authority, the school. Poor attendance was normal; for example, "The children of those days must have known what hard work was. Throughout the minutes the committee and teachers complained of lack of attendance. Apparently parents thought they were more useful on the farm" (1880s; Papakura). As late as 1901 the annual report of the teacher of the small rural school at Waione, W. H. Gould,* records: "Irregular attendance has, throughout the year, been a most serious drawback. There are a few parents in the district, who, it is deplorable to note, do not seem to recognize their responsibilities as parents. As a result a number of children are growing up in total ignorance of anything scholastic." In addition, roads were bad and attendance was largely enforced by the local school committee. The following description of Tokomairiro schools before 1877 is true of many other schools until the end of the century:

The fact that before 1876 parents were free to keep their children at home explains partly why in nearly all the earliest schools the boys always outnumbered the girls by approximately three to one. This unequal distribution is probably further explained, first, by the need of the mother to have help at home and, secondly, by the fact that the boys were considered more hardy and therefore more fit to undergo the rigours of travelling long distances to school in all weathers.

In small rural areas there is constant reference to children being away because it is wet, or late because the roads are bad. "River flooded, roads impassable, weather stormy, no attendance" (Waione Logbook, September 3, 1900). One logbook reports: "All early this morning, not one late; a record. Fighting late comers for weeks, as this school is fearful for late comers" (Horoeka Logbook, August 17, 1908).

With the incentives for attendance so low, truancy came

*Gould was to become the first Professor of Education at Victoria University of Wellington, and the present author commenced his studies with him.

quite easily to many children. Any passing event might attract them away from the school. This is not surprising, since at a time when recreational activities were sparse anything that did occur took on a certain "spectacular" quality, which it could not have done so easily in a modern community that was used to a regular round of amusements. For example:

St. Patrick's Day. The majority of the children were away at the Weber Sports. (Waione Logbook, March 17, 1904)

The practice of being absent on Friday afternoon is common. (College Street School, Palmerston North, April 24, 1893)

Seventy pupils succumbed to the attraction of the Fire Brigade procession. (August 31, 1895)

Tournament at Hokowhitu—very poor attendance at school. (March 18, 1896)

Fifty pupils absent at races. (February 24, 1898)

There were also times when the teaching staff aided and abetted the truant. A dull pupil might be told to remain away from school while exams were in progress in order not to lower the percentage of passes by his presence. The fact that truancy was everywhere a matter of seriousness is indicated by the existence of education board truant officers. Nevertheless, the amount of this truancy appears to have varied from district to district. Informants recall the "play" as follows:

There was not much. We were made an example of if we did, and got an almighty thrashing. Only the outlaw type of kid persisted. (1890; Gisborne)

Only certain boys. (1875; Wakefield)

Truant officers were unknown in the early days of the school; but there was little truancy, for the parents were always willing to hand the offenders over to justice. On one occasion might be seen a mother leading her truant son to school—on the end of a dog chain! The culprit was handed over to the headmaster. The cure was permanent. (1870; Invercargill)

In other districts the situation was apparently somewhat different:

Playing the wag was very common. We made for the bush, but it was difficult to time one's arrival at home correctly. (1875; Dunedin)

We called it "playing tally." (1875; Wakefield)

On any fine day. (1880; Tapanui)

In the early days of our school, truancy was very common. . . . If the pupils were absent, inquiry was made as to whether the absentees' names were on the Albany Street roll, and later on the policeman was asked to report on any "waggers." (1877; Palmerston North)

When we got into standard three some of us became badly infected with the spirit of lawlessness and disorder, or probably the trouble was sheer laziness. At any rate "wagging it" became a popular pastime, and I doubt very much whether the truants averaged more than three days a week at school. I know that in that year our party explored the banks of the Waihopai from Woodend to Kennington, made an exhaustive personal study of the sawmilling industry from McCallum's mill on Puni Creek to the recesses of Seaward bush where the men were at work falling trees, and got a fair idea of the flora and fauna of Cruickshank's bush, 'round where the woollen mills now stand—all in the time when we should have been in class. . . . It must have been torture for the good lady whose misfortune it was to be in charge of us; every now and again I pass her in the street and I feel inclined to slink 'round the corner in order to escape her accusing eye. Of course, detection and punishment followed, but we got hardened to that and it made no difference, and at the end came the inevitable result—failure. (1880; Waianiwa)

Although the concern here is only about truancy from the children's point of view, larger issues were clearly at stake.

The problem of time haunts developing societies; it is at the very heart of the transformation of agrarian habits, which do not emphasize precision and promptness, into habits consonant with city life and large scale manufacture. Every society since the industrial revolution began has had to develop a mechanism for changing the behaviors appropriate in a traditional society into those called for by modernity. (Katz 1975:32)

In New Zealand, as in other societies, the schools and their truancy officers were major instruments in this transformation. Katz's maxim that when 50 percent of the children are roaming the streets public schools become mandatory seems to have been borne out in New Zealand (Ewing 1960:40).

4 the playground

In the early days the small, official playground, particularly in rural areas, did little to restrict the play of the children. Most country schools were surrounded by open paddocks, hills, and sometimes bush. In some rural areas it was the custom to allow the teacher to keep a cow and a horse, which further extended the normal playground space (e.g., 1875, in Tahataki). It was only in the towns, and at a much later date in rural areas, that the effects of the "quarter-acre act" were felt.* Here is a glimpse of one of the more picturesque of these early rural playgrounds:

*The quarter-acre was the space to be given over to the playground in public schools.

There was a neat little school and teacher's dwelling, with the background of native bush in its various shades of green, bedecked in spring and summer with lovely flowers of the clematis, wild bramble, and many other varieties. Then there were the native birds each pouring forth its song . . . especially the tui and bellbird. . . . The scent of the flowers and the song of the birds remains with us still. Meandering through the bush there was a creek running into a watercourse which ran through the playground. In this watercourse grew rushes and native plants. In normal times the creek was only a murmuring ripple, but in the rainy seasons it rose to a turbulent stream, rushing over the footbridge and road, then dashing over a bank on the further side like a miniature waterfall, and then spreading itself over the flat beneath. (1870; Waianiwa)

Most of the first playgrounds, however, though they may have had their beauty in season, were very primitive. For example:

When the school was first built there was no shed, just the bare school in the middle of a paddock. (1875; Tahataki)

The only game we could play was Hide and Seek, as the surrounding ground was thickly covered with tall rushes right to the school door. (1858; Kaitangata)

On wet days a convenient flax bush was the only outside shelter or play shed. (1875; Owaka)

We had an immense playground in those days, and we used to roam all about the hills. One of our games was for a boy to go into a hollow and the others would go up above and roll stones over his head. That went on for quite a long time until an accident happened. (1850s; Green Island, Dunedin)

[The town belt of trees was also used as a playground]: Any day one might have seen dozens of boys, each hanging on to a calf's tail, being dragged up hill and down dale. (1860s; Dunedin)

There were no school games save marbles, as the school grounds were on the hillside, but the bush and the sea provided great experiences, and the peninsula permitted plenty of excursions on Saturdays. (1886; Pigeon Bay)

We had no lawns to mow, no garden plots to keep tidy. Neither were we troubled by visiting drill instructors, doctors, or dental clinics. Fingernails were not subject to scrutiny, nor were we brought to brook with the reproach "Did you nugget (shoeshine) your boots this morning?" (1870; Waianiwa)

In some cases it was the property adjoining the playground rather than the playground itself that determined the form of the play. Next door to the Balclutha school, for example, there was an orchard, and around this orchard hangs a history of escapades. Much to the chagrin of the scholars, it was replaced by a school garden in 1907. Next door to the Union Street Normal School, Dunedin, there were Chinese gardens, and furthermore there was no fence between the two. There are many records of lost footballs, stolen carrots and parsnips, and fights with the Chinese owners. Some of the playgrounds were of a decidedly dangerous nature:

One cannot but be struck with the difficulties the boys must have faced when playing their games on those slippery and precipitous hillsides. In March 1874, Moeller, when playing a game of Prisoner's Base, fell and broke his collarbone, and a son of Colonel St. John dislocated his ankle while engaged in the same game (Wellington Boys College).

In the winter many of these playgrounds were turned into a sea of mud: "The Committee this week put down bundles of manuka round the school to keep the children out of the mud" (Horoeka Logbook, July 14, 1905). And the rain did not always make its presence felt only in the playground: "Closed school this afternoon on account of rain coming in through the roof in a regular stream" (1880s; Whakaronga). Children, of course, made use of the various and notorious mudholes in and out of the playground when they desired to "fix" a victim.

A recurrent note in reminiscences on the playgrounds of the early years is the reference to drinking water. One is apt to forget, that children are as perpetually thirsty as they are hungry. Water was supplied at a spring, at nearby houses, in a tank or with a pump, and all these places were locations for escapades. For example: "Boys working their pump vigorously to prevent girls from getting any water, and girls retaliating." Or again, "We threw water at one another" (1870s; Waianiwa).

In wet weather, children generally would be allowed to play in the school or gather around the fire.

We would play Puss in the Corner, one in each corner of the room. There wouldn't be many present when it was wet, and the teacher would allow us to push some of the seats back for floor space. (1875; Tahataki)

We would play marbles on the floor in school. (1870; Takaka)

We had spelling bees, singing, made paper and string models. (1880s; Waianiwa)

Later most of the schools had play sheds, and the children could retreat to these in wet weather. Some of these sheds gained favor for special purposes. Generations of boys at Waikouaiti, for example, swung along the rafters in their shed until they became as smooth and polished as varnished wood. At Kakaramea Taranaki, holes were carved out of the wall between the boys' and the girls' sheds and billets-doux passed between (1870s). Then, as now, not only the sheds but also the latrines were used as a place for escapades in wet weather or fine. Some informants speak of the conveniences as filthy and evil-smelling buildings placed necessarily at an inconvenient distance from the school and, at best, camouflaged with perfumed roses and honeysuckle. Since they were often open at the back, it was possible to play disconcerting pranks upon the sedentary occupants.

A further feature of most early playgrounds was the strict segregation of boys and girls (1900; Waikouaiti). Many informants of one sex have only a hazy notion of what the other sex did in their playground. There was sometimes a high concrete or brick wall between the two playgrounds (1880; Tapanui). "We grew up like two races apart," says one informant. "Consequently, on the few occasions we did meet we were absolutely at a loss" (1895; Gisborne). Were the concrete walls meant to keep the boys out, to keep the girls in, or to preserve privacy? Whichever it was, even out of school, girls of all ages were well supervised and made little appearance in the life of the colony except on festive occasions. An informant, speaking of her years at private school in Wellington in the 1880s, said that girls of her social class were not permitted to play on the streets. They were transported to college and met at the stop by a female teacher who marched them to school. On one such occasion the marching girls suddenly came upon several men engaged in a brawl in the street through which they had to pass. "Young ladies, eyes down!" shrilled the teacher, and they all went solemnly past, ostensibly with their eyes to the ground. This piece of scandal was the talk of the school for days. Other informants recall: "In our school there were separate playgrounds, and play together was never encouraged" (1900; Lower Moutere) and "The wooden turnstiles which acted as gates at the old school were all cut and carved with initials. The boys went through one gate, the girls through the other. Brave was the boy who defied the school regulations and went through the girls' gate, but sorry was he if he was caught out" (1890; College Street, Palmerston North). In some schools, however, particularly one-teacher schools, it was only by playing together that the dozen or so children could get any play at all.

Children playing Leap Frog at Kaitaia School.

For example, in Tahataki (1875), Wyllie's Crossing School, Taieri (1898), and Rockville (1885) boys and girls would often play their cricket and rounders together, perhaps even their skipping. "Strange to say, our favourite was skipping, and the boys held a big tether rope and the girls formed in a queue, and as we followed to have our skip, the boys called us all by a pet name of their own, and some of them were not always complimentary" (1890; Upper Tutaenui, Marton). "In some cases, even at that early stage they played football together" (1890; Murchison). Today some of the happiest and most valuable accounts of school play life came from these little one-teacher country schools, whose whole population ranges from ten to twenty-five pupils.

We cannot describe here the many hundreds of games that took place on the playgrounds of the nineteenth century, but we will summarize and list some of the names of the formal games that children played. The full description of these games is of book length itself and appears in the author's *The Games of New Zealand Children* (Berkeley: University of California

Press, 1959), republished in *The Folkgames of Children* (Austin: University of Texas Press, 1972). The current work emphasizes informal play as opposed to formal or folk-game play.

It has already been mentioned that the girls of the day were in most cases segregated from the boys, and this did have its advantages. Because they were protected, by a wall, the girls were able to carry on their tranquil singing games undisturbed by marauding boys. Here was a pocket of elegance and formality, in marked contrast to the freely running assertiveness that characterized so many other plays of the nineteenth century.

The singing games (ring games) through which the girls wended their at times staid and decorous way were mainly those they had played at picnics or in the parlor. Having watched them played by youths and adults and even having participated in them themselves, the girls readily reproduced them in their playground play. In these years, Oranges and Lemons, Nuts and May, Green Gravels, and The Jolly Miller appear to have been the four singing games most universally known. Those that appeared frequently in the playground were: Oranges and Lemons, Nuts and May, Green Gravels, Jingo Ring, Draw a Pail of Water, Pretty Little Girl of Mine, Ring a Ring a Roses, Farmer in the Dell, Sally Waters, Poor Sally Is Aweeping, Drop the Handkerchief, and Bingo. Those usually played in the presence of adults but occasionally also in the playground were Jolly Miller, Three Dukes, London Bridge, and Duke of York.

The value of these games for girls, especially in small schools with a wide age range, was their egalitarian character. In these games children of all ages could participate. However, these singing games were not always played at schools by girls:

Oranges and Lemons would come in crazes, different age-groups having their own circle. We had also Draw a Pail of Water. (1890; Waikouaiti)

The Jolly Miller came later in the eighties, but not while I was at school. (1870; Wakefield)

The Jolly Miller, Pretty Little Girl of Mine, and others were played in the playground. (1875; Tahataki)

The singing games were played more often on the reserve next to the school. I remember especially Sally Waters. (1875; South Clutha)

We did not play any of the singing games at school but played them only at home and at friends' places. (1900; Palmerston North)

Green Gravels was played at school, and I have a feeling it might have been a bit sexy in parts. (1890; Nelson)

We all joined in Nuts and May at school. (1880; Timaru)

We played Nuts and May in the school grounds and inside school if it was too cold. (1870; Otago)

These reports show that it is difficult to generalize accurately about these games, but we do know that all the singing games mentioned below were reproduced by girls at some time in some playground. The great majority of boys, however, played these games only at parties or at picnics, except perhaps when they were very young, but even this generalization had its exceptions, since boys at some small country schools sometimes played, and still play, these games throughout childhood.

The singing and chanting games of the day can be divided into four groups: (1) circle games concerned with marriage, funerals, and pantomimic actions; (2) winding games, most of which are also concerned with marriage; (3) line games, again involving marriage. If these games represent any commentary on a young girl's outlook, it is not surprising that we must mention another group of games: (4) the couple games, in which, presumably, the goal of endeavor is achieved.

Two other kinds of games that played an important role in the girls' playground, along with the singing games, were chasing and dialogue games. In New Zealand, chasing or tagging games are initiated by the "He" player (called the "It" player elsewhere). Before 1900 there seem to have been fewer "He" games. This may be no more than a surface appearance, because the great variety of tagging and chasing games occurs mainly in the play of the eight- to ten-year-old age-groups, and this is an age that is easily forgotten by the reminiscer, who tends to remember only the more obvious and advanced games of ages eleven and twelve. Thus, the game of Tig (known as "Tag" in the United States) is always remembered, though its innumerable forms may not be. On the other hand, some informants claim that they never played Tig in its present haphazard forms, but only in a circle (in Cat and Mouse or Twos and Threes formation), "with the mouse running 'round and 'jinking' the cat by getting another player between herself and that cat-player" (1874; Tahataki). The circle formation might have been the more common form, since children would be likely to imitate it from picnics and adult practice. Furthermore, the less vigorous and circular forms of Tig might have been more suitable to the starched and heavy habiliments of the time, particularly for girls. It would also be the form naturally adopted by the older Tig players. However, the greater attention given to these formal Tig games can only have been a matter of emphasis. All the main forms were played then as they are today. The universal Tiggy Tiggy Touchwood and Hide and Seek, for example, were very informal, with a very loose structure. In addition, Fox and Goose, Bar the Door, Tom Tiddler's Ground, Prisoner's Base, French and English, and Puss in the Corner were all common. There are traces of other variants of a more formless type:

In Tig round the school, you "jinked" and turned back. We played it to warm us up, but it was a dangerous game. (1860; Taieri)

It was called Trip and Go (1875; Tahataki) [or simply] "Chase." (1900; Naseby)

As you caught the runners they joined your side. There was a lot of random tagging. (1870; Christchurch)

Clearly there were innumerable forms of tagging games, but they all had certain basic characteristics. In all these games players ventured beyond a "base" or "home" and then tried to avoid a He player whose aim it was to tag them and make them He. Sometimes they avoided the He player by holding on to some safe place (Tiggy Tiggy Touchwood), and sometimes they avoided him by hiding (Hide and Seek).

The He, of course, could be a fearsome creature and sometimes had awesome animal names (e.g., Wolf). Sometimes the He was blindfolded, in which case it was easier to taunt him. On other occasions the roles were reversed, because the game was played at dusk or in the darkness and that made the He all the more frightening: "You never knew just when He was about to seize you." There was something dangerous about the power He had. In some games, if He tagged you He poisoned you and made you lame. Further, because He was an awesome person, he had to be very carefully chosen, and so the mysterious counting-out rhymes were used. Despite his powers, however, his potency could be minimized in many games by the fact that the players helped one another fight against him (e.g., Bedlam, Relievo, Kick the Block).

In Puss in the Corner a player could avoid the He by staying in the corner. This was the He game played from the earliest years of school life, and play sheds seem almost to have been made for the purpose. Hide and Seek was also particularly suited to some of the very early rough playgrounds. "We used to play Hide and Seek amongst the flax bushes and niggerheads during our lunch hour" (1911; Blenheim). Occasionally unusual types of hiding games were played, for example All In or Taranaki. In this game there were two teams and a home base. One team, the "outs," went and hid, while the home team, the "ins," counted. When they were ready, the "ins" went and looked for the "outs." As soon as an "in" player saw an "out," he cried, "All in for Tommy Jones" (the "out" player who had been spotted). At that cry all the "in" players raced for home, and all the "out" players emerged from their hiding places and attempted to tag them. If all the "in" players could get home without being tagged, then the person seen (Tommy Jones), was considered captured, and he had to come and sit in the home base. And so the "in" team went on trying to sight players and then get home without being tagged. In that way, one by one, they caught all the "out" players. When they were very near the end and had all the "out" players except one or two, they would naturally send out only their very best players; they didn't want one of their own players to be tagged, because if one of their own players was tagged while running back to the home base he was said to be "out off." That meant that all the captured "out" players could go free again and hide. Then the "in" team had to start from scratch all over again. "It was quite popular and suited to smaller play spaces where there were a number of buildings and bushes to provide 'hides,' from which 'outs' could dart to tag unwary 'ins' trying to spy them" (1880; New Plymouth).

A favorite time for playing "He" games was at dusk.

Twilight tig was a game played on a cousin's lawn and garden which was dotted with shrubs. We played it before we went home after spending a day with them. It was played at dusk in complete silence after the first counting-out, so that it was difficult to tell who was He until perhaps you felt a touch on your own shoulder and knew that it was yourself. The effect of the silent figures flitting and dodging in and out among the bushes in the half-dark was eerie in the extreme, and I can feel it still. (1890; Dunedin)

Perhaps the most common of the outdoor dusk He games was

"Moonlight, starlight, Bogey won't come out tonight." We had several paddocks divided off by hedges, and the neighbouring children always congregated for games after their chores were done. We usually ended with Moonlight Starlight. As the bogey was at liberty to move 'round, one never knew where the next pounce was coming from. (1910; Nelson)

The fear of darkness could be played upon in other ways too. Children at Ohau in 1912, for example, played a game of Hide and Seek in which the prisoners were locked up in a windowless shed that they called "the black Hole of Calcutta": "It was rather thrilling to be there, though I don't know why." But the most exciting of all the games in the darkness was the games of Ghosts. This was sometimes simply a tagging game, but at other times it took more exciting forms. For example:

Three of us made a ghost from a hollowed pumpkin with holes in the pumpkin for nose, mouth, and eyes. The mouth had bits of stick in it for teeth. A lighted candle inside the pumpkin gave the right effect. The pumpkin was fixed to a pole about five feet high, near the top of which was a cross stick draped with an old pillowcase and a strip of woolly sheepskin. We recorded a number of frights with this apparatus, once or twice in connection with knick-knocking. (1890; Taranaki)

This was a universal play object among boys in those days, but ghosts were not always kept within the safe confines of play.

When I was about the age of nine a ghost trick was accidentally played on me. Even at that age I often had the duty of taking a horse to the paddock situated at some distance past an old Maori graveyard. On this occasion, night had just about fallen, and I wasn't a bit keen on that old cemetery after dark. Just as I thought I had passed all trouble, I was suddenly scared stiff. My head tingled. Just in front and about twenty yards away something white had appeared, and there was a distinct sobbing sound, a constant noise, though the white thing came and went. I never felt more like running for my life. But I didn't run. Shivering, I moved up to the thing, and as I cracked it with the rope halter and blustered "What's that?" a fairly strong breeze was moving the blind of a house not far away, and the light flashed intermittently on a big piece of stiffish white paper that had wrapped itself 'round a post and one part flapped in the wind making a noise that any imaginative boy of ten could make into a dozen horrors. (1890; Taranaki)

The best-known counting-out rhymes before 1900 were Ickle, Ockle, Eenie Meenie, and Onery Twoery. Between 1900 and 1930 One Two Three rose to equal importance. The most common rhyme at all times has been Eenie Meenie Minie Moh (or Eeenah Deenah Dinah Doh).

Carrying some of the mystery of chasing games and some of the ritual of singing games, girls' dialogue games were also characteristic of the girls' area of the playground. These were of two types: those that involved the capture or stealing of children by a witch (Mother Mother the Pot Boils Over) and those that involved the caricature and teasing of an old woman (Old Lady from Botany Bay). They involved verses chanted by children and witch, and then a pursuit and flight by the children. Other names for similar games were: Blacksmith (taking the function of the witch), Fox and Family, Digley Bones, The Jampots (because children were swung between witch and mother to determine their value), Jack a Lingo, and Who Goes Round My Stone Wall.

Girls of those days were not without games of skill, even though they had fewer such games than did boys, perhaps because girls were more occupied with household tasks and had less freedom to roam, experiment, and explore. Theirs was a more ordered and decorous way of life, and the types of games they played support this generalization. There were more games of a quiet nature and more home games. At school, however, in addition to their singing, dramatic, and tagging games, they had skipping, Hopscotch, and Knucklebones, which were of great importance in the girls' play year. Other games generally played more by girls than by boys were hand-clapping games, string games, guessing games, and parlor games.

On the other side of the wall—the boy's side—the games appear to have been both more active, rough, and complex. Boys also had chasing games, but the most typical of these was Bar the Door (sometimes called King Caesar), in which one boy in the middle attempted to tag the others as they ran across. When tagged they joined him in the middle until all were caught.* Sometimes taggers joined hands to chase everyone

*The game had over fifty names in New Zealand and is described in detail in the author's *The Folkgames of Children,* p. 491.

else, as in Ballahonie and Ballyhooley. Or the players being chased ran through the base, freeing all the other players by kicking the can, the block, the tin, or the *homaiacky*. Since older boys played these games they could be quite rough. Thus in Punch King (a variant of Bar the Door) the middle player simply punched the running player three times on the back. At Collingwood (1900) the cry was "King Caesar Sinio, one, two, three," but in this case the running player could avoid being tagged by holding his hand on his head. A similar practice is reported from South Clutha (1875): "When King Seeny attempted to crown the player with the cry 'One-two-three, you're the man for me' the player attempted to escape by punching and biting the He's hands in an effort to keep them off his head."

The best example of a crowning ceremony is one that was called Kinging. In this ceremony the captive was patted on the head while he lay flat on the ground with other players astride him. If he managed to move during the ceremony, then the rhyme must begin again: "King Seeny, one, two, three, you're the very man for me. Keep him quiet, hold him down, pat him thrice upon the crown. Blackball, blackball, one, two, three, Joseph Jackson, you are He" (1895; Canterbury). There are no reports of elaborate crowning ceremonies later than 1900. It was probably displaced by rugby tackling or frowned upon when playgrounds were supervised. The practice may also have lost its importance when the custom of wearing school caps began to die out. As F. L. Combs (1939) said, "when no boy, however, otherwise disreputable, would dream of flouting the decencies by not wearing a cap," it would be of some importance not to have the dirty hand of another boy on this symbol of one's dignity. Undoubtedly a main reason the game of Bar the Door (the most popular name for this kind of game) has been so popular in New Zealand is the fact that it was so adaptable to the rugby code. It was almost inevitable that the tackling habit of rugby football would carry over into Bar the Door. And in many schools where the ground was suitable, forms of tackling, (not always very orthodox) were substituted for the tagging. It often happened that some disliked player would be allowed to come across last and then the whole crowd of players in the middle would "down" him, piling on top of him. Thus, if a running player fought too hard on his earlier trips, he would be likely to meet a time of reckoning later, when the mass of players in the middle combined to return the injuries. In some cases the tagging was done with three punches, which is said to have led to many fights, especially when running players felt they had been punched too exuberantly. Tackling forms of the game were often known as Scragging or Collaring (by mothers as "the clothes-tearing game"). Other variants of Bar the Door were Gag or No Gag, and Punch King. In Gag or No Gag (sometimes known as Gag or Smuggling the Gag) there were two teams. One player of one team hid some object on himself such as a pocketknife or a stone, and when his team ran through the other team in Bar the Door fashion the other tried to guess who had the object and catch that player. When they did succeed in catching the right player, then it was their turn to carry the object, the gag.

Punch King was similar to Bar the Door, but more violent.

The game was called Punch King Sinio. . . . Five were left uncrowned. . . . The five had their backs to the wall, and woe betide any luckless mite who dared to come within reach of their punches, so indiscriminantly were they delivered. Any punch was legal, rabbit or otherwise. Many retired hurt in silence to nurse their bruises; not a few were placed hors de combat by blows below the belt. As soon as the five showed the least signs of exhaustion, the pack exultingly rushed in and all was over. . . . It was really the only regular outlet for boyish exuberance we had. (1876; Wellington)

The game began by one team lining up with their backs to a wall and another team attempting to pull them out over a line placed about a yard from the wall. The pulling team could only pull, but the defending team could punch. In Otago in the early days Punch King was known as Goosey.

If Rounders is reminiscent of girls, summer afternoons, and picnic fun, then Shinty, a boys' game, reminds us of some primeval time.

One other pastime which accorded well with boyish spirit was Shinty, a prehistoric version of hockey, one in which boys of the cave-dwelling age would have revelled. It was played without restrictions as to the sticks used or the height or direction of the swing made when swiping the ball. The popularity of the game would become a craze. In the heat of the willing contests, someone would suffer serious damage and Shinty would be proscribed. Few indeed escaped without hard knocks and losses of skin. But under the pressure of eager spirits the embargo would relax until another casualty imposed the ban. So it went on, and it was not till rugby football took hold that Shinty vanished from the playground. . . . I suppose we used fifty different types of clubs. It seemed we never got 'round to play until the playground got good and muddy. . . . Shinty was my favourite game at school, and perhaps I was the cause of it being stopped. I knocked Jack Lopdell's eyebrow off and brought him to his knees. Perhaps it was then he decided to go into the ministry. (1870; Waianiwa)

Shinty required sticks—any shape sufficed—and Black Jack's palings were very suitable, even if obtaining them involved encounters with Black Jack. Occasionally iron-shod sticks were used; the wonder is that more heads were not broken. The cry now rings in my ears, "Shinty one, hockey two, shinty three, and away." Sid Tarlion, though a duffer at spelling, was a demon with the stick, adding at least one opponent's finger to his war trophies. (1900; Invercargill)

It was well named: All the skin was off our shins and there were often black eyes. (1870; Taieri)

The cry "Hockey one, shinty two, cherry three and away" was a war cry more than anything else. (1900; Waikouaiti)

In most places Shinty was the roughest and least regulated game of hockey played. Generally the two ends of the paddock, road, or playground were goals enough, but in some cases Shinty was the more sophisticated game, with special goals and other rules, while Bang the Tin (1875; Dunedin) or Hurling (1875; South Clutha) were the haphazard forms of the game. In areas in the North Island the name "hockey" alone was used (1885; Bay of Plenty). In South Clutha one interesting practice was that in Shinty the players teed off from the middle of the field after each goal had been scored. And they decided who would have first choice of the innings by using "the rules of contrary": The two captains caught hold of a bat, and someone else said, "By the rules of contrary, when I say let go, hold fast, and when I say hold fast, let go," and the one who didn't do the contrary lost his choice of the innings. As with Rounders the children made their own equipment: "Manuka roots for sticks and macrocarpa nuts for balls" (1880; Tua Marina); "A supplejack root was pared down for a ball" (1895; Collingwood); "Crooked sticks were cut from the bush, and instead of a ball we used a lump of wood or even a stone" (1870; Anderson's Bay). Sometimes they displayed even greater initiative in gaining their ends: "I sawed the wooden end off the bedstead and filed down the rough edge. It was a great ball and lasted for a long time, even though I did get a hiding for it" (1909; Colac Bay).

In this era there were no major sports. True, some games were relatively more important than others, but none received the attention commanded by the major school sports of today. The year brought instead an ever-changing round of seasonal activities that included games of all types. The most widespread summer game of both boys and girls was Rounders. In some areas boys also had cricket, in which case Rounders was more often played by the girls. Shinty (or hockey) was the most important winter game for boys. In the last two decades of the nineteenth century, however, cricket and rugby gradually replaced Rounders and Shinty as the playground games of boys. Rounders continued as the mainstay of girls' summer play even after the advent of tennis. Girls cannot be said to have had a major winter sport until after the advent of basketball, although they did have a major winter game of skipping.

The greatest number of skill games of this day were boys' games. Games that were both widespread and more distinctively girls' games could be numbered on one hand (skipping,

Hopscotch, Knucklebones). Other game seasons that had almost as much importance as these major ones were as follows:

Winter: Shinty, skipping, Hopscotch, Whip Top, King Seenie, Prisoner's Base, hoops, sliding, and, on a lesser scale, stilts, Cockfighting, Duck Stones, parlor games.

Spring: Follow the Leader, Egg Cap, soldiers, Fly the Garter, Leapfrog, Buck Buck, Peg Top, bows and arrows, kites, and Mud Slingers.

Summer: Rounders, Tipcat, swimming, Hares and Hounds, Paper Chase, Chevvy Chase, shanghais, Butcher's Bat, Cat's Cradle, climbing, balancing, walking, and fishing.

Autumn: athletics, races, pole vaulting, Hop Step and Jump, marbles, Knucklebones, Stagknife, Buttons, Conkers, Pitch and Toss, peashooters, bells, sledges, Rough and Tumble, Sacks on the Mill, and King of the Castle. These seasons are only approximate; there was marked variation from one school to the next.

PRE-1900

The games listed below are recorded in several different provinces, so we can therefore assume that they were all widespread before 1900, although not necessarily played elsewhere. A great number continued to be common in the period from 1900 to 1920. Those for which there is little record after 1900 are: Sally Waters, Jingo Ring, Last Pair Out (or run), Punch King, Chivvy Cheese, Chibby, pole vaulting, Duck Stones, Lazy Stick, Cunning Joe (Cronje, Cunjo, or Cunny), Buttons, Buck Buck (Jump Little Nagtail or Monkey on the Bridge), Queen Anne's Dead, Ickety Bickety, Tip Tap Toe, Dumb Grambo, How Many Miles to Babylon, Queen of Sheba.

Games for which there is also little or no record after 1900, but which were not so generally known before 1900 are the following (games whose name only was remembered by the informant are marked with an *x*). *Otago:* Carry My Lady to

London (x), Jack a Lingo, Babbity Bowster (x), Wallflowers (x), Oats and Beans and Barley (x), Marry Ma Tanza, Follow Old Mum to Market, Kick Post One, Peggy, Trip and Go, Horney, Mingle the Bonnets, Hop the Hats, Pinch, Dooking for Apples, Cum Je Cum, Nivvy Nivvy Nack, Hot Cockles; *Canterbury:* Down in the Valley (x), Bold Jolly Lads (x), Boys and Girls (x), Green Grow the Leaves (x), Three Little Ships, Baloo, Baloo Balight, Tursie, Hop the Hats, Block Hammer and Nail, Judge and Jury, There Was an Old Woman, Buttons; *Golden Bay:* Here's a Prisoner, Duck Under Water, Would You Lend My Mother a Saucepan, Cap It, Hopping Base, Hop Peg, Bumpers, Horney; *Wellington:* Merry-go-rounds, Mummy, Blackthorn, Run the Ball, Cocky Hole, Cap Oh; *Taranaki:* Dumpy, Hopping Base, Hats, All in Flicks, Telegrams, I Love My Beau with an A, Putting an Eye in the Peg; *Hawkes Bay:* Fool Fool Come to School (x), Brother Ebenezer (x); *Auckland:* Wallflowers, Aunt Sally Has Gone to Paris.

5 *a naïve world*

Considering the rigid curriculum, the strict, and often harsh discipline, the rough playgrounds, and the rugged roads to school, it would be surprising if the play of the children was a picture of only sweetness and light. It is to be expected that their play would reflect the crude conditions of the school and the school environment, and this fact must be emphasized, lest one wonder why the story that is to be told is not an idyllic one of children gamboling on the rural green. Many adults expect such a picture, and in that they have been encouraged by some children's literature, including that by such notable authors as Lewis Carroll, Robert Louis Stevenson, Walter de la Mare, A. A. Milne, Rudyard Kipling, and Kenneth Grahame. Nevertheless, of all the chapters in this book this is the most "idyllic," for it deals with children's make-believe games, those games in which the more imaginative side of children's nature is expressed.

In make-believe games the children of the nineteenth century were on the whole less sophisticated than their counterparts of today. Older children played at games in which present-day children would scorn to indulge, or at least in which only the younger children of today's playground would willingly participate. This lack of sophistication was due primarily to the fact that children then were not influenced by the commercialized modes of recreation that play a large role in the life of children today. Their lack of sophistication was also due to the smaller number of available toy materials and, consequently, a greater implicit demand made upon the children themselves for improvisation in their informal play. One of the players said, "Even the big boys did not think it beneath their dignity to play at marbles, Hopscotch, Horses, or Rounders" (1870; Anderson's Bay).

Horses is an example of the way some of the games of the day were derived from aspects of adult life that are no longer of great importance, although the example of the movies still keeps horses in the forefront of infant school play. In general, however, with the passing importance of horses, coaches, and bullocks, games based on these activities have slipped down the age scale. In the nineteenth century they were an important part of the life of both men and children; thus in 1890 it is noted in a school logbook, "The beautification of the grounds was handicapped by the fact that all the trees planted had to be protected from the children's horses." Informants recall:

We played horses even in standard five. We would careen 'round riding a stick and using a switch. There would be horses everywhere, and a lot of horse talk, or at least our idea of it. (1890; Gisborne)

Horses were played with some children as horses (with reins, usually knitted ones, decorated with little brass bells) and other children as drivers. At another time with our cousins we had horses of sticks of toitoi, the greasy heads making effective manes for the horses which were decorated with coloured wools and ribbons. (1890; Dunedin)

Another popular toy was made from a small branch of kauri. These branches, when cast off by the tree, have a disc-shaped enlargement at the end that was attached to the trunk. With the aid of a pocketknife, a boy could quickly carve the disc into the shape of a horse's hoof. He would then take his imaginary horse into his hand like a walking stick and would be delighted to see the miniature hoofprints in the sand or soft earth. (1870; Waipu)

The senior boys were the horses, the lightweight juniors were the jockeys—and races followed. A development—the horses were blindfolded, the jockeys steered the horses by their ears. I, as a jockey, either failed to steer well or my horse was so intent on his running that he did not obey the steering and ran into a tree. Result: a bleeding nose. (late 1880s; Greendale, Dunedin)

Another play unknown at a later date was the widespread Bullock Teams:

It was easy to make a team of working bullocks from pieces of supplejack, with their opposite branches doing duty as horns. The manufacture of yokes, substitutes for chains and model sledges gave a boy the pleasant feeling that accompanies successful achievement. Leading the team by a piece of string was the next step. (1870; Waipu)

We joined bottles together with flax ends and dragged them along the road on the way to school in imitation of bullock teams. (1870; Waikouaiti)

It was no uncommon sight to see a bullock team twenty strong in the playground, and we knew the boys best suited for polers and leaders. (1885; Waianiwa)

And then there was Coaches, which also faded into obscurity:

On a cold and frosty morning we would have a dozen in a row as a coach, hands joined behind backs. (1900; Waikouaiti)

For coaches two children linked arms behind each other's backs while standing side-by-side. Then they ran along imitating a pair of coach horses. (1900; Moeraki)

Trains is a game that has persisted:

We had a rope. All players held the rope with one hand. The first child was the engine whistle. They ran along in a line. (1900; Moeraki and Oamaru)

We each held on to the coat of the one in front. As it gathered momentum the train swung sharply 'round the school, much to the consternation of the rear. It was nothing to see twenty boys sprawled across the playground by the centrifugal force. (1885; Dunedin)

Other pastimes included miniature ploughing matches, which were held on the roadside. "The furrows were turned by pocketknives or other small flat tools. I remember Bob Grieve constructing a miniature swing plough, which he brought to school and tried out" (1880; Waianiwa).

There was plenty of stimulus for games of Circuses and Concerts, for as early as 1857 Foley's Circus made its appearance in New Zealand. "We used to sew up some old coal sacks and do handsprings and double somersaults on them. We would get into little trunks to perform" (1875; Dunedin). For an example from the 1870s in the best Booth Tarkington tradition, consider the following story of Invercargill:

The section on which Jim Kingland's home stood in Eak Street ran to Tay Street, opposite to Adam Little's timber yard. Mr. Little's white horse, a placid old creature, was a valued adjunct to the yard. Jim had imagination, and he saw in the combination of yard and horse a circus if you please. He got some sacking, taught the horse to do a few simple stunts, helped himself to some timber, and pitched his tent at various points about the section. Once he got it up against his father's dwelling. It was used by some youthful smokers and the reek drifted indoors and Jim had to shift camp. Then he and his associates made a rare find in the timber yard— a fine span, a ship's mast in fact. It was too long, so taking Mr. Little's consent for granted, they sawed off ten feet or so, then rigged 'round the pole a quantity of canvas. They also achieved a platform and with the help of some of the older girls in the vicinity ventured to give an entertainment—admission, a piece of slate pencil. This was the charge till some canny souls cut their admission to a mere stub, whereupon the management altered the charge to a marble. . . . Of course, a circus needed a band, and kerosene tins were promptly requisitioned. The music evolved might not have satisfied a Siddall or a Wills, but it drew a crowd, who one night enjoyed an unrehearsed effect—the platform collapsed.

Concerts both impromptu and prepared also had a part in the play, especially in birthday entertainment. Then there were the bands: "We played on mouth organs, combs, Jew's harps and accordions. A piece of paper was put around a comb and blown or sung into. The boys in our street had contests against those in the next" (1890; Dunedin).

The Salvation Army came in for its share as a play source:

The Salvation Army was quite a new institution in those days and many a rotten trick including stale eggs and cabbages was played by the elder toughs of the town on the small company of odd folk who held their meetings at the "pub" corners. I have no recollection of any boys taking part in this typical intolerance—perhaps they had no eggs. But just as a circus, the

races, a tangi or an ordinary funeral, a stock sale, or even the
riding of mares by women provided the base for much of our
acting, so the Salvation Army became one of our choice models.
Occasionally there would be a gathering of the clan, and we
would parade the back streets (ten to fifteen of us), with kerosene tins for drums, tops of tins for tambourines or cymbals,
hollow cones of brown paper, several combs wrapped in tissue
paper, and squeakers. Those were made of two pieces of tin or
zinc between the slightly concave sides of which a piece of tape
was tightly stretched and the ends firmly bound together with
tape. Between the taped ends the pieces of tin were bare and
slightly apart. When properly blown the instrument could make
a noise like that made by an angry kaka—quite good enough
for rhythm but hopeless for tune. The band played a number of
tunes and shouted over and over again words that sometimes
parodied the original words. Here is one I remember a part of:

"Oh, you must be a lover of the Lord, of the Lord,
Or you won't go to heaven when you die, when you die,
Oh, you must wear a collar and a tie, and a tie,
Or you won't go to heaven when you die."

Once or twice we "did the block," but I am afraid our collection
was even more inadequate to our supposed needs than the Army's
was to theirs. A Guy Fawkes appeal was much better supported.
The Army was considered either irreverent or a pest. (1880–90;
New Plymouth)

This boyish make-believe is better understood when it is known
that the adults of the day were up to similar pranks. For example,

---

In the early days of the Salvation Army, opposition "skeleton
armies" were formed by larrikins, often with the active encouragement of the publicans. These groups had their own "captain,"
carried flags bearing skull and crossbones, and would attempt to
break up both outdoor and indoor meetings of the Salvation Army.
They pelted Salvationists with rotten eggs, flour, mud, and even

such things as dead cats. Sometimes they would corner a part of the Salvation Army hall and disrupt meetings by singing parodies of well known Army songs. But their plans for breaking the Army went astray when numbers of them became converts. (*Evening Post* [Wellington], April 16, 1951)

At home there were make-believe games with *toy soldiers:* "Hero worship was demonstrated in our games of tin soldiers, which we played endlessly. The rule was that Bobs (Lord Roberts), on a white horse, was never allowed to be knocked down by the shells of an enemy, and whichever side drew him had to be victorious. A sense of guilt accompanied any accidental knocking of him over" (1910; Waitara).

Most important of all the boys' make-believe games were the cowboys-and-Indians games. The interesting fact about these games is that New Zealand children constantly played at "Indians," but seldom at "Maoris." "Generation after generation of New Zealand boys have fed with shining eyes on the stories of European and Indian Scouts and have scarcely realized that these men have had prototypes in their own land" (Mulgan 1944:59). One informant recalls:

Cowboys and Indians was the main game in this series, and there was no trouble in getting boys to take the part of Indians. They were scarcely regarded as enemies. It never occurred to use Maoris, though Maoris were playing with us all the time—I mean it never occurred to us to play "Maoris and Settlers." (1904; Petone)

This situation can be attributed to the fact that children's literature (and subsequently films) was filled with the exploits of the Indians. From 1870 onward the adventures of the arrow-shooting, scalping West spread across the world. Thus, E. S. Turner, speaking of the innumerable boys' magazines that came into being toward the end of the century, says:

Sooner or later, a fictional hero had to pit his wits against Red Indians. Dick Turpin was shipped to America by the Blue Dwarf and found himself caught up in some stirring adventures with the Mohicans. Jack Harkaway had numerous blood-thirsty encounters with redskins. . . . Sexton Blake undertook at least one enquiry on behalf of a Red Indian Chief. . . . And the boys of Greyfriars (Magnet) were as certain to be embroiled with Apaches on their trips to North America as they were on their trips to Paris. (1948: 233)

New Zealand had never seen such glorification of the militant relationships of the Maori and the pakeha (non-Maori). The shamefaced attitude to the Maori wars and the veneration of the anomalous Waitangi did not lead to the growth of a literature extolling the victories of "self-reliant" colonial against the ravaging Hau Hau.* Had the glorification of the Indian and of British soldiery elsewhere in the world not existed as a counterinfluence, it is conceivable that white children would have taken to games of "Maori and pakeha." There are a few records of children having played these games. For example:

Father's sister played at Red Indians at Waipu for a long time after the arrival of their ship from Nova Scotia, but the game was frowned upon by the strict elders of the Gaelic community. During the Maori wars the Red Indians became Maoris, though it was the same game of hiding and stalking. (1860s; Waipu)

I can remember some of us making a Maori camp on Primrose Hill, Paeroa, then covered with a dense growth of manuka intersected by survey tracks. (1900; Paeroa)

*The 1840 Treaty of Waitangi guaranteed Maoris the sovereignty of their lands.

Other ideas for games of this sort came from the events and literature of the time. Of great importance to the children of the day was the Kelly Gang, a group of notorious Australian robbers who visited New Zealand, in the 1880s and 1890s.

When Fred Jackman led the Ravensbourne Kelly Gang what stirring times! He was so enthusiastic in his tin helmet that he was quite a power among the scholars. What Mr. Kyte thought of the escapades we shall not tell. A broken leg ended Fred's career as Kelly. (Ravensbourne)

At Paeroa, with the forest at our doors and the exploits of the Kelly Gang our favourite bedtime story, we played bushrangers endlessly. (1900)

Some parents of the day used Ned Kelly to frighten young children into going to bed, just as others used the boogeyman or Wee Willie Winkie. Robin Hood, Jules Verne, the Wright Brothers, Ivanhoe, Tom Sawyer, and *Arabian Nights* all had an effect on make-believe combat games. Other current influences can be seen in the following recollections:

Russians and English with tussock and clod fights. (1880; Hampden)

Indians, stalking each other through patch and swamp. We had different tribes of Indians and made wigwams from flax sticks. (1880; Timaru)

De Wet and Boers. (1900; Dunedin)

When the Ohinemuri River spilled a flood of yellow water over the swamplands each winter, we were pirates with tin-lined boxes for our pirate ships, and many were the fierce Lepantos we fought. (1900; Paeroa)

Then there were the preparations for the great battles fought in Lindsay's paddock, the flax swords and koradi spears. How we girded on our swords and smote the French at Waterloo. (1870; Waianiwa)

On another occasion, there had been a bit of blood working up for days between two factions of boys. After holding a League of Nations meeting (although not called that then) we decided to settle it with the sword. Buck Wilson was the captain on the one side and I on the other. Some thought Wilson's side won and some thought it didn't. During the fight, Porky was pressing Whirlie McNaughton very hard until Whirlie forgot the League of Nations rules and hit Porky round the ears with his sword. I think that ended the fight. (1880; Waianiwa)

The make-believe games of the girls were, on the whole, of a gentler hue. The most important of these, of course, was Houses. Throughout the country in all historical periods, there are reports of children playing Houses in the presence and shelter of trees, particularly pine trees; perhaps there is something houselike in the nature of pine-needle softness. Informants recall:

All through primary school we played Houses with old, broken crockery and dolls. (1895; Catlins)

All the girls would bring flowers for their houses under the pine trees beside the school. (1895; Waikouaiti)

We played it in the flax tussocks and got into a row because we tied together the tussocks and flax for seats and the horses were tripped by them. (1885; Hampden)

Dolls were an inevitable part of the same game.

Like most children I preferred the plainer dolls, rather than the elaborately dressed ones, and the china heads to the wax, which got scratched and melted if left in the sun. We had, of course, dolls' tea parties with visiting friends. At one time there was a vogue among some of our group of cousins for tiny little black dolls about one and a half to two inches long. We made minute dresses for them and beds out of matchboxes. We had also a doll's house for which we made some of the furniture with assistance from my mother and a nursemaid. We made some of the things with matchboxes, and a set of tables and chairs out of blue-gum nuts, with pins stuck in for legs and for the backs. The backs were wound 'round with wool. (1890; Dunedin)

Even in that less shop-infested age, the game of *Shops* was nevertheless of great importance to young girls.

In our backyard we set empty cases a few yards apart. One child pulled a dobbin to imitate a grocer's cart. In it were leaves and tins which we made believe were stores. If there were only a few players, a child had to run ahead of the cart and be housewife in the shop. (1895; Moeraki)

With my sister as shopkeeper, we used to ask for the most impossible things, and of course the change was never right. (1870; Christchurch)

Dressing up was also as universal then as it is now:

Girls dressed in clothes of their elders and played with or without the aid of small tea sets, prams, dolls. They dressed up cats very exactly and very amusingly, especially when they thought no one was watching them. They copied the speech and gestures of visiting adults. No peculiarity was missed. (1880; Taranaki)

Schooling was also mimicked: "One would be teacher. I had a roll book and added fictitious names to make a sizable class. I used a piece of clay or charcoal for chalk" (1900; Moeraki). And it was commented on in rhyme:

Mr. Low is a very good man
Who tries to teach us all he can.
Singing, spelling, arithmetic,
He never forgets to give us the stick.
Mr. Low is a very good man,
He goes to church on Sunday,
He prays to God to make us good,
And gives us the cuts on Monday.
                    (1910; Palmerston)

Sometimes the teacher as portrayed in rhyme was diabolical rather than merely hypocritical:

Ole Pa Watson's a very good man
He goes to church on Sunday,
He prays to God to give him strength
To whack the kids on Monday. (ibid)

The girls probably played at more fairy-centered imaginative games than they do today, and these games tended to be played at home rather than at school. "We girls were very fond of playing witches, even to tying on a broom with which to fly. I lost two small front teeth after taking off from our back steps. Being great believers in fairies, my girl friends and I spent much time dressing. We wore lace curtains, not forgetting the wand and star" (1908; Auckland).

Religious training also probably had a greater effect on play than in later years:

On wet Sundays, dolls and cushions were led through a reverent
service of worship, and each had to repeat their golden text and
verse of hymn. . . . We once had to bring in a load of wood, so we
made a walk all 'round the lawn to represent Pilgrim's Progress.
The woodshed was the place of the cross where Christian dropped
his burden, the wood. . . . Every dead sparrow was given a reverent
funeral with the singing of "Safe in the Arms of Jesus." (1905;
Warkworth)

Because memory plays nostalgic tricks, or perhaps because
it is selected minds that do the remembering, it often seems
that it is the material of this chapter that gets remembered
rather than the material of the next which deals with more
barbaric kinds of play.

6 *barbaric pastimes*

Just as memory for the past tends to be selective in an idyllic fashion, so it often seems that current theories of play are uninformed by much acquaintance with history's often very severe nature. It is said, for example, that play is to be defined by the fact that it is free, voluntary, spontaneous, and an end in itself. As the material of this chapter shows, however, play was often only free in the sense the players were free from the teacher to carry out their own particular kinds of terror. Most of the play on school playgrounds was made compulsory by one's peers. One substituted the authority of other children for the authority of adults. But then this is the way it has been throughout history where most village or tribal members have done what they had to in festival and game along with their fellows. Through the larger haul of mankinds' history such play has usually been obligatory. Defining it as voluntary is a twentieth-century ethnocentrism owing its origins to the contrast between leisure and factory work, and to the identification of the capacity to play with the privileges of elite groups. What distinguishes play from other frames of living is not any voluntariness, but rather its passionate and exciting character. Play is a part of the Dionysian order of human expressiveness, rather than the Appollonian order of rationality. In addition to the roughness of many of the boys' traditional games, there were other ways in which boys could show a bellicose spirit. Most schools, for example, had a regular fighting pit, either in the school or in the paddock next door. It was to this area that the boys retired, out of sight, when the pressure became too great for the civil order of childhood: "We had an arena surrounded by black logs and blackberry bushes" (1895; Nelson). "There were hawthorn hedges 'round a gravel pit" (1900; Palmerston).

In the late nineteenth century individual and gang fighting seem to have been at their peak, a reflection, no doubt, of the ruggedness of the time—a time to which W. Pember Reeves (1934:231) could posit the question "How's trade?" and receive an appropriate answer: "There ain't bin a fight for a week." There is evidence that some teachers of the day with Stanley Hall the famous American child psychologist saw value in this "noble strife," although that was not always the case: "Two boys were punished for fighting in the school ground. They were encouraged by about thirty others, who shared in the dividend at a somewhat lower rate of payment."

Often the fights were arranged for the entertainment of the older boys.

They were arranged by the school bullies. (1895; Nelson)

You even had to fight your boy friends if it was arranged for you. (1895; Waikouaiti)

Small boys were induced to fight for sport. (1880; Waipu)

There was nothing organized for us, so we organized fighting. (1875; Dunedin)

Fighting was arranged in a paddock. If one flunked it, he was crowned. The victor patted him three times on the back and spat over his head—usually aiming too low. I never remember seeing any boy consent to crowning, even when threatened. Sometimes he was held. Otherwise, it was the ultimate humiliation which no one could stand and retain his self respect. (1900; Petone)

She learned further during the course of an incredulous investigation that every boy had to fight twice a week to retain respectability. Opponents were selected by a committee, and the fights took place on Wednesdays and Fridays. It was "too, too much" but perhaps not surprising when one looked at the fathers. (1890; Kaikohe)

Yes, now, as I come to think of it, the part of the school that I remember best were the fights—not dogfights in the play shed or such like crudities, but the formal, full-dress ceremonial affairs carried out as only schoolboys could. There was always in the background a "promoter"; he was the only one who seemed always to escape the punishment which fell on fighters and onlookers alike. The ring was a clearing in the bush, densely surrounded by rangioras and laurels, and there was always a strong smell of moist earth and rotting leaves. The two contestants removed their coats and reluctantly and carefully rolled up their sleeves—they really didn't want to fight at all, but honour and the "promoter" were adamant. The seconds fussed around; the onlookers selected comfortable seats on rotting logs and lighted up their collection of Old Judge butts and dock-leaf cigarettes. The referee stepped back onto a bunch of stinging nettle and the fight commenced. One or two swinging air-shots, then a contact, a bleeding nose, and then calamity arrived—calamity in the shape of the head teacher with a long supplejack. (1900; Pongaroa)

But the fights were not always arranged. Sometimes they arose casually, often in connection with football. Or "they arose out of arguments amongst the barrackers" (1890; Charleston). Girls are not often mentioned in connection with fighting, but there were some exceptions: "I saw many fights in the gravel pit amongst the boys, and on one occasion my sister scratched the face of one boy who was apparently winning in a fight with my brother. Sometimes girls fought in their own way—hair pulling, etc." (1890; Moeraki).

Group differences would also become a basis for group quarrels; some of these have already been mentioned in Chapter 2.

The personal and the arranged individual fighting were dwarfed by the mass fighting of the Reds and Blues. Can you imagine twenty Reds pitted against twenty Blues, making use with straps with buckles on them, with waddies, with six-foot manuka sticks, confronting one another in real battle array and at a signal, and with the use of rallying calls, entering the fray determined to overcome and rout the enemy? Blood flowed, heads and bodies suffered, until one or other side was overcome through sheer exhaustion and casualties! This section fighting assumed such ugly proportions that authority, in the shape of the headmaster, stepped in and prohibited it. (1880; Queenstown)

In towns the same sort of group fighting was usually known as gang-fighting.

Different gangs took different sides in the Paper Chase. (1900; Riwaka)

Each gang had a corner of the playground. Captured prisoners were held by force and by force alone. There were torn shirts and fingers bent back. When enough prisoners were caught, they would break out by force. (1915; Forbury)

When there was a gang quarrel we lined up in two lines in the gravel pit for an all-in fight. (1900; Nelson)

Some of these gangs (and the girls' groups or sets too) had their secret language and/or codes. For example:

Our particular form was to take the first syllable only of a word or if a long word perhaps take two syllables and add "ara." Thus, to take a sample, "Are you going to the pictures tonight?" became "Ara yara tara the para tara t'nara?" In my mother's day they used the form "irigo" in place of "ara." The same sentence was rendered: "Arigo yurigo girogo tirigo thirigo pirigo tirigo nirigo?" (1903; Petone)

The first and last syllables were distorted. Thus, time became "tut-i-mum." (1895; Collingwood)

I remember many such languages. One gang would attack another for daring to speak its language. (1915; Christchurch)

Some of the children of our school used to talk gibberish. It consisted of removing the first letter from each word and tacking it on to the end [with "ay" added]. Thus, boot became "ootbay." And lend me your pencil became: "endlay, eemay, ouryay, encilpay." (1895; Waitara)

Every gang had its secret language. No self-respecting gang could speak without "iry" at the end of a word. "Weiry, williry, goiry homiry!" Ordinary members would have this "iry" language, but the leaders would also have a letter language. For "you" they would say "Y-pip, o-pip, u-pip." (1875; Dunedin)

We removed the first consonant, added it to the end of the word, and added "way." Boot became "ootbway." These languages were considered worthwhile, but they took too much trouble for us to take them too seriously. (1885; Gisborne)

As we have seen, the individual and gang fighting of the day was frequently quite harsh, and the younger and less virile members of the playground must have often been terrorized by those stronger than themselves. But the harshness did not stop there. In many places there were also initiation ceremonies. Ducking under the tap was the most widespread of these customs, but there were others with a more unique flavor. Of these, King of the Golden Sword, well known in Wellington schools, was probably the most interesting: "The new boy was made to face the fence with his hands behind his back. There was a long ceremony about his crowning and entry into the school, and then finally the golden sword (which had been dipped into the latrine) was pulled through his fingers" (1890, Mount Cook, Wellington; Taita and Clyde Quay). Another initiation rite was Pee-wee Some More Yet: "The initiate was blindfolded and ordered to 'pee-wee some more yet' into another boy's cap. The cap turned out to be his own" (1890 Mount Cook, Wellington). One cannot help but be struck by the number of times the forbidden parts of the body were involved in these ceremonies. For example:

We would take the boys' and sometimes the girls' trousers down and then spit on their privates. (1900; Hutt)

One very interesting initiation ceremony was to take the new boys down to the stables and wait till a horse was urinating and then spin him under the stream. (1900; Petone)

He had to eat half a tin of pipis. (1900; Rangitoto)

We peed in his cap. (1900; Thomas)

He was invited to a tug-of-war with his cap. The cap was held in the teeth of the initiate and the teeth of one of the big boys. Hands were supposed to be behind backs. While the struggle was in progress, the big boy urinated over the initiate, who could not see the operation because of the hat but learned about it only gradually and with surprise. (1870; Takaka)

Other plays with similarly assertive but not quite so harsh notes were daring, slanging, scribbling, nicknaming, smoking, teasing, and torturing other children. There were no stereotyped forms of daring apart from the pranks mentioned above.

Daring could arise at any time. J. M. Thompson says in his
Bush Boys of New Zealand (1905), "The other boys had practically dared him to carry it out. That is enough for a boy. Dare
him to do anything and he will do it, if it is do-able." It was a
thing in itself which is further illustrated by F. L. Combs's
remark in the *Harrowied Toad* (1939): "Neither threats nor
appeals elicited an admission of guilt. He frowned and alleged,
'Henry Marcus dared me.' This seemed irrelevant but gang-
sters have their own mental processes." Scribbling often came
under the heading of obscene practices, and little can be said
that keeps within the laws of legitimate publication. There is,
however, one case of such poignancy that it simply cannot be
omitted. It was the year 1900 Dunedin and the children had
been sent out into the playground to write a poem:

It was an exceptional circumstance, and they made the most of it.
When they returned, the girls glibly recited their poems about the
wind in the playground, the flowers, and the sun. One group of
boys, however, had nothing to show. When asked what they had
done with all the time they had, they merely hung their heads,
tongue bound, and said nothing. Naturally, they were punished for
their laziness. In fact, however, they had been busily occupied
while in their playground. For although most of the boys had
commenced on their own poem, one boy had crowded all else out
of their minds with a verse which began "I've got a dog called Jack,
and he's got a cast-ironed cock," etc. After that, the whole group
devoted themselves to this poem. The final product was outstanding, but they could hardly let the teacher see it. It wasn't that sort
of a poem. In the lunch hour and after punishment, they still felt
the effects of their creative effort so strongly that they wanted to
do something with it. Some boys suggested that they should try to
get it in the weekly paper. Others laughed at the suggestion and
said the only way was to publish it themselves. But then who had
the money for that? And who'd take the rap anyway? Yet, they
couldn't let it go. It wasn't a thing like that. Finally, one boy had
a brilliant idea and so they all duly proceeded to that place and
inscribed it for all time on a wooden wall.

The sickness that was supposed to follow smoking appears to have been an exceptional rather than a normal occurrence. Most anecdotes, probably of a moralistic and cautionary origin, indicated the contrary. Arnold Lunn's statement in *The Harrovians* (1913) that "in defiance of all tradition they had not been sick" describes the more typical state of affairs. Where there was any sickness, it often followed from the fact that the children had treated the smoking as an endurance test, a competition between the smokers. It could, however, result from an overdose of cigar or bad tobacco or pipe. For example, "We found a pound of bad tobacco and all had some during the lunch hour. We were all sick and the school had to close for the day" (1900s Takaka). In earlier days, the older boys at primary school probably attached more importance to this activity than children did in 1950. Because smoking was severely punished it was all the more a venture. "We used to get tobacco off the Maoris, who grew their own. The teacher would give us a hiding when we entered school, because he could smell the tobacco on us. But that didn't matter, we smoked it just the same" (1900; Takaka). But then, until World War I, smoking was essentially a man's habit, not a habit of adults as a whole. The most common homemade tobacco mixture mentioned in all reports was that made out of dock leaves. One elderly informant reports that it was "as good as some of the tobacco today" (1875; Wakefield). Almost everything was tried by children. Some other mixtures mentioned were dock stalks, dock seed, fur at top of fern trees where ferns come out (two puffs nauseated), rag, clover, and dock leaves, fuchsia bark, and manuka bark with a little bit of cinnamon (which gave it a nice scent), dried fern leaves, straw, dry supplejack (very hot), poplar root (good if dry, but too hot), rim of butcher's basket, dock and manuka with a drop of methylated spirits, totara bark, dried tea leaves, bamboo cane, dried pith from elder trees, dry grass, dried maize leaves, pine needles, dried bullrushes, and, last but not least, "dried horse dung cut plug." Pipes were made of various materials. There are reports of clay pipes, bamboo and acorn pipes, old hard cabbage stems, reeds, empty fern sticks with burnt-out corks, the gum bole and a straw, and many others. Wrappers were made from newspaper; the tissue paper came from drawing books, toilet paper, and so on.

Most commonly, children of the day, both boys and girls, expressed their hostility through teasing tricks, teasing expressions, and teasing rhymes, although, as one identity has it, "it was always essential that tricks involving pain or ridicule for other boys should be staged by the more expert barbarian warrior so that there should be no subsequent 'thumping,' 'bashing,' 'lamming,' or 'neck-screwing' handed out by the victim." Some of the tricks of the day were Kick Donkey Kick, in which a player was blindfolded, led around, and allowed to kick other children. Finally, he was led up to a door and left there to kick at it until some person came out (1895; Moeraki). Other examples of tricks are:

A pin in the toe of one's kicking boot, a piece of stale meat in a rival's pencil case, rice shot through a peashooter, a push over a bending back. (1899; Waitara)

"What's a ship do when it comes into harbour?" "It ties up," and then flip out their tie. (1915; Dunedin)

We'd get a boy to play the Golden Rule. We all put our caps down and then had a race around the building. One boy lagged behind and removed all the caps except the cap of the newcomer. He was allowed to win the race. When he arrived at the end, he found his cap full of horse dung. (1870; Dunedin)

Putting the seed of the oat down a person's neck. We called them animated cats. (1875; Dunedin)

We would look at a girl's hair for a moment and then say in a shocked voice, "You have things in your head. They are white and they bite." On her replying, "Oh, I haven't," we would jeer, "Oh, haven't you any teeth?" (1910; Palmerston South)

We took hold of a person's arm and, rubbing it, said, "Skin a rabbit, skin a rabbit, chop him off here!" and with the word "here" dealt the person a blow on the inside of the arm opposite the elbow. (1895; Rockville)

One of the most common methods of attack was the teasing rhyme. Most universal of these was:

> Giddy giddy gout,
> Your shirt's hanging out,
> Five miles in
> And ten miles out.

"And every effort was made at the first sign of disaster to make the relative distance quoted more or less correct. We would pull their shirt out. A whole mob would rush 'round after the boy, chanting aloud the rhyme." In such a situation, there was only one effective response:

> Sticks and stones may break my bones,
> But names will never hurt me.

Most of the teasing rhymes centered around children's appearances. For example:

> Skin a ma links
> And lanky legs
> And big banana feet
> Jammy face. . . .

> Green eyes, greedy eyes,
> Brown eyes, pick the pies,
> Blue eyes, tell lies.

Other teasing rhymes referred to children's habits:

> Baby baby bunting,
> Set the cat a hunting,
> Round and round the porridge pot
> To get a piece of dumpling.

Tell tale tit,
Your tongue shall be slit,
And all the little puppy dogs
Shall have a little bit.

Cowardly, cowardly custard,
You ate your father's mustard.

Follow old mummy to market
To buy a silver basket,
When she comes home
She'll break our bones,
But follow old mummy to market.

The same aggressiveness manifested in children's play within the school was displayed outside it. In many of these plays, the children actually focused their hostility on adults themselves, which is not surprising considering the way grown-ups sometimes treated children. Children tended to pick on certain types of adults, however—foreigners in particular. These adults represented for children adult society at its weakest link. Here they could express their antagonism toward adult society without being fully culpable, for after all, were they not merely giving overt expression to popular prejudices held by their parents? The matter was not clear-cut, however, because the adults themselves were not consistent in their own attitudes. They did have a distaste for foreigners, but that distaste might not always be admitted. Boys were sometimes caught in the crossfire between these two attitudes.

Another amusing incident we recall took place in the old days when Indian hawkers were a plague going 'round the district. The senior boys of the school took a great delight in throwing mud at them. One day one of these hawkers marched into school and reported them. . . . When we were all assembled in Mr. Duncan's room, the Indian hawker standing beside Mr.

Duncan, he picked up a flower from the mantlepiece, smelt it, and then gave us a little homily in the following strain: "This, boys, is God's handiwork. A thing of beauty is a joy forever." Laying his hands on the shoulder of the Indian hawker, he resumed, "One of God's children. The cowards that threw mud." Pursing up his lips in his severest manner, he continued, "The boys who threw missiles, the devil's work. Hold out your hand." From memory I think he started at the top and finished at the bottom, soundly thrashing every boy from the fifth to the seventh standard. (1870; Green Island, Dunedin)

More often than not, the adults picked upon by the children were Chinese, a fact not unrelated to the belief held by many whites in the 1870s that the immigration of the Asians represented a threat to their own economic welfare. There appears also to have been a hint of unconscious sexuality projected into the subterranean accounts of the bodily enjoyments supposedly indulged in by Orientals behind curtained doors. It was a kind of projection perhaps not unrelated in children to the fear that if the "Chow" caught them pinching his peas he would take to them with a great flashing sharp knife. Unlike insults toward other foreigners, which were mainly of an aggressive and physical kind, insults to the Oriental were often of a symbolic nature. For example, one spat through crossed fingers and then rubbed the spittle into the ground with one's foot, an insult that would, it was said, bring down dire Oriental vengeance if performed in the face of the local greengrocer. Or one threw one's cap on the ground, clasped the hands in front and bowed the head, and trotted around it on tiptoe in a shuffling manner that was supposed to represent the Chinaman's gait. If this didn't suffice, then the following insult in schoolboy Chinese would most certainly bring the "Chink" on your trail:

Tu la marnie
Dubble I tite tie.

Girls could combine veiled insults with skipping:

Ching Chong Chinaman, bought a toy doll,
Washed it, dyed it; then he caught a cold.
Sent for the doctor; doctor wouldn't come
Because he had a pimple on his tum tum tum.

Or they could shout, as boys still do today,

Ching Chong Chinaman,
Born in a jar,
Christened in a teapot,
Ha ha ha.

Or, again, in pigeon Chinese:

A cabbagie, a carrotie,
Turnie up the lettuce-ie.

The Jews got their share of banter, and they too were eternalized in a skipping jingle:

Iky Moses, king of the Jews,
Sold his wife for a pair of shoes.
When the shoes began to wear,
Iky Moses began to swear.
When the swearing began to stop,
Iky Moses bought a shop.
When the shop began to sell,
Iky Moses went to H-E-L-L.

The same rhyme has sometimes been attributed to Nebuchadnezzar or to Pontius Pilate. Another was:

Get a bit of pork,
And stick it on a fork.
And give it to the Jew boy Jew.

People of German extraction have probably experienced the greatest amount of physical aggression at the hands of New Zealand children and youths, particularly during World

War I. In the last century, Roman Catholics were regarded in some places as "a byword and a hissing" (e.g., in the Nova Scotian settlement of Waipu). But often the children's attacks were focused on "odd" types of people rather than people of a specific ethnic group. There are reports of attacks on old bachelors, old spinsters, inebriates, but particularly on "mean" people who would provide excitement by giving chase when insulted—which shows that half the joy in these games lay in the thrill of escape involved in fleeing from the offended adult.

But children did not always attack society at its weakest link. Sometimes they tackled the archetypes of authority themselves. We have seen how they would tackle the teacher, and there is record of them trying out the policeman: "Many will remember how they delight in whistling 'Bobby Bird, you can't catch us, Bobby Bird' to the local constable" (1890; Blenheim).

There were many other characteristic tricks or pranks of the day, through which children directly or indirectly vented their feelings at the expense of older people as well as young. A common forbidden activity of the day was hanging on to the back of horse-drawn carts:

In those days, butchers' and bakers' carts drove from town. They were not in the habit of dropping spoils to delay us, but we were in the habit of hanging on behind. They would lash at us with their whip over the back of the cart, and once I caught the stinging cut of a lash on my ear. In retaliation, I called out, "Butcher, baker, candlestick maker, they all jumped out of a rotten potato." The man on the cart turned his head to tell me "Heh! young man, if you're not more polite, I'll take the whip to you." To keep up my end, I informed him I'd knock his head off. He stopped his horse, leaped down, and gave chase.

Many will remember our butcher in those days. He must have been the best-natured man alive to put up with us, as he did, hanging on the cart, following up, and crowding 'round as he served his customers. Our cry of "Give us a sausage, Joe" was seldom refused. We were always playing tricks on him, and only once did I ever see him lose his temper. We used to endeavor to pull his horse to a stop when he was going up the hill where the old school now stands, but he would use his whip to shake us off. One night we prepared for him by having a piece of fencing wire with a hook on it which we hooked on to his cart, and being out of reach of his whip, we succeeded in bringing his horse to a standstill. But then an explosion took place. I don't remember his words, but there was fury in them. He was down among us playing his whip in real earnest, and it was only a matter of a few seconds and we were over the fence and going for our lives. It was a case that time of the last through the fence being scabby. (1880; Otago)

Sometimes the children's fate was worse:

The coach to Dunedin used to stop at Fagerty's Hotel for watering the horses, which were glad of a spell, and then we got ready to hang on behind. The boys who could not get hold of a strap or something would call out, "Whip behind," and one ill-natured driver did it, too, as the coach went on. Once one of us tripped, and a heap of boys fell in the wet and mud. Dick and Bob Runciman and my little brother Dick were covered with the slurry from head to foot. We got them cleaned somehow and went on to school. (1868; Green Island, Dunedin)

There were other tricks, some even peculiar to certain localities, others common throughout the country. Of the first type:

We would imitate a rooster in the evening and set all the chucks [hens] in the valley going. (1895; Takaka)

I used to crawl up a culvert when I saw a horse coming, with the result that the horse would rear up to a stop at the culvert or jump over it. I had many a hiding for this. (1895; Nelson)

Ringing in the bell in the fish shop as we returned from the Band of Hope. (1910; Warkworth)

We would get a big sack. One would climb into it and then another would stand by the sack and ask passersby to help him carry it, much to the amusement of the hidden person. Naturally, it was done mainly at nighttime. (1910; Masterton)

About 1910, we had the practice of sending comic postcards to people. For folks who had no sense of humor, they must have been maddening. (Moeraki)

One common prank was Knick Knock. In this game, children knocked on someone's door, then ran away, but it could be played more elaborately:

In Tick Tack we stuck a pin into the middle sash of a window; a button was suspended from this on a piece of cotton. Then a long length of cotton was attached to the smaller piece and led away to the gate. The cotton was pulled every now and then and the button tapped against the window. It was nighttime, and folks would pull up the blind and peer out. Some more adventurous spirits would come out and investigate and would maybe get entangled with the cotton. Then the culprit would run away to some other house. (1900; Moeraki)

Usually a small youngster would be cajoled into this. (1885; Gisborne)

J. A. Lee in his *Children of the Poor* (1939) mentions the game of knocking on doors. It was known also as Tip Tap (1885; Waikouaiti). Another widely known trick was Jingle the Penny: "We tied a string to a penny with a hole in it, then hid behind a hedge or on top of a verandah. As a person stooped to pick it up, we would whisk it away" (1895; Ngakawau). Sometimes the same trick was played with a button or by throwing a nail from a height so that it sounded like money and caused passersby to look for a coin. The trick was not always a roaring success; often the scapegoats found the disappointment a little too much for them: "Once a lady took to us and beat us with her umbrella" (1914; Palmerston). A similar trick was Rats, in which a piece of fur off a woman's coat or a piece of rag was used. People would jump because they thought it was a rat. "Men would strike at it with their walking sticks and ten to one break them" (1890; Charleston). Another type of a similar nature was the Dummy Parcel: "There was a practice of making neat parcels and dropping them 'round the roads. Some of these were over a foot long. Those who made them would then hide and see who took them home. Everyone likes something for nothing, but I don't know what the finder said when he found the parcel contained dry grass, stones, mud, and cow dung" (1895; Moeraki). A similar but more vicious trick was Ooh My Toe. One Wellington boy of 1900 would put a brick in a bun hat and wait for the idle foot to kick it, and then wait for the name of the game! More often the gag took the form of a stone in a brown paper bag. One identity reported that his toes are bent to this day because he kicked such a bag with his bare foot (1890; Charleston). Again: "We would stretch a rope across doorways, empty people's ash cans on their verandahs, and tar doorknobs for unsuspecting hands" (1900; Dunedin). The poor ventilation of the day presented other possibilities. The trick was to fasten tight the door of one of the old pioneer huts (or of a schoolroom), then block the chimney with a sack and wait for the people inside to be smoked out. At Moeraki in the 1890s this was a favorite prank, of which there are several accounts:

It was done mainly to cantankerous old men. When water was thrown down the chimney, the ashes would fly up and nearly choke the inmate. The door would be shut tight so that the old chap could not get out. On one occasion, it was tried on an old chap who had been drinking. He was sitting by the fire. Meanwhile the wags had found a ribbon fish on the beach. It was fourteen feet long and a foot wide. They cut it into one-foot lengths and carried it to his hut and then threw it piece by piece down his chimney into the open fire. Naturally, the old guy thought he was getting the D.T.'s. He tried to get out, but the door was tied. He, in desperation, cut a hole in the back of his hut, which was partly made of sacks sewn together, and set out for a distant neighbor's.

On another occasion an old foreigner was the chosen bait.

The scene was an old fishing village. Each hut had a wide-open fire and a low chimney. One old chap who was very cantankerous was singled out to be teased. The boys played all manner of tricks on him. This night they made tiny pieces of paper up into balls, each ball containing a little gunpowder. These balls they tossed down the chimney into the half-dead open fireplaces. The old man, an Austrian, said afterwards, I lie in bed and puffet my pipe. Tommit my cat, he lie by the fire. All at once "fiss bung," and Tommit hit the bloody roof. I not get out fishing for a week. Every time I stir the fire "fiss bung, fiss bung" all the bloody time.

The schools had their share too. At Owaka in 1870 the schoolroom was 20 by 12 feet with two small windows and a clay chimney. From two different sources comes an amusing story of how two boys who were asked to get wood for the school fire piled on plenty of green sticks. On their way outside, presumably to put away the ax, they fastened the door on the outside and placed a bag over the chimney. Soon the room was thick with smoke, and it was only after some hard bargaining regarding the matter of reprisals that the culprits agreed to allow the choking occupants to get into the fresh air. But the culprits weren't always so lucky:

Then there was the time that the two young boys were sent out to burn the rubbish. Some logs were smoking badly so they carried them under the ventilator and blew the smoke up. All was quiet for a while when all of a sudden the children yelled, "The school's on fire," and started a stampede, until the master looked out of the window and saw the cause. The fire was not so hot then, but the seats of these young gentlemen's trousers became quite hot a bit later.

One of the most universal boyhood attacks on society was throwing stones: "We used to throw stones on the roofs of old diggers who were on their own—mainly because that enabled us to make a good getaway" (1895; Charleston). Occasionally it was the schoolteacher's roof that suffered, sometimes the thrower himself: "Caned W. K. for throwing stones. This boy is a persistent thrower of stones, and on this occasion struck another small boy over the eye" (1910; Papatawa School Logbook). Occasionally the activity had its humorous side:

An incident comical to all except J. H. occurred one day. A neighbour's fowls, learning from acute observation that the midday spell at school brought to them golden opportunities, paid regular visits to us as we ate our meal in the playground. One day, one of our favourite chums, Jim Hayward, in a thoughtless mood, threw a stone at a young rooster, thus ending its school days. To cover up the crime, and believing that dead roosters tell no tales, we threw the bird under the school. But murder will out, and later in the day the angry owner arrived on the scene and ordered Jim to crawl doglike under the school to retrieve the fowl. While he was obeying the irate lady, acting as the agent of Providence, which we are told "shapes our ends," proceeded to belabour poor Jim on the part of his anatomy for the purpose. James thought the company of a dead bird safer than that of an angry woman whose patience gave out before his. (1870; Waianiwa)

Equally universal among predatory boyhood was orchard-raiding, and to a lesser extent pilfering and "pinching" of other sorts. Perhaps it is true, as Lee says in *Children of the Poor*

(1939:144), that "children like the birds, the field mice, possums, see fruit on trees as something to which they have proprietary raiding rights. Stealing fruit is a great social game."

How one could recall the orchards, the pea paddocks, and the hen roosts robbed with brigandlike bravado, and the thrashing which befell the robbers when complaints were brought to schoolmasters, the pinching of crayfish from Jim Crossley's fish cart, which remained unattended by the Criterion stables while Jimmy was quaffing a tankard of Dodson's ale at the nearby hotel. (1900; Blenheim)

What would school life have been without Robertson's bush and the fear of Mrs. Robertson? We roamed through the tracks in it and in season enjoyed the lawyer berries. We also feasted on the white berry of the stinkwood, the brambles, and the fuchsia, climbed the white pine trees for their luscious red berries, and ate the green gooseberries on the trees that were quite plentiful through the bush. We climbed the totara tree beside the clearing for no other object than to climb down in double-quick time when we heard Mrs. Robertson in her own particular accent calling, "What are you boys doing there?" (1870; Waianiwa)

We would crawl half a mile on our stomachs to pinch a turnip. It was a great adventure, but we didn't really care much about the turnip. (1885; Nelson)

Some of the raids and pilfering had direct relationship to the state of the raiders' appetites. Just as there was more scope for raiding orchards in those days, there was also, on account of hunger, more incentive for it. Consider the following episode:

On the homeward way one evening, as the baker's van drove swiftly past us, the door flew open and a loaf of bread fell out. We ran for it like a lot of hungry fowls. One chap got it. I grabbed half of it from him and sold a piece of it to one boy for six fishhooks, giving another a bite at the remainder for a few marbles. The loaf was polished off in quick time; our long walk home made us hungry enough to make short work of a windfall like a loaf. (1880; Dunedin)

He and the boys used to annex the goats owned by Mr. Pinner's parents, take them into the bush, milk them, and drink the milk. (1880; Ravensbourne)

It was a common trick of ours to kill a fowl. We put feed outside of the wire netting. When the fowl put his head through to eat, we hit him over the head with a stick, then reached under the netting and dragged him away. In the bush we made a fire until the stones were red hot. We covered the fowl with clay, and put it on the red hot stones with a wet sack over it. As a result, all the entrails and the feathers fell out and we ate the rest. (1880; Dunedin)

Besides their direct and indirect attacks on adults and their institutions, the children would often take a tilt at the conventional standards of adults. Some of them were no less interested in the obscene and the taboo than are some of their 1950 counterparts, although it is doubtful that in an age of poorer communications such things as obscene rhymes could spread as quickly as they can today. But there were exceptions: "To get new swearwords, we used to go to the Te Aro wharf and hear the cattle landed and get our vocabulary very much enlarged" (1870; Wellington). One informant who spent his primary period at Naseby, a gold-mining district in Otago described the manner in which the boys at his school competed among one another to tell obscene jingles and stories: "The boy who could tell a new dirty jingle became the hero of the day. We often chanted these in groups to the girls to make them laugh or to disgust them." Examples like this last one are as seldom paralleled today as they were exceptional in the 1890s.

In the stories, Pat and Mike always held a central role— not to forget of course, the scatalogical Mustard.

The majority of primary-school obscene rhymes referred to

the excretory processes, and the most universal of the more innocuous versions were the two that began "Ink, dink, pen and ink" and "Red, white, and blue, you dirty kangaroo." In the later primary years and at the secondary level, sexual interests predominated and were celebrated extensively by limerick and parody. No old boy forgets "Down in the Valley," "Abdul a Bull Bull Amir" or the "Marble arch."

There was also a place for experimentation, and it is clear in this connection that the romantic sexless conception of boy-girl relationships portrayed in some literature about children is a little removed from true life. Sometimes this interest was expressed indirectly. As Betty Smith says in her *A Tree Grows in Brooklyn,* "a few hypocrites devised such evasive games as 'playing house' or 'doctor,'" though indirect games did not need to be a mere camouflage. Several informants told of games played by boys and girls in which they imitated the sexual intercourse of animals, for instance, roosters and hens and bulls and cows. Most reports of actual experimentation and mutual inspection come from rural areas; the vast proportion of "symbolic" expressions of the same interest—rhymes and stories—come from urban schools. Among boys, especially secondary-school boys, "zipping" that is, the ripping open of another's pants, was universal, although New Zealand boys did not make a habit of collecting the buttons as did English boys.

Urinating competitions and competitions in what have been termed "unfortunate sounds" were also widespread, the latter generally after lunch or after a special preparatory diet of dried fruits and nuts. There were victories to be had in this too: "I remember the champion of my class. His great ambition was to 'play' through 'Fight the Good Fight' but he could never get further than 'Christ.'" But it was a practice that had its casualties. Occasionally then, as now, a breach of conventional standards came before the eyes of the teacher. For example, the following recordings in several school logbooks:

Thrashed severely, A. H. for interfering indecently with the girls. (May 1901)

Today I punished a boy . . . for using obscene language in the playground. The punishment was administered with a light cane over the buttocks. (1901)

Mrs. P. called at the school this afternoon to investigate a complaint of using bad language which Mrs. W. had laid against her son. The boy admitted the words complained of, but the girls had given him some provocation by teasing him. As he is only eight years of age and this is the first time a complaint has been made, it is probable he did not understand their impropriety. He has promised better behaviour. (October 1904)

Here then are some of the more brutal, the more furtive and the more inversive orders of children's play. These protest plays express peer dominance, invert the status quo and create a community of players impelled by the harsh adult order to generate their own harsh worlds. One joins the action or is crushed, rejected or scapegoated. If we wish to reach for universalist definitions of play we do better to discuss excitement or passion (which can be negative and cruel) as well as inversions of the normative social order. These form a better basis for such definitions than notions of freedom of choice, nonseriousness, positive affect, egalitarianism, and flexibility.

7 out of school, out of doors

Pioneer children spent their time exploring their surroundings rather than playing formal games, and this continued to be true after compulsory schooling was established
and formal games began to be played regularly on the school
grounds. What was striking about their play was the way
they looked after themselves and made their own play
materials. When one reads accounts of their constructive play
with shooters, projectiles, and motile objects, their experiments and explosions, their nature play and play with animals, dams, flowers, grass, and trees, their swimming, skating, their hunting plays, bird-nesting, rabbiting and eeling,
one cannot help feeling that where these children were sufficiently well fed and were not overworked and narrowly educated (as was so often the case) the rural play life of the day
was admirably suited to the development of their natural in-

interests, their initiative, and their independence.* For example, the child playing out-of-doors had to have some tools to work with, and the primary piece of equipment was a pocketknife. As a play object, the knife was the all-purpose tool of childhood. It was used in school for erasing inkblots, sharpening slate pencils, and carving initials, and out of school for Stagknife, Pegknife, whittling, carving, and making shooters, shanghais, and whistles. The best type of knife, it is said, was the "pampa" knife made in Sheffield, England, which cost one shilling. It could be used for many purposes and yet remain sharp for months:

With it we cut our names and initials everywhere possible, though chiefly on telegraph poles, any trig station available, the front of the town hall, on different parts of the bridge, on the edging of the wharf, and on school desks. During the First World War, boys began buying a similar curved-blade knife, only this time they were made in Japan. (1910; Wellington)

The primary piece of equipment made with the pocketknife was a shooter: a shanghai. Shanghais have been the all-time most popular improvised weapon of New Zealand boys. Occasionally they were known as catapults. After a careful search, a suitable "prong" would be cut from a tree and trimmed; apple trees and willow trees were often chosen. To each side of the prong was fastened firmly a piece of boot lace 3 to 4 inches in length. To this, 8 to 9 inches of elastic was tied; both round and flat elastic were used, but the round elastic was preferred—and could be bought at the local store for about sixpence. It is said that it took a good man to pull 4 to 6 inches of that elastic. When there was no money to buy the elastic, as

*Although the sources for this chapter, like the others, were multiple, I wish to pay special tribute to Mr. W. H. Clark of Wellington, who contributed several notebooks written especially for this purpose. He was a man of prodigious memory and concern for times past in New Zealand childhood. Any unassigned quotations are his and refer to New Plymouth during the years 1880–90. In addition, references to Waitara and Taranaki are his.

was generally the case, a woman's garter or a baby's feeding tube acted in its stead. Two short pieces of boot lace were attached to the elastic; these were joined by the "holder," which was an oval piece of leather about 1⅛ inches long and 1 inch wide, taken from the tongue of an old boot. One informant recalls, "They took all day to make and half an hour to break." Stones were most frequently used for missiles. These were carefully picked off the riverbed, and the best were about half an inch in diameter. They were kept either in the pocket or in a specially made pouch like a marble bag. The more fastidious would buy a shanghai bullet mold and spend hours melting down lead and pouring it into this mold. "At the end of the day half a dozen would be made and then fired away in five minutes" (1875; Dunedin). All the animals in the neighborhood were prospective targets. Cats and dogs, but more especially birds, rated as high priority. Informants talk of going out as boys for a day's bird-shooting with shanghais. Special targets were made of bottles and tins and of paper in a school slate frame. Occasionally there were gang wars and at times, windows were broken. "All the boys had them at school. We used them constantly, in and out of the playground and on the way to school" (1900; Waikouaiti). Sometimes a boy would be caught with one and the whole lot would be confiscated and lined up on the mantlepiece.

Slings were not used as much as shanghais. They consisted of a leather pouch 3 inches by 2 inches with string about 2 feet in length attached to each side of the pouch. The first string was gripped by the fingers, the sling twirled around the head, and then the second string, which had been held between the finger and thumb, let go. But slings were erratic and therefore not as popular as the shanghai. Another variety was the leather sucker-type. A boy would get a piece of sole leather from the boot-maker, then put a string through the middle of it and soak it in water. If this was later pressed down on a stone or other small object, it would lift it out of the road. These stones were then swung around on the sucker until they flew off. In yet another type of shanghai-sling the elastic was attached to one stick—not a forked stick—and then also attached to a pouch which held the missile. It was fired partly by pulling the elastic (as with shanghais) and partly with a slinglike downward swoop of the arm.

But a shanghai or sling was not enough by itself. In season every boy also had to have a bow and arrow. The construction of these absorbed immense amounts of time. The bows were made of supplejack, green willow, broom, bamboo, umbrella ribs, and corset wires; the arrows of toitoi, dock, bamboo, pampas, slithers of Australian hardwood "pinched from the school fence"; the arrowheads of nails.

We used shoe nails for the points of our arrows. We'd pick them up in the blacksmith's shop. We'd get it in the neck if we had a proper nail. (1890; Waikouaiti)

At a later stage we sharpened our nail heads. One boy received such an arrow through the lobe of his ear. An irate parent withdrew the arrow and boxed the ear into the bargain. (1890; Gisborne)

I made a crossbow once out of broom and a piece of wood with a trigger attached to the wood, but this was not general. (1905; Naseby)

I invented a bow that I have not seen anywhere else. It was made of umbrella wires arranged to make a bow about four feet long and bound tightly with fishing line. Though not so long as many of those made of supplejack, the bow could drive a toitoi reed (bound with a little cotton at the notch end, and with a sharpened nail into the head and firmly bound there) a distance of two hundred yards. Only one mate was let into the secret, and in my time he did not split. Others tried the toitoi arrows, but they were not effective without the nailhead, and nobody struck the bamboo idea. My mate and I used to play Indians against each other with these distinctly dangerous arrows in a big boxthorn-bound paddock owned by his parents. I wonder now how we escaped serious injury, as I once killed a cat with one of the arrows. (1880s; Taranaki)

The willow bows made in the spring were preferred, and with these bows the boys played Ned in the Blockhouse, the Blackfeet Versus the Crows, and shot arrows at paper and other targets or enemies. "We called ourselves the William Tell boys. We didn't take our bows to school, though we took our slings concealed in our pockets" (1880; Tapanui). Opinions vary as to the success with which the progeny of Tell and Hood scored hits on the local bird life.

In addition to the shanghais and bows, a variety of other shooters played an important, if smaller, part in boyhood. There were the clay shooters, which were based on the same principle as the ubiquitous ruler and chewed paper pellet. The end of a spring willow stick or piece of broom was stabbed into the end of good apples or potatoes (rotten ones would not stay on the end), and the stick was swung with all possible strength to send the missile a long distance. More often than not, mud was used: "We would pelt a roof from a concealed spot a long way off. The mud went at a terrific speed" (1900; Hampden). The same practice has been known more recently as Bula Bula (1925; Invercargill).

Popguns were made from a straight piece of elderberry wood about 8 inches long with the pith removed. The boys who owned an elderberry tree were the envy of all the others. The gun was fitted with a ramrod bound at one end with rag to make it tight. Paper was chewed into two wads, which had to be wet. One was pushed in one end and the other in the other end. The ramrod was pushed a short way into the rod and then pushed quickly against the stomach. Out would shoot the wad. By this process the second wad would take the place of the first and would, in turn, be shot out after a third wad had been inserted. "I used a marble once. It was a perfect fit. The compression was just right. I was staggered when it broke a window thirty to forty yards away" (1895; Waikouaiti). Usually, however, these popguns would fire only a few yards. They were essentially indoor weapons. Quill guns were made in the same way. A piece of stick was used as a ramrod, and the ammunition was potato, carrots, or parsnips, into which one end of the quill could be stabbed.

Spring guns were made of an elderberry tube with part of

the pith cut and a slit in the bark. A spring from an old corset was bent up by hand at one end of the slit, and when the spring was released it shot a missile out of the hollowed portion of the tube. The ammunition of stones, wheat, or grain lay up against the bent spring before it was released.

Peashooters too were made out of the elderberry tree. The elderberry must certainly have been a highly treasured tree. Once again the pith was taken out, and any suitable small objects were used for missiles, the most-reported being elderberries, wheat ("it is better to suck it straight off your hand into your mouth than to take it through the spout"), mouse peas, and hawthorn berries. Seeds of any sort could be used, however. "Our shooter was a piece of cane bamboo, and in the early days at the silent pictures we fired them at bald-headed men. As soon as they came in they'd be scratching."

Water-shooters were not used as much in those days as they were later, when children had the commercial toy at their service. There is, however, occasional report of squirting water through a peashooter or out of a punctured tennis ball or rubber breast-bottle tube of the old type. These were known as "sausages."

A constant in-school shooter, but one without much power, was the dart. The paper dart was for gliding to the other side of the classroom; the dart made out of a split pen knib was for sticking into the ceiling. These darts, together with the wads of chewed paper shot off the end of a ruler, were the children's chief contribution to the interior decorations of the day—that is, when added to the ink splashes and the holes and initials carved by idle pocketknives.

Next in importance after the shooters were play objects that children could themselves project across or into space. These were the projectile toys, chief among which was the kite.

Kites took all day to make and a few moments to smash, but at least there were no electric wires in their way. (1875; Nelson)

The frame was made of light wood in the form of a cross. The four corners were joined up with string and the whole area pasted over with paper. The loop in front which we used to adjust its angle was called the bridle. It had the usual tail composed of rolls of paper joined together to steady it. We used to send messages (sometimes called messengers) up to the kite by slipping a piece of paper or cardboard with a hole through the centre onto the lead string. We would watch the wind carry them up. Then one day a friend brought us a box kite from Wellington, the framework of wood covered by a light, strong material. And she was a beauty! So steady, and flew further and higher than any other kite that I have ever seen. We used a whole ball of binder's twine obtained from an upholsterer. It was very light and strong. (1899; Waitara)

At a later date a large shipment of Japanese kites arrived here, very much like the shape of an aeroplane made of tough scarlet paper and with a cane foundation. These would also go high when skillfully handled. They had no tail and could be flown by running with them. (1890; Nelson)

There are reports of strenuous days spent with enormous tailed kites fighting the high winds, of kite string made with flax when no other string was available (1870; Taieri), and finally of fights between kites when one kite attempted to pierce the other with its head.

On occasion the boys went through a spate of whip-making, usually prompted by the passage of bullock wagons through the township and the reading of Australian and American stories (1880; Taranaki).

The ordinary whip was a plain three or four plait, always in green flax, but occasionally someone would do a twist. A good specimen of a twist was greatly admired, but to get the required evenness it had to be held so tightly as to make the hands ache terribly; and it was difficult to hold the twist in order except by hand. Plaiting did not need the tension of twisting and could be left and taken up again, day after day. The ideal whip was about twelve feet long, though we used to hear frequently of someone somewhere else who had done a full-length stockwhip of twenty to twenty-five feet. Although our ambition was always to accomplish this feat, we seldom did more than twelve. Life is too short. The three-plait was easy to do and very quick, over and under, over and under, taking the outside strands right and left alternately and crossing them over the centre piece and under the opposite strand. A couple of yards an hour was not an uncommon rate of progress. The four-plait was more difficult and slower, but it made a real workmanlike and solid job. Anyone with a four-plait whip, evenly done and of six or seven feet in length, could command almost anything in the child's world in exchange, though usually such whips were retained because the envy and admiration it aroused was beyond price. A whip that was seldom seen because it required patience rather than skill was made by crushing gently the green parts of the flax without injuring the fibre, and then carefully scraping off all the pulped parts, leaving the soft threads of fibre. This was then rolled and rubbed in a cloth to remove even the colour and washed with warm water and soap. The result was a fibre soft as silk and pure white. This was usually three-plaited and, owing to the trouble of preparation, about four feet was about its maximum length. I can remember only about four of these whips in my childhood. Handles were of supplejack, and the way they were attached was important because the whip could easily slip off. The big boys usually did the job with that condescension which only a big boy can produce properly. Many expeditions have I, in company of boys, made to swamp for flax, where beautiful six-feet blades grew, and even now the bitter acrid smell of flax takes me back a long way and arouses memories of how we used to eat the wax from the joint of these flax blades. How bitter it was, and how we pretended to like it so often that finally we did. Even now I seldom handle flax without tasting, yes, and liking, its unpalatable flavour. (1903; Petone)

The whips were used for a variety of purposes, for example, to whip a tin off a post or a small stone off a larger one. The one who could do it from the greatest distance and without shifting the support stone was the winner. Not infrequently whips were used to show one's opinion of an undesirable associate. Most

important, however, were the whip-cracking competitions—
Who could make the loudest noise? Cracking with an up-and-
down movement was easy, but it was a real achievement to
crack by swinging the whip round the head and then changing
direction. This would produce an earsplitting sound.

The fastest method of self-transport in this era were the
sledges, which were of all kinds. Some had runners and cross-
bars. The important skill with the runner variety was to know
how to jerk up the front over the sheep tracks; otherwise, one
would pitch headfirst over the front when the runner stuck in.
Sometimes these sledges were found ready-made as, for example, when boys used a heavy but short wooden ladder with
sharp points. Others were made from the curved board of a
barrel with bars across to hold the seat and feet: "These slid
well and were fast, but more important, they were light to
carry. They went extremely well on the dry hillside or after
they had been greased with lard or candle-grease" (1890; Akaroa). Others were made simply of boards.

In the old cemetery in Trafalgar Street we used boards which
became very slippery with use. We either sat on them or lay down
and went headfirst. At one time in our own garden we had a shorter
slide, and each of us had our own sledge made from boards taken
from an old derelict house nearby. These had a footrest nailed
across one end and each had a name. Mine had "Hinemeni"
painted across one end. (1880; Nelson)

Simpler still were the nikau palm leaves—the cabbage tree.
One sat in the bowl and another pulled it down the hill by
the leaves. In more recent years boys have often found a
piece of old roofing iron even more accessible than the cabbage tree.

If boys could project their power across and through
space with shooters, sledges, and kites, they could also fill
up the same space with noise. The known could overcome
the unknown. Foremost among the noisemakers was the
whistle.

Before the spring sap rose in the willows, we would carefully select sticks suitable for making whistles, cut off a short length, and run a knife 'round it at one end. The bark on the longer end was then tapped sharply all over with the back of the pocketknife until it could be drawn off without damage. Then a notch was cut in the white stick pith and a shallow edge made from it to the end. The bark was then slipped back on and the proud possessor whistled all the way home. These whistles were spoiled as soon as they became dry, so every now and then we would slip off the bark and thoroughly lick the white stick before putting it on again. (1900; Lower Moutere)

Sometimes the sticks were soaked in water. This helped to lift off the bark. Occasionally they were painted and varnished to preserve them for a longer period. Whistling was also produced by a circular piece of tin bent in two with a hole through it; with grass stretched between the thumbs; with a leaf in the mouth, and with two fingers in the mouth.

Another noisemaker, and one of some anthropological repute, was the bull-roarer, which was made of a piece of wood about 15 inches long and 1 inch wide. Notches were cut in it, and it was attached at the end to a piece of string. When it was swung around the head it made a roaring sound. "It was connected in our minds with Ned Kelly and the bushrangers" (1875; Dunedin).

The "snory bones," as it was called at Moeraki in 1900, was made of a piece of string on to which was threaded a button. The button was moved along to the centre of the string, which was then held in both hands and twirled until the string was sufficiently twisted to be "wound up." If the string was then suddenly pulled hard, each hand opposing the other, the rotation of the button as to the string unwound would make a strong buzzing sound.

A certain shell found on the beach could be made into a kind of horn if holes were made in certain places. It was like a miniature conch shell and it made two distinct sounds. Horns were also made from bullock horns. The tip was cut off at the small end, then pressed to the lips at the side of the mouth. When the shell was blown into, it made a booming sound. In neither of these sound-producers, however, could the sound be varied much. A "conch shell" made with the cupped hands was much more popular, as it could produce a greater variety and volume of sounds. The thumbs of the two hands were placed together in a vertical position. The right hand was then clasped over the left, and the left folded around the side of the right. The palms of the two hands were hollowed but closed all around. The thumbs were bent to turn their first knuckles into a mouthpiece. By blowing through the thumbs and varying the opening made by the fingers of the left hand, some very distinctive sounds could be made. These sounds were used as signals that enabled mates (friends) to give each other urgent calls, warnings, and scraps of agreed information.

The thick, fleshy end of flax blades were cut off about 2 feet 6 inches long and partly split down the middle. These were known as flappers. One side was bent to form a hinge, which enabled the top side to crash against it when the two were flapped together.

Another outdoor interest of the time was in fires and explosions, which were always an attraction. There was ample scope for both. "I used to delight in going over the back country and lighting fires," says one informant (1870; Richmond); the adult pioneers gave the children ample examples for this sort of thing by burning off the bush. The magnifying glass was used to make fires then as well as now, but it was, like the pocketknife, a multipurpose toy. It could be used for its legitimate function, to peer at stamps, or it could light paper in the sun, burn initials on wood, be used to torture small animals enclosed in boxes, or to "burn" the arms of one's fellow or rival gang members.

Probably of greater interest were the explosions that could be contrived with gunpowder. Miniature brass cannons, no less than shanghai elastic, were sold in the shops for threepence and sixpence. Since most houses had a gun, and live and legitimate targets were often to be had from the doorstep, there were ample gunpowder and used cartridges available. Therefore explosions were frequent. Many accounts of explosions all have their own fascination.

We used to obtain a discharged .303 cartridge case, file a "touch hole," ram home a charge into the breach, fill up with a paper wad, sprinkle some small pieces of powder over the touch hold, apply a match, and then run. The cartridge would fly in one direction and the missile in the other; some resorted to tying the cartridge firmly to a wooden base, which held it in position at the time of discharge. (1899; Waitara)

One day at school I goggled the eyes of the boys in one of the back desks (the old style that imprisoned six or seven pupils) by pulling from my pocket something they all knew about but probably none had ever handled—a loaded cartridge. A note "I'll show you at playtime," was passed along. And when the break came and all had handled and had a good look at the treasure, "Do you want to hear it pop?" was sufficient to have about half a dozen to follow me through the broken palings of the fence into an old Maori cemetery that adjoined the school grounds. The cemetery was totally neglected and tall, dry cocksfoot covered most of the graves, but there was one where a big mound of concrete marked off the burial place of some Maori of higher rank. "Get behind me and watch what happens," I said, as I seated myself on the stone. Then, holding the cartridge between two fingers and thumb, I tap-tap-tapped the business end against the edge of the concrete. Presently off she went with a bang that half deafened us and knocked one or two of the youngsters off the side of the tomb with fright. A few exclamations, and it was a quiet and rather pale set that sneaked back into the playground. Only the fact that my father was a very particular sportsman and used brass cartridges for his smokeless powder (I often refilled them) saved my fingers. (1880; Taranaki)

Sometimes, however, the schoolteacher heard the blast. This was the case at Mangatainoka when the pupils let them off in the school shelter shed. He could hardly avoid hearing that. At other times he caught them in possession. Here are some entries from the Ngaturi school logbook of 1901. The familiar methods of schoolmaster detection are carried through to their customary climax.

September 15:   Found boys in possession of blasting powder, fuse, etc.

September 17:   Asked Messrs. Hansen and Martin to protect their explosives from boys who were bringing them to school.

September 18:   Noticed explosion in bush at dinner hour. Detained boys for a week at dinner hour.

September 19:   Told that fuse had been taken from under bridge. Held an enquiry. Found Allen Brown was the one who had taken it. Punished him severely. Children forbidden ever to leave the school ground on any pretext.

September 23:   Complaint from Mr. Brown that his boy had been the scapegoat for the others. Held another enquiry: found that Allen Brown had been the chief culprit, though another had assisted.

[*Report of inquiry held on September 23:*]

Boys who were within five yards of barrow at time of fuse cutting [eighteen names given]. Eye witnesses to the actual cutting [four names given] who all swear Allen Brown was the culprit. Did Allen Brown have any boy assisting him? The four eye witnesses all answered in the negative. Did any boy see James Stewart touch the fuse in any way? No. Nor any other boy? No. How was it A.M. and B.O. were so close and yet saw nothing? They both state they were on the bridge looking in another direction. Whose knife did A.B. use? James Stewart's, confessed by him. (Question to J.S.) Did you know at the time you lent Allen your knife that he intended to cut the fuse? Yes. Signed. . . . James Stewart was punished as an accomplice.

Despite the tendency to use real gunpowder for their explosions, boys also made them without gunpowder. One method was to put two or three matches in the bottom of a cartridge in paper and then fill the cartridge up with clay. This was then held over the fire on a wire. Combustion and air pressure blew out the clay, and the "gun" could be aimed at targets. In more recent years a similar sort of gadget called a "bolt bomb" had been widely used by New Zealand children. Some wax match-heads are put into a large nut and two bolts are screwed tight into this nut from either side. When it is thrown on the ground, the friction explodes the matches and parts the bolts violently.

Having covered the common homemade outdoor play objects, we now turn to other outdoor activities. For example, as Rudyard Kipling declares, in *Stalky and Co.,* in summer all right-minded boys build huts. And at Wellington College in the 1880s the boys were as "right-minded" as Kipling would have them be.

At the back of the college was the same dense scrub growing on the high ground, with a *little Pinus Insignis* dotted here and there. It was amongst this scrub, and sometimes in the gorse, that we constructed manuka houses of whares, into which we used to retreat and hatch mischief. Some of these "houses" were elaborate affairs, having a roof and walls of interwoven manuka. The floor was usually levelled and made comfortable with bundles of scrub. The charm of these retreats lay in their privacy.

Not all the huts and forts of the day were as well made as the one in this account:

Our hardest and most sustained work was put into building a fort. Between the school and town on a piece of first-class unoccupied unfenced land was some of the thickest gorse I have ever seen. My townmate and I made a narrow, low, winding tunnel, with one or two offshoots at the sides ending in dead ends, leading into the middle of this big gorse patch. There we cut some of the gorse for a space of about ten feet by ten hacked up by the gorse and pulled it out piece by piece. Two poles from the bush were let into the ground upright and tied back to the gorse at each end. A rope slung from pole to pole supported a piece of old sailcloth for roof and was tied back to the gorse at the sides. The walls were then lined. Many trips were made to the swamp for raupo. This was straightened, tied in half a dozen places to make little bundles about one and a half inches thick and long enough to reach from the ground to the sailcloth roof. They were tied close together one by one to the gorse at the back all 'round the hut. The flax tying was reinforced by split supplejack lathes interlaced. (We'd seen plenty of Maori whares. I'd spent a holiday of three months in one once.) Then the floor was dug out, about six inches deep with a piece left about two feet wide all along each side and about one foot wide at each end, the two-foot strips for beds and the one-foot strips for seats. The dirt from the excavation was piled up against the raupo walls to raise the beds and the seats, and then it was flattened. The seats had a covering of cut-down sacks, and the beds had a good thickness of dry fern and a sugar-bag pillow holding the soft toweled heads of the "bully-bulls," the raupo heads. All this was done in great secrecy, and care was taken that no evidence remained near the entrance. The fort was used for "koreros," toy-making (tops, whips, bows and arrows, etc.) and for feasts. Food was brought from home, including herrings we had caught, cooked, and put into vinegar. But "bullies," mushrooms, and whitebait were among the things cooked in the fort in old fruit tins on wire tripods over two or three ends of candles stuck on a board. Drinks were heated up in the same way. Only two or three others were ever "let in the know," and then only after the gravest promise of secrecy and a "one, two, three, cut out my throat if I tell a lie" promise. These visitors were blindfolded some distance from the entrance, and both before entering and after leaving the hut they were whizzed 'round on their feet and rolled over and over on the ground. We never saw during two or three years any evidence that the hut entrance, blocked with gorse, was ever discovered. The hut was destroyed one year when the whole patch went up in smoke. (1900; Waitara)

Tree climbing was a major pastime and took innumerable forms. Apart from simple climbing there was, for example, "crossing" the plantation on the treetops, and Rough-riding, in which one player sat on a fir tree branch while the others took the end of it and pulled it up and down and then let it go flying up in the air. The player who could stay on the longest was the rough-riding champion. Of a similar nature was Buck-jumping, in which individual players rode a macrocarpa or gum branch to see who could rise the highest. The branches near the end were trimmed to provide a seat. Then there was Tree-diving:

I discovered, partly by accident and partly by trying to come down headfirst, that if one chose the right place—not too close to the trunk where the limbs were too thick or too near the end of the branches where the "give" was so great that one tended to slide outwards to disaster—one might dive headfirst fairly fast through the boughs, guiding oneself and regulating speed with arms and legs. It was only possible to do this trick with macrocarpa. (1900; Waitara)

It is clear that much of the joy in fruit-hunting or bird-nesting lay in the risks involved in the tree-climbing part of those activities.

To succeed in getting the eggs of kingfishers or wild pigeons, to climb some of the taller "giggy" trees, to crawl on hands and knees on narrow branches or by means of supplejacks over areas of dark brown or black slush, if the bush were a "wet" one, where a fall would mean a horrid mess if nothing more, or to pass from one treetop to another to save coming down, did mean a bit of pluck and made an appeal to which healthy boys gladly responded. (1900; Waitara)

A tree branch could also be used in place of a parallel bar. There the children could do Sitters, in which they held on to the trunk and fell over backward. There were forward and backward "sitters." In addition, there was Head Over Turkey, which is self-explanatory. Another name for these sitters was Fainting. There is even record of team forms of tree climbing:

I often think that had our fond parents but known the plays that their boys were engaged in their hair (the parents') would have stood on end, turned grey, or fallen out. A ploy would be Hide and

Seek on a moonlight night when a number of us would visit a plantation of sixty-feet pines. There would be, say, six hiders and two seekers. The hiders would scale up the high trees, give the signal, and the seekers would try their best to find and tig the hiders. Coming to the foot of a tree, the seeker would spy a hider and proceed to climb the tree after him. The hider, knowing he was spotted, would climb higher and higher, with the seeker hot on his trail. To avoid capture, the hider would crawl further out on a swaying branch, and just as the seeker was reaching out his hand to grab him, would release his hold, and, trusting to sheer luck, drop, hoping to have his fall broken ere he reached the hard ground. Perilous, yes, but 'twas real fun. Coming in for supper, tired and hungry, no wonder Mother wondered where and how her boys had their clothes covered with gum, gum, gum! (1880; Queenstown)

Apart from the orthodox swings, children made their own swings in the bush or out over cliffs. Supplejacks and willow branches were used. At Denniston, children swung out over the cliff on the chains from the old mine trucks. As they progressed in courage, so they graduated to a lower knot in the chain. There are also many records of children swinging out over banks on ropes or vines. For the smaller children, the five-bar gate was swing enough. At Waikouaiti, generations of boys swung along the rafters in the shed until they were polished like varnished wood. The shed was 25 feet long and the rafters 2 feet apart. The boys would put resin on their hands to harden them for the competition, which was to see how many times they could go backward and forward along these rafters before giving up. Many homes had the conventional seesaws, but boys with imagination would make their own: "They were made with the thick straight branches of trees lain across logs or across the middle or top rail of a post and rail fence, or by using after working hours, stacked timber on what was considered common ground."

In the early days, banquets or dinners were among the most favored forms of adult entertainment. Almost every occurrence of any moment—the visit of cricketers, the annual football match, the visit of the Duke of Edinburgh was accompanied by a tremendous feast. In fact, one often feels that the sport was not itself the main event, but rather a glandular preface to the feed. No doubt hungry colonial children shared this feeling. It appears that the children then were more often urgently hungry than is the case today, when there is an ever-ready supply of school milk and "chews" available. But then as now, the children were able to deal with the delights of gustation in fantasy. One of the ready sources of food for hungry children was nature herself.

As the spring advanced, we would take the fresh young shoots of willow and peel and eat them. Broom shoots were also relished, but our favourites were the young stems of the briar rose. These were difficult to gather and to peel on account of their various numerous large thorns. I don't remember a knife ever being used, and there was a sense of triumph in exhibiting a six-inch length of the sweet, luscious pale-green stem, denuded of its bright red skin and thorns. We sucked honey from various spring flowers, but the most prized was a low-growing and a very prickly native heather with flowers about half or three quarters of an inch long that grew on the stony plain. There were masses of it which we called rice-plant because its masses of sweet, juicy white berries spread out near the ground resembled polished rice in appearance. A plant that we called "wild birch" (because its leaves resembled birch leaves, I suppose) had red astringent berries that we enjoyed. It grew among the manuka scrub. We tried many kinds of berries and used to say, "Anything that the birds can eat, you can eat." We knew better than to eat the tutu, though we greatly admired it. I remember taking a handkerchief full of the tutu berries home once, to mother's freely expressed horror. (1900; Lower Moutere)

Of all the natural foods, however, the kei-kei, or "giggy" as it was commonly known, was the best.

Every year during season, two or three times a week, sometimes more often, a great deal of fun and fodder was got from
raids into the giggy bush. The giggy is the flower of a sort of
thick-stemmed vine that grows about many of the big trees in
some parts of our North Island forests. When fully ripe, the
giggy looks something like a magnolia with its white petals and
stamens sticking up in the middle. There are two kinds growing
on the same tree. The soft stamens of one of these are cream-
coloured and covered with creamy-yellow pollen. This we called
the "lady" or sometimes what the Maoris called it, *tawhera.*
The other, the "gentleman" giggy *(tiore)* had harder brownish-
green stamens. When young, the giggy looks like a young
maize [corn] cob in its green sheath, only in the giggy the outside green leaves are much longer and stiffer in texture. The
value lay in the soft, white petals which, when the giggy is
quite ripe, are juicy and sweet. They were much prized by the
boys of the village. Boys operated as units or, if efficient mates
were at hand, as gangs of two or three. No boy would gang up
with a "passenger." Should two agree to work together, one
would call the "first pick," then climbing would begin. The giggies were detached from the vine after they had been carefully
closed so that all the outside leaves could be gripped in one
hand. Then with a sharp jerk downwards or to the side the
stem of the giggy was snapped. The giggy was then tied 'round
with one of its long leaves and slipped stalk-first over the side
of the tree to the ground. Due care was taken to note the probable landing places. Few were lost or misclaimed. Boys seemed
to know their own giggies as they knew the best bush track
and individual trees. Mates gave mutual help by calling attention to beauties which they spotted from adjacent trees. Some
of the giggies were found low down, but others had to be
climbed for, even to the height of forty feet or more. Some of
the best were in dangerous positions and could be collected by
only the most venturesome climbers. This climbing would naturally encourage quite sturdy appetites, and no doubt it was not
uncommon for several of the choicest giggies not to find their
way to the common pool. There was usually much shouting
from tree to tree regarding gains and prospective gains. Any

fairly long silence might mean that a boy was "kai-ing" or "scoffing," and occasionally warnings were given very righteously against any such meal. When on his own, a boy ate some of his second-best. When twenty to forty giggies had been added to the pile, "picking" would begin. All the giggies would be untied and placed for inspection. The first pick would take a careful survey and then choose one, noting another for second choice if he got the chance. Then his mate would pick, and so on alternately through the collection. The giggies varied in size and ripeness. Everything else being equal, "gentlemen" were preferred to "ladies," because the pollen from the fingers of these gave one a very ticklish throat after half a dozen were eaten. After picking, each boy, if he had not already had a surfeit, ate two or three of his worst to lighten the load. Then, to prevent loss on his way out, he fixed his swag by carefully tying one long leaf 'round each giggy to close it safely and then plaiting the ends of the long leaves of each in turn so that this swag looked like a string of huge onions, points of stems down ending in long pigtails of strong, plaited leaves. The swag might weigh as much as twelve to fifteen pounds, though in the height of the season only the fewer very best giggies were taken home. Smart lads always had an eye on the future too. Any half-open giggies were carefully tied up with one of their long leaves. This was supposed to discourage the rats and certainly meant that such a staring invitation as a fully ripe, open giggy would not be present to rival marauders. Late in the autumn, the giggy bush gave us another call. The *tawheras* that had been missed had dried and shrivelled, and the white of the *tiore* had decayed, but the fingers of the "gentlemen" had swollen considerably and now provided us with New Zealand "pineapples." The really good ones were eight inches long and two-and-a-half inches in diameter. They were wrenched out in the same way as giggies. These "pineapples" were never very much sought after by the general public. They needed what might be called an acquired taste. They were tricky eating too. You bit off all the outside hard, nobbly but not prickly covering, and then gnawed the soft, sweet flesh to the bone. I've written a screed on giggy-hunting. It made such an appeal to so many of us, and there are perhaps few of the boys nowadays who know anything about such fun. I've hunted the Wellington bush many times in different places to put my children, and even my grandchildren, onto the track, but I have not seen a giggy for sixty years. I am not at all sure of the botany part of the description. (1880; Taranaki)

Giggies are also reported from the West Coast of the South Island, Canterbury, and North Auckland. "The summer ones came in November and the winter ones in June" (1885; Ngakawau).

Other natural foods were elderberries for soup, tea, and wine, lawyer berries, whiteberries of the stinkwood, brambles, fuchsia, red berries of white pine trees, karaka, konini, and tawa berries, berries from the African boxthorn, sunflower seeds, "little apples" (the seed from a weed), "nuts" (the seed of wild mallow), nectar from the nasturtium and honeysuckle, honey from the flowers of the flax plant, shivery grass, oxalis, Scotch thistle nuts, and shamrock stalks.

Another method of satisfying the appetite was outdoor cooking, for example, potatoes and pipis. Sometimes this cooking took unusual forms:

In a small mining village in the king country, Mangopeeki, about a dozen of the children came to school by train. We had to wait several hours after school for the train, and in the winter one of our favourite games was Sausages. We would all pool our pennies and buy sausages from the local butcher, then go down to the mill furnace, which was a slab fire in the open. At the edge of the fire, which always burned day and night, there were glowing embers. We had long, pointed sticks, and a sausage was placed on the point and held over the embers, and when we thought one was done it would be carefully laid on a sandwich kept over from lunch for the purpose. If someone had no pennies, pieces were bitten off several sausages and given to the poor one. This was a very exciting game, for often the sausages would slip off the stick and into the fire. If it was retrieved, it was very ashy and so had to be taken to the nearby river to be washed before a further cooking. Sometimes the sausage caught fire before it could be stabbed out. Those that lost their sausages in this manner were not allowed any bites of the others but could, if they liked, toast the sandwiches, which in most cases went the way of the lost sausage. I cannot ever remember any of us getting tired of the game. (1910)

Perhaps the most common activity of the day for boys (and one of the most common ways of satisfying the appetite) was some form of hunting, whether bird-nesting, rabbiting, hive-hunting, or fishing. In this Tom Sawyer age, bird-nesting was subsidized. The rates varied.

At Hampden the rate was eighteen pence per hundred eggs, at Timaru, two pence a dozen. At other places as much as three pence a dozen and, by jove, a shilling for four dozen was great money for us in those days. I invested my egg money in marbles and Jew's harps; but, of course, the money was only paid out for the eggs of grain eaters. The birds were shot with guns and shanghais, or trapped with bird lime and other traps. To catch them with bird lime, the lime was put on willow sticks which were lain over the cage of the call bird, or "cally." When the bird alighted on the stick, he stuck fast.

There are several records of this method being used after 1900 to catch goldfinches to sell to private people and, in Wellington, to the zoo. Sparrows could be caught half a dozen at a time with a sieve trap. A round sieve raised at one end was supported by a stick to which was attached a fishing line. Oat and chaff under the sieve drew the birds. When a number were underneath the sieve, the line was jerked and the sieve fell.

Round the feedboxes of the horses dozens of sparrows and a few linnets collected whenever there was anything doing. I caught many in the traps made with bricks, two for sides, one for the end, and fourth raised on an angle between the sides and supported by sticks so as to fall against the end brick. A bird hopping on the balanced stick to get the crushed oats would cause the lifted brick to fall on himself. (1880)

We set traps for wekas, which we gave to an old Chinaman to eat. The trap was a cage with a door which was suspended by a stick caught under a staple. The other end of the stick was jacked under a hook of wire which hung inside the cage. On the wire inside was a piece of meat, and when a weka pulled the meat the door closed automatically. Kakas could be caught by snaring them. I was quite adept at snaring kaka by calling them to me. My method was a flax noose at the end of a stick which I used to pop over their heads, and then what a noise arose, and bites too, but the fun was worth it. Much of the birding was done for egg collections. I had dozens of eggs "blown" and strung on stripple cotton hung in festoons in my bedroom. Sparrows, larks, linnets, goldfinches, thrush, silvereyes, and yellow-hammer were the commonest in my collection. I had a few kingfisher, tomtit, fantail, and quail eggs and of the morepork, tui, and pheasant only two or three at most. I cannot remember any miner eggs, though the birds were plentiful enough. I spent hours watching the beautiful pukekos among the "rapau" or stalking proudly on the grassland near the swamps and tried often to track the wekas but could never find their nests. Hawks, wild pigeons, bittern, wild duck, shags, and pipers, which were all well known, completely baffled me. I had a kiwi for two or three weeks, closely guarded as I thought, but such a helpless bird couldn't expect to last long under the best conditions I could contrive. I cannot recall seeing starlings, blackbirds, hedge sparrows, or chaffinch in Taranaki in those days [1880–90]. I knew them first in Horowhenua, 1890–1900.

After these accounts it seems strange to hear of the boys at South Clutha between 1875 and 1880 who one afternoon treked four or five miles to see some sparrows, and of the boys at the same place who found the first blackbird's nest and made a charge of a penny a head to see it. This was, of course, in the days when these birds had been only recently introduced in the country.

There was also much hunting with dogs and gun. In the cases where boys did not have guns, they hunted rabbits with dogs alone, or if they were lucky, with ferrets. At Palmerston South in 1896, rabbits were bought by rabbit-buyers at two pence each. One informant reports that between standard four and standard seven he did little else out of school except catch these rabbits in traps. He put the traps out at night by lantern and collected them at daylight. He claims to have made an average of one pound a week at this practice, but this was the exception rather than the rule.

For the enterprising there was occasionally honey for hunting. The falling of a tree in the bush with a hive of bees in it and the taking of honey provided an exciting adventure.

We used to light fires, but as we had no way of controlling the smoke, it would go everywhere but where it was wanted. The enterprise resolved itself into an endurance test. I can still see Angus Wallace chopping like mad in the midst of a swarm of bees and, when he could stand it no longer, retreating at the double from the scene. Jack Wallace would then seize the ax, rush to the fray, get in as much as possible as long as he could stand it. There always appeared to be some boy brave enough to pick up the ax as soon as it was dropped, and in this way the tree was felled, the hive reached, and the bees were robbed of their store. But how dear it was to the robbers.

Fishing in one form or another was common. Here is an account of some interest:

There was not much organized stealing by boys in 1880–1890 in our part of Taranaki. All that I can remember outside the private "pinching" of home delicacies was associated with what to some of us (two whites and one Maori boy) was a major Saturday craze, namely, fishing. Herrings, by the way, two or three at a time could be caught in the river at the blood chute from the freezing works, and sometimes a kahawai or two. But it was too easy. The mouth of the river Waitara supplied a little more excitement, more kahawai, small sharks, and an occasional snapper. Once I caught a stingray there, too, much to my amazement. I had never seen one, nor had my mates, and we hadn't the slightest idea what it was. It certainly seemed a monster to be respected. We dragged it in triumph to the township and there learned that it was a "stingaree." And "stingarees" they remained for some years. The main thrilling objective, however, was to fish outside the "bar" where there was more chance of catching snapper and where the sharks were large. But this exploit meant a boat, and boats were by no means easy to get, and were difficult to manage in any case. A canoe, however, was simple. The Maoris had canoes on the slopes near the water's edge and they were secured with rope only. On the way to the bar we would pass the Maori kumara and watermelon gardens, and our Maori associate would say, "Pull in, I got no dinner." He'd scramble up the bank and disappear, but soon came back cuddling a large watermelon. There was not the slightest objection on our part to being receivers of such ripe, pink treasure. But only one of these trips was taken; the risk was too great. Their place was too public, and we were too near the owners of the canoe. On several occasions we tried the more private upstream course, where we had the springboard for a depot and a bit of cliff one hundred and fifty yards away for a decent hideout. A canoe was not essential to navigation. Sometimes there would be a "fresh" in the river, and logs came down in hundreds. One year the river looked like a Canadian "drive," only most of the trees were whole. On that occasion the beach was strewn with logs for miles on each side of the river. The whole town collected firewood. Our house had enough to last for three years. Boys did not lose any such opportunity of throwing out a grab at the end of a rope and securing suitable logs. It was seldom that a swimming season passed without there being two or three community logs capable of carrying six or eight youngsters who traveled across the river and up and down using a much prized homemade paddle. When not in use the logs were made safe by twisted flax or rope or a piece of wire fastened to the springboard or to strong stakes driven into the bank. A good log hauled up on the bank during the winter lasted more than one year. Here again, canoe borrowing (we always took the canoe back) was considered more of a frolic than a win, though it would have been very difficult to get our parents to come to that conclusion had they known. I cannot pretend that our watermelons "borrowed" were not stolen for their own sake alone.

Eeling also took place:

In tidal rivers when the tide is out, the entry and exit holes of eels are clearly visible in the mudbanks. The method is simply that of putting a hand in each hole, feeling the eel inside, and pulling it out. A grip with the middle finger over the top and the second and fourth fingers underneath is a firm one. Very large numbers can be caught in a very short time. Where holes are very large, discretion is the better part of valour. The most suitable costume for this game is the nude, and several of us would spend an hour or two roaming the tidal banks in the nude pulling out eels. We have met parties much older than ourselves similarly clad. Mudbanks can be very messy. In swamps a piece of plain wire attached to a stout stick is all that is required. By frequent poking, eels can be felt by the quivering of the stick. The eel is then pulled out as before. In soft, muddy places they can be felt with the feet. In rivers nighttime is the best. A torch made from sacking or the stalks of flax flowers provides a suitable light. A gaff is needed to pull out those attracted to the light. (1910; Kaikohe)

We used a lighted tyre to attract the eels. We fished eels with a rod. A bait of worms were strung on cabbage leaves, and wiwi was used as a hook. (1900; Nuhaka)

Crab fishing was done at night:

A light was used to attract the crabs, and they were hooked out with a piece of wire turned up at one end. (1920; Whangaparoa)

We dived for paua, sea eggs, and crayfish. Crayfish pots (called *pouraka*) were set at night. Crowds of families would go down at the early morning tide and fish them out. We would compete to see how many sea eggs we could bring up at one time. This was done in shallow water. We felt 'round with our feet first, then dived to bring them up. The same was done with crayfish. We felt their holes with our feet, then dived to bring them up. The eggs could be eaten raw. Some old folks would eat them whole. (1900; Horoeka)

Quieter children, and especially girls, would play outside with grass and flowers. Some, for example, knew flower games:

In the pansy family game, you need a pansy flower, preferably one with different coloured petals. You pull each petal off and describe the dress each daughter wears to the ball. Generally the eldest daughter is the largest petal at the top, and she wears a lovely purple velvet. The others are not quite so grand. When they have all gone off in their gay dresses, there is only the poor little old grandmother left. There she is sitting all alone with her feet wrapped in a blanket. If you are very careful, you can pull the blanket off and see her two little legs.

The violet has the same story, but the daughters are all dressed alike. Informants from Nelson during 1880–90 told of other similar imaginative plays:

The periwinkle was said to have a tiny paintbrush in the centre. The young shoots of the hawthorn and the tiny cheeses of the mallow seeds were said to be bread and cheese. We would peel and eat the young pink briar shoots and chew the stems of wild aniseed.

Daisy chains were made in two ways. The flowers were threaded on cotton, or a hole was slit in each stem and the next flower was threaded through. Periwinkle flowers were also threaded. Briar berries made lovely necklets. With them on, you became the queen of the fairies.

Peep shows made of flowers were arranged behind a small sheet of glass and covered with paper with a window cut in it. "A pin to see my peep show," we said.

Grass, too, had its possibilities. There was the Tinker Tailor game with rye grass, in which the children selected a husband or a future by pulling off the ears of the grass. They said, "Tinker, tailor, soldier, sailor, rich man, poor man, beggarman, thief." They chose their clothes for a wedding, "Silk, satin, cotton rags," or a carriage, "Horse, carriage, wheelbarrow cart" (1903–14; Petone). And sometimes they used the same grass for less elevated purposes:

"We picked grass to choose which lavatory cubicle we would use" (1930; Musselburgh, Dunedin) or "We used goose grass to put up boys' trousers. We had a joy watching their discomfort as the grass worked its way up." (1910–15; Nelson)

Animals provided scope for play. In country areas, Hide and Seek, bows and arrows, and polo were sometimes played on horseback. And in rural areas there were many pets. In fact, in the more rural conditions of the time, pets may have been more common than they are today. One correspondent contends that there were more dogs in Christchurch before World War I, and considering the increase in traffic since that time, this seems likely. Another writes that as a boy in

Wellington in 1870 he had for pets cats, ferrets, guinea pigs, weasels, and stoats, an unlikely collection for the Wellington child of 1950. Another informant from New Plymouth of the 1880s says:

I cannot remember learning to ride. Except during school I was as much on horseback as on foot. I knew every road, Maori track, shortcut, and farmhouse for miles around. Often on a Saturday there was a horse to be ridden to New Plymouth to Newton King's saleyards. During the first fifteen years of my life I must have ridden, if only once or twice, as many as fifty or sixty different horses. And how different they were—as in looks, so in temperament. Like humans, no two were alike. As I recall some of my experiences with them, I wonder that I am still alive. Three horses of our own were permanent friends. Two cows for three or four years gave me sufficient experience of "getting the cows in," milking, and churning. This was considered work, of course, not distasteful but sometimes restrictive. But the dogs were a delight. We had pointers, one or two (and sometimes a family), a little yellow cattle dog and her pup, and three greyhounds. These made up the biggest dog-score at any one particular time; but the show champion pointer, a collie, and one greyhound seemed a part of the household always. How intelligent and faithful they were. What a contribution to a boy's education they made. I shore only one sheep, and because of my fear of cutting the animal and of the mass of piripiri entangled in the wool, it proved an extremely difficult job, a slow and painful job. And the shorn sheep looked like nothing on earth, or so the grinning shearers said. The fleece was certainly worth four shillings and threepence a pound.

Minor pets were experimented with:

My mother had guinea pigs for a time, but their continual families were a problem, and after a dog or cat had twice got into the hutch and created horrible carnage, my mother said they must go. (1895; Dunedin)

We had an opossum once, but it mysteriously disappeared. I always suspected mother, as the cage was by the washhouse door and the smell was offensive. (1890; Akaroa, Christchurch)

Insects too could become pets:

Raising silkworms was a popular hobby. We would have paper cones pinned on the wallpaper in our bedrooms while the silk was being spun, and we would be very proud of our own pale-green or cream hanks of silk. Prior to that stage of silkworm culture we would have a cardboard shoebox with holes pricked all over to let in the air, and inside would be the silkworms feeding ravenously on mulberry leaves. If there was a mulberry tree on any property, so there would be children hovering 'round until the coast was clear to take leaves home to their silkworms. If we could not get mulberry leaves, lettuce had to do. (1908; Auckland)

Animals and insects could be used for games of other sorts:

We used to tie tins onto dogs' tails any evening after dark just to hear the row they would make. Once we tied a dog's tail to the cord of a steam-tractor whistle. The whistle blew, the dog ran, and the cord, catching in the fence, kept the whistle going. Soon the church bells began to ring and finally the fire-engine turned out. This was the usual method of sounding an alarm. (1895; Carterton)

Then there were the inevitable chicken, ant, caterpillar, lady-bird, beetle, and snail races, but the following was less customary:

Passing the shed one day during interval, I heard squeals of mirth from a little group within, and on investigation found

that a new game had been invented, a race meeting in miniature. A series of parallel courses had been chalked across an
inclined board, one for each player. The actual contestants,
pediculi [lice] were started off scratch, as it were, at the bottom
of the board, and were encouraged and guided toward the
finishing line at the top by straws wielded by respective back-
ers. Any which refused to run paid instantly with their lives
and were promptly replaced by reservists.

There was that boyish attempt to imitate the gamecock
fighting of their fathers, which is mentioned by Neville Harcourt in *The Day Before Yesterday,* and another account:
"Their teacher learned with the disgust of a pious Victorian
maiden lady that her diminutive scholars caught hawks in
traps, clipped their wings, and threw them into the local turkey
pens. The turkeys usually won, but it took an hour or two of
rollicking entertainment. Miss Wrigley discovered the admission to 'The Horrors' was paid in marbles" (1888; Kaikohe).

A universal animal play in the North Island, but known
also in the South Island, was a game variously termed
Butcher Bats, Butcher Boys, or Penny Doctor Beetles. In this
game, straws suitably moistened at the end with spittle were
placed down insect holes and flicked out when the insect bit
the end of the straw. The player won who could flick a beetle
up first. Another common practice was inflating frogs with a
straw, which were then floated on water or stoned. Such cruelty plays to animals or insects were legion. They could crop
up anywhere: "Mr. Rowe's ducks sometimes explored the
school grounds attracted by scraps and crumbs of food lying
about. They had to take the risks of the playground in the
way of a well-aimed stone or being caught with a bit of bread
on a pinhook attached to string—dry-land angling" (1870;
Waianiwa).

Lacking horses or other means of transportation, walks
had a certain vogue. There were the informal rambles of the
younger boys, which they themselves would hardly have clas-
sified as "walks": "We enjoyed going on a Saturday morning

ramble to watch the work in foundries, factories, and on the wharves" (1900; Mount Cook, Wellington). And there were the walks of the early teens. Thus F. M. Leckie (1933) says, "During these years, walking entered largely into our recreations. We formed ourselves into small parties, and visited the neighbouring boys on the coastline, and other places of interest within easy walking distance. On Saturdays and holidays one met with such parties in all directions." Occasionally a schoolmaster might take the boys on an expedition on Saturday or during the holidays (1870; Wellington). Much younger children still had their own "play" versions of orthodox walking: There was, for example, Ghost Walking: "All the schoolchildren ghost-walked in my country-school days. The movement was sideways with the feet held close together. Some of the girls were incredibly quick at it. As it was done in bare feet, it was supposed to be noiseless. It was also competitive" (1887; Paeroa). And then there was "Chinaman": "It was just a sort of follow-my-leader, but the trot was in imitation of the itinerant Chinese fruit vendors, of whom there were so many in the Auckland of those days. An interesting thing is that an old West Coaster told me he had seen children playing it on the Greenstone and at Red Jacks, both old Chinese diggings" (1900; Parnell, Auckland).

In most places swimming was the major summer sport, but on the whole it seems to have been restricted to boys. Girls seldom shared freely in this pastime. The adult attitude to girls' swimming is expressed in the following apparently innocent but rather ambiguous rhyme (1900; Palmerston North):

> "Mother, may I go out to swim?"
> "Yes, my darling daughter.
>   Hang your clothes on the gooseberry bush
>   And don't go near the water."

At coastal places the sea was used:

Ravensbourne has a lovely harbour, and safe bathing has been indulged in since early times. . . . Fifty years ago [1877] boys

bathed in all the bays, and the train passengers got free entertainment at the time, and the youths of the district spent almost
the whole of the hot days on the beach by the "beacon" and
Gillander's Beach or down at Bull Island, where cockles were
gathered, cooked, and eaten after the swim was over.

Inland, one of the major enjoyments of the swimming season
was reckoned to lie in building the hole. Usually some creek
had to be dammed up for this purpose. Where there was easy
access to a good hole or to the beach, most boys soon learned
to swim of their own accord, even though their strokes were
somewhat haphazard. One informant records making a cork
jacket and teaching himself in that manner. Another tells
how the older boys would drive the younger ones into the
shallow end of the pool, and then when they seemed confident
make them dive into the deep end near the bank. Others
learned (or failed to learn) less pleasantly: "I remember
Angus Wallace trying to teach me to swim by his way of it
and letting me get under so that I shipped a mouthful. Anyone who had had that experience knows the sensation of waiting what appears to be an eternity before he is able to breathe
again." And so they learned to swim—although not all, it is
hoped, like Uncle Jim:

> Down in the duck pond
> Learning how to swim.
> First he does the overarm
> Then he does the side.
> Now he's under water,
> Swimming against the tide.

One of the sidelights of swimming was the race to the water-
hole.

There were some records put up in stripping for the water, all the
buttons being undone as we ran for the pool; and, having no boots
on, we just shook off our clothes when we got there. As we were

not encumbered with either bathing suits or towels, we were in the water within half a minute of getting there.

Once in the water, there were innumerable games: swimming, ducking, diving, handstanding, looping the loop, and many others.

On one occasion when the seniors wanted me for some purpose, they found me bathing, but I refused to come out. I was good in the water, and they did not venture in after me. For a time I had them beaten until they were struck upon the idea of getting some big gorse that had been put down next door and which was dry. By setting fire to this and throwing it at me, they drove me out and captured me. (1870; Waianiwa)

There were other types of summer water play: water fights, play with boats, rafts, and dams. "We made boats out of sticks or pieces of flat board about six and a half by two and a half inches, and put on tow masts and tied a piece of string to the front and spent many happy hours sailing them in the creek or in the horse trough" (1890; Amberley). But toy boats made from flax sticks and flax leaves were the typical New Zealand homemade boat toy. Stella Morice says in *The Book of Wiremu*, "He then sharpened the ends and hollowed out the pith until he made a whole fleet of canoes." Rafts of wood or kerosene tins have been known wherever there has been water on which to float them. On Regatta Day on the Avon, all the boys of any merit launched their improvised tin and wooden boats.

Watermills were made to operate in the local creeks:

There was a creek on the farm. One year we decided to dam it to get enough depth for a swim. From immediately after breakfast until about three o'clock one day we worked, nude, most of the time in water below the knees, dragging and piling logs, cutting, and fitting sods and stones. It was a reasonable success, and so was the sunburn which was the "very worst ever." The immediate result was two days in bed for both of us and later exercises in each trying to pull the longest piece of skin off the other's back. The dam paid, however. One could swim, and there were crawlers to be caught by day and eels in the evenings. The crawlers and the eels were sometimes cooked in an old tin. There was not much meat in the crawler, but the eels were always voted first-class, better even than the mussels and cockles we cooked on the beach. A bridge was also made across the creek, a swing bridge made of rope and interlaced flax and interwoven willow sticks of about a finger thickness. The bridge was tied to trees on each side of the stream. But it was no easy bridge to walk upright on, and there were a few falls into the creek. (1890s; North Island)

In some circles there were trips to the beach:

Various neighbouring families met at the beach for the day, weather permitting. We set forth on a sledge pulled by a draught horse with the dog tailing up in the rear. A buggy seat was fastened to the sledge for mother and any visiting lady. A kerosene case (or more) was loaded on with previously cut sandwiches (salmon ones were favourites), cakes, apples, tea billy, and the etceteras, never omitting bathing costumes, towels, and tins for fan shells. We each had a lovely collection of these. We spent hours collecting the shells of all colours along the tide line. On wet days we would sort them, licking them to bring out the colours. We'd then have competitions to see who had the three best greens and the three best yellows, stripes, purples, speckled, etcetera. Mother would come in to judge. On the beach we played leapfrog and cricket with balls out of kelp. From the kelp we also made sandals, cutting out an oval and then cutting a T-shape on the top surface. We'd run our fingers inbetween the upper and lower surface to make room for our feet and then put them on. We went white-baiting in the lagoon. Dad would set the net blocking the side with stones while we children went upstream armed with sticks with pieces of tin dangling on the ends. We shook these in the water and chased the fish downstream. In this way we caught hosts of "creekies" (minnows) and bullies and sometimes enough whitebait for a fritter each for tea. As well, we went fishing for "guffy" from the rocks. Often we caught a crayfish and at low tide sometimes several. At low tide also we collected mussels. These we boiled in salt water and ate (except the tongue and beard). They were delicious. We collected many paua [abalone] shells, which we took home to put 'round our gardens. They made a nice edge. Then, of course, we swam, sunbathed, dived, jumped the breakers, rode in on the waves, surfed on boards, and played "Old Daddy Sea Can't Catch Me," running when the waves came ashore and trying to race them in. There were sandcastles, forts, and houses too, decorated with shells, flowers, and seaweed. Most of all we loved a day at the beach immediately following a storm, as we generally found sea anemones, seahorses, sea eggs, and the like. Making sandballs was another beach art of ours. We would make a firm ball of wet sand and then roll and bury this in dry sand, smoothing and working it until it was really firm and wouldn't break till it hit its target. Then we picked sides, made sandballs for our lives and commenced the fight. (1890; Akaroa)

We played games in the local beach. We ploughed the beach, built sandcastles, and fished off the rocks and out of punts. On the sand we wrote and drew, made kelp shoes and skipping ropes. On the sea we skipped stones and thought we were clever if they struck twice or more. At the water's edge we paddled, splashed one another, and bathed. (1900; Moeraki)

In the winter in the South Island there were outdoors activities that went with snow and ice. There are naturally reports of snowballing, making snowmen, and tobogganing, but most exciting of all seems to have been the skating on the local pond:

In wintertimes we would get hobnails put in our ordinary school boots for skating. Without that surface the leather would drag. A good heel plate was a help also. Some who were braver than the others would test out the ice on the pond. They were the ones who received the ducking and the thrashing. The difficulty was that the edges were always thin because of the shallow water there, whereas it was thicker out in the centre. It was necessary to slide out quickly over the edge and risk getting back. It was a terrible thing to go through because it was so difficult to get them out. The lagoon ice edges would nearly always break. (1895; Waikouaiti)

There was the time Kate Wallace went through the ice into two or three feet of water well out in Robertson's pit. Every time she tried to get out again the ice broke, and in this manner she really smashed her way out, to the delight of practically the whole school. Once Joe Pink was out on the ice on the pit across the road from the school. When it began to crack he tried to save the situation by getting down on his hands and knees, and he went through in that position up to his neck. (1870; Waianiwa)

On August 4th, 1904, a heavy snowstorm occurred, and as this was an unusual occurrence at Stoney Creek the teacher allowed the school to indulge in some snowballing. He reported afterwards that all were wet but happy.

Our favourite snow competition was to see who could build the largest snowball. Once we made one so large that it rolled away from us and tore down the main street. It smashed into a front door, went right through, and proceeded to melt within. (1900; Cromwell)

But the best account of snowballing and snow-throwing comes from Invercargill, at the bottom of the South Island:

Many old boys, and girls too, will remember the great snow fight in the open vacant section in Don Street, adjoining the master's residence. The previous snowfall had caused a little trouble. A certain gentleman was passing down the school side of the street.

The boys had their "ammunition" in their hands. In a most dignified manner he strode past, but he made the fatal mistake of shaking his folded umbrella at the boys and warning them not to throw snow at him. The challenge was accepted at once, and the pedestrian found the other side of the street handy for his retreat. Then others were attacked and complaints were made. As supervisor I had to take immediate action to check these attacks on defenseless persons. With that ulterior end in view, a battle was arranged next day: Sides were chosen, distances were marked off, ammunition dumps were prepared behind a barricade of massive snowballs each four feet in diameter and each the work of twelve boys. The impatiently awaited signal was given and the "Snowdown" fight began. Exultant shouts when a good shot was made, and shrill shrieks when a prisoner felt the icy ammunition down his back, soon attracted a crowd to watch the varying fortunes and misfortunes of the combatants. I am pleased to add that the aforementioned gentleman came and witnessed the fun, and probably 'twas he who, on passing Kingsland's bakery, suggested hot buns and cocoa, a ration much appreciated by the boys. Casualties that day comprised seventy wet and thirty torn jerseys, beside two hours loss of schoolwork. Advantages gained: a fixed future battleground; an honourable understanding to attack only in self-defence; approval of spectators; a general pardon by the headmaster. (1873–1923)

These accounts call our attention to children's self-reliance and their capacity for innovation in their rural environment. They do give support to the notion that children used to be more enterprising in these ways in the nineteenth century than they were to become in the twentieth. Although, as has been seen, it was an enterprise with respect to natural things and the outdoors, rather than an enterprise in matters of a symbolic order which was to come later. And again it was an enterprise which was associated with a harshness and aggressiveness of life, much of which was also to disappear.

8 the nineteenth century: an overview

A rural kind of play was characteristic of nineteenth-century children, including hunting, shooting, raiding orchards and gardens, climbing trees and hills, and subjecting themselves throughout to very considerable physical risks. Beyond the often stringent demands of home and school for hard work and obedient behavior, children also occupied an interstitial world in which they pursued many kinds of furtive behavior. It was as if the harsh demands for adaptive social behavior left them more disposed to cruelty, teasing, obscenity, prejudice, and fighting, as well as rebellious pranks upon both the weak and the strong. Survival in the power struggles of playground and neighborhood required fisticuffs, initiations, and torture.*

*One must concede that this acount is based on the oral and written reports of both men and women. Since women have traditionally been less permitted or willing to ackowledge baser kinds of behavior, the differences between the sexes in this account might suffer some exaggeration.

With the advent of public schooling in the 1870s, the relatively sparse provision of formal games was suddenly supplemented by a great confluence of folkgames inherited from former generations of children and youths. Separated in their playgrounds, the girls on the one side practised formalized and decorous pastimes, while the boys on the other side engaged in the vigorous and the uncouth. Neglected by adults, both sexes improvised play objects and organized a game life of considerable complexity. There was a vigorous autonomy, a passionate excitement, and a furtive rebelliousness all at the same time, and an almost naive involvement in imaginative play about horses, ploughing matches, circuses, trains, cowboys and Indians, and with grass and flowers.

Examples of the range of games played in some schools before 1900 follow.* The examples chosen are those about which records appear to be fairly complete. Nevertheless, even these cannot be considered exhaustive.

South Clutha, 1875 (male)

Fire on the Mountains, Sally Waters, Marra Ma Tanza, Rounders, Chuckie stones, Stagknife, Tipcat, Chevey Chase, Jolly Miller, Hot Cockles, Cockfighting, Pitch and Toss, Tip Tap Toe, Hurling, Shinty, Buck Buck Buck, Leapfrog, Hopscotch, Cat's Cradle, Wiggle Waggle

Tahataki, 1879 (female)

Bar the Door, Nivvy Nivvy Nack, Pinny Show, tops, Leapfrog, Blind Man's Buff, cricket, Rounders, football, catching and bouncing balls against wall, Hopscotch, marbles, Jingo Ring, Trip and Go, Hide and Seek, Twos and Threes, Bingo, Drop the Handkerchief, Puss in the Corner, Tig, Green grass, London Bridge, Honeypots, Forfeits, King of the Castle, Hickety Bickety, Sacks on the Mill, Jolly Miller, Kiss in the Ring, Nuts and May, Pretty Little Girl of Mine

*Taken from interviews with the following people: South Clutha, Dr. James Brugh of Dunedin; Tahataki, Mrs. Johnstone of Dunedin. Stillwater, Mr. Isdell of Greymouth; Taranaki, Mr. W. H. Clark of Wellington.

Stillwater, Nelson, 1885 (male)

Smuggling the Gag, Fly the Garter, Rounders, tops, marbles, Fox and Hounds, Bar the Door, cricket, hockey, Paper Chase, Duck Stones, skipping, kites, stilts, Hopscotch, Cockfighting, Hide and Seek

Taranaki, 1890 (male)

Cockfighting, Stagknife, tops, Bull in the Ring, Hopping Base, stilts, wrestling, Fly the Garter, King O'Seeny, kites, marbles, Follow the Leader, whips, hoops, Paper Chase, skipping, Eggs in the Basket, Finger Stones, Knock Backs, Hopscotch, Puss in the Corner, Kick the Tin, All In, Hide and Seek, Twos and Threes, Filling the Gap, Prisoner's Base, Oranges and Lemons, French and English, Rounders, Last Couple Out, Kiss in the Ring, Sally Waters, Nuts and May

Boys at Central School Nelson.

A PICTURE OF RURAL CHILDHOOD: GROVETOWN, BLENHEIM, 1870–85*

"Grovetown at that time was a small farming community. The greater part of the land was bush, flax, and swamp. It was two miles from Blenheim. There was nothing but bush there when we first arrived. Later there was a hotel, a wheelwright, and a blacksmith, although stores continued to come from Blenheim. Before I was sixteen years of age, I had been on a relation's farm, sewing, ploughing, stacking, thatching the stacks, reaping, digging potatoes, market-gardening (we grew pea seeds for a town firm). Before school in the mornings there were cows to milk and pigs to feed. On Saturday also there was plenty of work to do. One of our special jobs when very small was to keep the cows moving so they could get new grass. As long as they were kept moving, the ranger couldn't take them. In the holidays there was harvesting to do. At twelve I was tying up corn and stooking it. In February-March the schools were closed down for about three weeks because no one went in any case. It was the hop-picking season and the parents took their children away with them.

"For a girl there were always innumerable household jobs and cleaning: weeding the garden, feeding the fowls, and collecting their eggs.

"At school we played hockey with sticks and ball made out of manuka. Sometimes an old lady would make us a ball out of wool. A rubber ball would go too far at one hit. There was no football. It arrived suddenly in 1885. We played the town boys at cricket, sometimes using solid wooden bats. There were few spring-handed bats about. At lunchtime we frequently played Prisoner's Base. We played marbles, Ring, and Eye-drop with taws, glassies, stonies, and agots. Although boys and girls were not separate in the playground, Knucklebones was a boy's game [this is unusual]. We aimed to see who could get the most knuckles on the back of his hand. We played also Mumblepeg, flicking the knife from the back and front of the hand, from the

*From an interview with Mr. and Mrs. Cheesman of Wellington, who both spent their childhood in Grovetown.

fingertips, and from the head. In winter there were tops, which we hit with flax whips. There were acres of flax handy. The whip was three feet long and made of flax strips. There were also Peg Top, Bull in the Ring, Follow the Leader, and circus acrobats on the trees, but we did not do handstands. There were no kites. We had stilt races and competitions to see who could climb up the highest. Some were so high we couldn't get on them without the aid of a tree. We used them in the flood waters, of which there were plenty. In the floods also we often played, skating the stone. We bowled hoops with a stick, not with a hook. The latter was altogether too inferior. We made a whistling toy out of a round piece of tin with jagged edges and with two holes in it and a circle of string through the holes. When the string was twisted and released, the tin spun 'round and whistled loudly.

"At the school the girls had a special croquet green, skipping (no rhymes), and a swing (for the girls only). Rhymes were used chiefly in picking-up games. Girls did not play marbles, Knucklebones, or tops. Rounders would be played by girls and boys together on cold days. Hopscotch was played only by girls, and that only of the kicking Hopscotch types. We also played Blind Man's Buff. At school we had a lot of 'drilling' from the teacher, who was a Frenchman—drill, such as walking, standing upright, arms swinging upward and sideways, etcetera.

"It was very difficult to get a teacher in those days, and our teacher was half drunk most of the time. I remember a boy who threw a slate at the teacher and walked off leaving school. Plenty of us played truant. It was easy because there were always some absent in any case. Some of the boys were wild characters; their parents were of no class, just working men with little bits of farms. Even the men couldn't get together long without fighting. Half the time there was no foundation at all for a fight. It was just that there were a few always looking for a scrap. Some of the rougher boys would pick on you going to and from school for no reason at all. They'd have a down on you and tell you so. They'd try and give you a crack when you weren't looking.

"On the way to school there was Tipcat, Leapfrog, and Whip Top, as already mentioned. We raced our tops down the road, lifting them twenty to thirty feet at a time. We had to get there before the tops stopped spinning on the worn gravel road. If it stopped we would start it again by whipping it, which we preferred, or by spinning it with a twist of the fingers.

"Outside school, bird-nesting was a high priority. We received twopence a dozen for sparrow's eggs from the Road Board, as the sparrow destroyed the corn. We climbed the trees to get their nests. With a good nest we blocked the hole and let the nest drop to the ground. The eggs were not hurt. When the tree was a hard one to climb or we couldn't drop the eggs to the ground, we took them in our mouths. At first we blew the eggs before taking them along to the city council men. He said, however, that he wanted them whole. So next time we went along we took a few rotten ones with us and 'accidentally' broke them in his presence. After that, he asked for them blown again. We collected many hundreds of eggs per year. In a good poplar tree, there would be a dozen to two dozen nests with five to six eggs in each nest. We also killed dozens of the birds with our shanghais—a band of rubber, two pieces of bootlace, and a pouch. Later we shot dozens at a time as they settled in their hundreds on the corn after threshing.

"Some Saturdays or a holiday, such as the Queen's Birthday, we would have a Paper Chase or Hares and Hounds in the bush. Generally the two hares would end up in a tree in the middle of the bush somewhere. Once in the bush there was plenty to eat, lawyer berry, fuchsia, blackberry, honey from the flax. There was a lot of honey in a big flax stick. We would suck the juice out of the toot (tutu) leaves through a cloth in order to get only the juice. The berries were poisonous. In school we would 'chaw' wheat. It was worth a hundred lines if we were caught. In summer there was swimming to be had in the Wairau (tidal and warm) and in the Pawa (snow and cold). On Sundays we went to Sunday school and rode horses. We often had horseraces, especially on the flat land by the Maori pa. We were present at the pigeon and sparrow shoots. They caught the sparrows in big nets and let them out of boxes for the gunmen. At the pigeon shoots, we hung 'round the boundaries hoping to pick up any pigeons that had gone out of bounds. We played Hide and Seek 'round the stacks after thrashing.

"There were plenty of pranks too. We hung cotton reels onto doors at nights and then pulled them with cotton. We made dummy ghosts out of hollowed pumpkins with eyes and mouth in them and with a candle inside. One night we combined this with a sheet and so frightened two boys that they ran away through a paddock for all they could go and tripped over a horse rope. The horse reared up and they really thought their end had come. Our favourite trick was to ring the school bell on New Year's Eve. Although threatened with dire punishment if caught, we did this several times by attaching lacing twine to the bell, which we then pulled over a willow and down into a neighbouring potato patch. Gates were always lifted off on New Year's Eve. Dock leaf was our tobacco.

"At school our chief sport was racing, and this was because we had racing, jumps, Hop Step and Jump at the school sports. They had all these at the school picnic in a paddock lent by one of the farmers. There was a free lunch and a lolly scramble. They played Oranges and Lemons, Nuts and May, Jolly Miller, and Three Dukes. Also Merry-go-rounds in which the one in the center would call a name, kiss the person selected, and change places. Occasionally we would have a school picnic train excursion to Picton or Massacre Hill (Wairau).

"There were no birthday parties at all, only school and Sunday school picnics, nothing else. Several families might have a private picnic. Occasionally a party of men and boys would go shooting. The school was used frequently for dancing in the winter, including square dancing, polkas, waltzs, and schottisches. A man with a fiddle played the accompaniment. Some of the young lads in their early teens would practice 'buck dancing' in an old house. On Christmas Day there would be a display at the Maori pa with afternoon tea provided. Attached to the hotel there were Ninepins. These were going all night for the men who wanted them. Put a bob in and the winner shouts the beer. Side bets were also put on. Later their place was taken by billiards. There was no tennis, although lots of people had croquet lawns. Cattle shows arrived in the middle eighties.

"In the evenings there were occasionally magic lantern shows, usually with a Russian scene starring the blowing up of Russian boats. At home we played Hide the Thimble, Postman's Knock, Musical Chairs, Pitch and Toss with halfpennies, and Shove Halfpenny. In Shove HalfPenny squares are drawn on the table. One knocks the halfpennies into these squares from the side of the table with a smack of the palm of the hand against the halfpenny as it projected over the edge of the table. The one who got the most halfpennies in the squares won. On winter nights there was Crib. My father said this was an education and made us play it. There was also sewing, school lessons, talking, and reading (there was a library at Blenheim). Most of the time, however, we went to bed at dusk and were up at six o'clock.

"We had lace-up boots with copper toes so you couldn't kick the toes out, tweed suits, and moleskin trousers. The latter were worn in winter and did not wear out very easily. For winter also there was a 'fore and after' cap which could be pulled down over the ears. We didn't take this off as it was too cold in the frosts. We also wore woolen underclothing or cotton shirts and jackets buttoned up to the neck."

A PICTURE OF UPPER STATUS URBAN CHILDHOOD: CHRISTCHURCH, 1870–85*

"We had an extensive amount of play at home. We made wooden swords with a sharpened end and a crossbar hilt at the top. We wore cocked hats made from a newspaper, so I suppose we fought a few battles. At one time we had a fad for sword-fighting with a basket protection 'round the hands. We played at Red Indians, largely, as a result of reading Fenimore Cooper. We enacted Ballantyne's novels. I remember playing at *The Gorilla Hunters* and *The Little Duke*. Others who had an influence on our play were Scott, Dickens, and Verne.

"For toys we had lead soldiers, cavalry and infantry, in the different regimental uniforms, also some fearsome-looking cannons with which we mowed down with considerable ease long rows of the opposing army. For the greater part, however, our soldiers were made of cardboard. We cut the figures out of

*This account is composed from two sources, a report received from Geo. Von Haast and an interview with H. Von Haast.

paper and then pasted them on cardboard so they would stand up. For toys also there were wooden Noah's Arks with wooden figures representing animals.

"At home we also played shops with my sister as shop-keeper and asked for the most impossible things, and of course the change was never right. I remember also that after we had gone to bed at nights we made an impromptu pulpit and standing up in our nightshirts we would preach a sermon. I am afraid the 'reverend gentleman' was somewhat irreverent at times. This would often result in a pillow fight, of which the domestic authorities took a dim view.

"There were our own made toys, bows and arrows, slings, shanghais, and tweakers. We manufactured various articles such as paua-shell hearts, coconut and silver rings, and various articles from kauri gum. Owing to my father's museum interests, I was an ardent collector of bird's eggs, plants (pressed and prepared), battered coins, and curios generally. I was fond also of chemical experiments in which I made oxygen and hydrogen in a strong bottle wrapped with a towel and then applied a lighted match with the resultant loud explosion. I ground sulphur and chloride in a mortar until it exploded and many more, but my interest was mainly in the spectacular side of chemistry. In the backyard we rigged up a gymnastic bar and did performance on it. Most people, more or less, had a swing. We also had a private croquet lawn in the backyard, and all the boys as well as the girls played this game. It was an amateur game and not highly specialized; practically everyone who had the space for it had a croquet lawn. Tennis came in the late eighties. We also had one of those 'bone-shaker' bicycles, a rough wooden contraption that squeaked a good deal.

"There were many other things to do at home. As there were five in our family, we used to act plays and bring in friends and relations to watch our performances. We played at tea often with little miniature cups and saucers. We played with dominoes and cards, particularly at Black Peter, which was a form of Old Maid. If we lost at this, our father would give us a black moustache of burnt cork, and the younger ones on receiving this would cry. The family did a lot of singing at home 'round the piano, particularly minstrel songs and Old English folk songs. In addition, there were glee- and part-singing evenings. At home we played Cat's Cradle, sack races, three-legged races, Rounders, and stilts.

"We had various lessons to attend. There were colour-painting lessons, flute lessons, and dancing lessons in the early teens. The latter were presided over by a dancing master who played the violin, called out the directions and somewhat scathing comments from time to time. The square dances were all done to regular steps like the minuet and gavotte, not like the square dances of later years, such as the lancers and quadrilles which were danced in a lackadaisical fashion, anything being good enough. At a later state we rode in buggies to innumerable dances in the country.

"There were lots of parties, mostly birthday parties. There would be ten to twenty of these in a year. All the guests brought a present for the birthday child. Nowadays the visitors all seem to get presents! We played Animal Vegetable Mineral, Musical Chairs, Postman's Knock (at a later state—twelve to sixteen), Twos and Threes, Kick, Hide and Seek, Puss in the Corner, Blind Man's Buff, Consequences, French and English, Green Gravels, Ring Ring Rosie, and at Christmas parties always Oranges and Lemons and Nuts and May. Sometimes there were magic lantern shows at these parties. There were also social parties held in the gardens in the afternoon at which all the games were played. At an older age there were certain gags we put on at parties, for example, Rockets, in which all the boys stood in a row and initiated the *sss!* of a rocket and the *oooh!* as it came down. They would slap their knees, *pad pad pad,* as it came down. Another was Sneezing, in which the whole lot said 'Hish hash hosh' quickly together.

"There were other entertainments. As children we were not allowed to attend the sixpenny evenings, nor were we permitted to the garden parties at which the adults played croquet, drank tea, and talked. Punch and Judy shows were sometimes available in the streets but had to be paid for. There were the Anniversary Day Sports in Latimer Square, which included races and a greasy pole. All the sports at these meetings were professional sports. There were no amateur sports then except the school sports. When the amateur athletic clubs were founded later, the public sports died out.

"At the private dame's school we went to, we played hockey with sticks and a block of wood in the street, King of the Castle on a hillock, Prisoner's Base in the street, and another game in which we charged up the street with our hands linked catching each other. There was also a lot of random tagging, Stagknife (throwing at each other's knives), Tipcat in season, very little Hopscotch, but some Leapfrog, Follow the Leader over rough ground, Honeypots, acrobatics. We imitated Blonden of circus tightrope fame. We did this on every fence available, in particular a corrugated iron frame with spikes, upon which we expected every moment that we would fall down and get our testicles ripped out. Other games were Rotten Cricket with a stick, Tip and Run, Hares and Hounds, and occasionally Paper Chase. These were succeeded by football practice when it arrived later, and marbles and spinning tops. All these games were very fugitive. They came for small periods and then went away. There were no gangs, although in our early teens we formed a cricket club which we called the Robin Hood Club.

"At the dame's schools there were the usual tricks. For example, you tripped a fellow up: 'What did you trip me up for?' 'I didn't trip you. I put my leg out and you fell over it.' Throwing darts into the ceiling was also a custom.

"Being a day boy at Christ's College, I was not initiated. There was fighting in the playground, at school, and at Hagley Park often. At Christ's College when it snowed, there was always a snow fight between the boys and the 'louts.' One college boy lost his eye from a stone imbedded in a snowball. At college we played the early football with as many a side as you liked and no stopping when the scrum collapsed. If a ball was caught on the full, it could be run with. Otherwise it was all dribbling. At college, too, all the boys dug holes in the riverbank called 'sausage holes.' Here they cooked their sausages in the dirt.

"We wore an Eton jacket for smart occasions, together with knickerbockers, stockings, and shirt. The shirts we wore always had stiff collars, and we were afraid of getting them dirty, which was a nuisance. At school in summer, we wore straw hats and in winter, caps."

The above two reports both bring out clearly the effects of different social classes upon the play and entertainments of children. On the one case, for example, there are no children's parties. In the other case there are many. These pictures serve also to give an idea of the distribution of games between the school and the home. In the first case, practically the only traditional games are played in the school environment. In the second case, the school games are supplemented by many others that are played at home. In both pictures, however, it is clear that the school playground was the main place for playing traditional games in these years. Many informants have said, "We only played games at school." The school playground provided the constant playing pitch and the constant group of children in sufficient numbers for formal games to develop. It was there that in the later years of the nineteenth century many of the traditional singing, tagging, and skill games came into their own.

This first period in the history of the play of New Zealand children was a period in which many influences affected children's play: the possibilities for adventure presented by the natural environment; the crude social and physical milieu; the Maori wars; the community events of entertainment, sports, picnic, and party; the rugged conditions of school life, both inside the school, on the way to school, and on the school playground. It was the frontier period in the history of children's games.

Never within the last hundred years have children been less stimulated and equipped by adults for their play, a state of affairs which was due partly to Victorian attitudes and partly to the exigencies of the pioneering economy. On the other hand, never have children been so completely free from adult influence in their play. They had a play neglect that resulted in many intricate and complex developments within their games. There was a quaintness and delicacy in their singing and imitative games, just as there was much "graceless self-assertion" in their other games. And that neglect had another important consequence too. It meant that even though they were generally denied the opportunity for initiative within the classroom, they did, with their hosts of self-made play objects and invented games, train themselves in the arts of enterprise in their playgrounds. In this way they were able to prepare in themselves that initiative which the world of their day demanded but which the schoolroom of their day seldom gave.

Finally, it is clear that although New Zealand children in these years did not have the repertoire of singing and traditional games that the children of Lark Rise (Thompson 1945) had, for example, they did have a far greater scope for hunting skills. These children at play were miniature frontier settlers and the symbol of their play life was not Oats and Beans and Barley but the shanghai.

2 the control of children's leisure 1890-1950

9 *setting the scene*

The history of the worldwide change from the negative Victorian attitude toward children and their play, to the sympathetic attitude that exists today, is too complex to be told in full here. Unless we recognize this change in attitude, however, and its ultimate influence on New Zealand adults, the story that follows is in part unintelligible. This change had its onset in the final phase of nineteenth-century recreation, that is, during an upsurge of interest in organized sports, an interest which was later confirmed and accentuated in the twentieth century by large-scale commercialization.

During this period new attitudes toward play and recreation were being formed, attitudes that can be traced back to the physical ideals of Johann Bernhard Basedow, Johann Guts Muths, Friedrich Ludwig Jahn, and Pehr Henrik Ling and later, in the British Isles, to Ian Maclaren; to the military needs of growing nation-states; to a consciousness of health that arose out of deplorable metropolitan and industrial conditions of child labor and out of the experience of war. As a part of the same change, attitudes toward children's play were changing, attitudes that can be traced to the educational ideals of Jean Jacques Rousseau and Friedrich Froebel, to a humanitarian interest in children, to the rise of popular schooling, to the child-study movement arising out of these and the new "evolutionary" science of the day. Whatever the circumstances, it is clear that adults became aware of the existence and problematic behavior of children on a scale that had not hitherto existed.

Although the American scholars of the day had different ideas about the meaning of this child nature (G. Stanley Hall phrased it in terms of recapitulation; J. Mark Baldwin in terms of dialectical imitation; E. L. Thorndike in terms of reward; and John Dewey in terms of instrumental actions, "learning by doing" [Cavallo 1981]), all agreed that cooperation, particularly team sports, was the answer to the problems of character-building for the vagrant masses that had to be assimilated into the reluctant and overly academic school systems of the time.

These new positive attitudes toward play and sports began to appear near the end of the nineteenth century, but they did not have their full effects in New Zealand until after World War I. The period from the 1890s to the 1950s was a transitional period in which the new ideas gradually sifted through to educational ideals and practice. During this period adults began to take a positive interest in children's play, and by so doing they influenced that play in terms of the prevalent ideals of the adult culture. The chapters that follow trace the steps by which the worldwide transformation of adult attitudes to children and their play resulted, in New Zealand, in a transformation of the actual nature of the children's free play itself.

Before so proceeding, however, it is important to emphasize that, in New Zealand, settlements were still sparse and the population thinly scattered. The total white population in 1900 was approximately 700,000; the Maori population was 45,000. The largest towns of the day—Auckland, Wellington, Christchurch, and Dunedin—had no more than 60,000 persons. Most towns were much smaller, and the towns that served farming communities contained a few hundred people and were, in general, desolate places with a few churches, the school, grocery store, and public house. There were no traditional centers of village life. The pub was not the social center it was in England. In what follows we will note the difficulties in organizing recreation and how sparsely it was attempted. At that time, even more than today, New Zealand was a country focused on agriculture and the opportunity to own and farm one's land. The last part of the nineteenth century saw the country consumed with the struggle as to who should own that land, and various tax and government purchase schemes were followed in order to break open the large land-holdings. At the same time, efforts were made to recover from the worldwide depression of the 1880s, which led to sweat labor in the cities as well as widespread unemployment. For some years, departures from the country exceeded arrivals. Revival was in part due to the development of refrigeration and the rapid expansion of the frozen-meat industry through the 1890s; meat soon replaced wool, wheat, and gold as the major export. In addition, a more liberal government in the 1890s pressed through factory acts, old-age pensions, loans to workers, health insurance, superannuation schemes, and the right to vote for women (1894). Dairy farming was facilitated by refrigeration, the invention of the cream separator, and a technique for measuring the butterfat in milk. With little or no resources, a working man could become a dairy farmer. His children, along with many others in country areas, would be up and working by four or five in the morning and sometimes would fall asleep on their books at school.

In the intermediate-sized hamlets of several thousand people, the situation might be more stimulating, but not dramatically so. For example, Lower Hutt, a small town of 2,000, was at the turn of the century little more than a country outpost (Millar 1972). Although joined by railway to the capital city of Wellington (some twenty miles distant), farmers still drove their cattle through the streets, boys swam naked in the local river, and picnickers came by train on Sundays to bathe in the Hutt River. There was a Druid's Lodge and a Friendly Society, which were among the few means that persons could use to ensure against illness and old age, and several churches. The town was surrounded by sheep farms, dairy farms, and market gardens, the latter often farmed by Chinese who were frequently exploited by politicians and attacked by Europeans as the first wave of the "yellow peril" reputedly bringing vice and disease. Bicycle-riding and a race club flourished through the 1880s and 1890s, and these vied for attention with religious revivals, temperance meetings, and the occasional circus. In the 1890s the picnic grounds became a business, and there were several that provided food (buns, ginger beer, and lollies), tennis, bowls and concerts, merry-go-rounds, and swings. In 1892 hundreds went to Hutt Park to watch Leila Adair rise 300 feet in a gas-filled balloon. The amateur swimming club began in 1897. There were pigeon shoots in the back of the Central Hotel, and in 1898 a cycling track was established on the Petone Recreation Ground after two cyclists had been fined five shillings each for driving furiously through the streets of Lower Hutt. A post office was established in 1891, the first telephone in 1897, and in 1899 nightsoil arrangements were made on a city-wide basis. The gravel road was first tarred in 1897, and local citizens were required to cut back the hedges and trees that hung over this street and to close down their adjacent sheep-boiling works and move back their pigs, which were creating a public stench alongside the road. Somewhat later, farmers were urged to arrange the mating of bulls and cows in back paddocks, because although it was a necessary activity it was immodest. In 1919 the council attempted to persuade farmers not to allow such a vulgarity to be indulged in on those paddocks facing the main thoroughfares (Millar 1972). If an isolated country school in a rural area can be regarded as the typical setting for play in the preceeding sixty years (1840–1900), a small town like Lower Hutt is probably the more typical setting from 1900 until World War II.

10 *adult recreation*

The picture painted to this point is one of children at play not much directly influenced by adults, but the break with tradition and adult influence was never complete. The adults of the day harked back to their memories of the homeland for a lead with their recreation and entertainments, just as they harked back to the homeland for a lead with so many of their other social institutions. In recreation as well as, for example, education, they attempted to carry on nostalgically something of the traditions of the land they had left behind them.

In the British Isles the period between 1840 and 1890 was one of transition in popular recreation. In this period there were still important remnants of the traditional village types of recreation; there was an upsurge in the number of new professional and spectator recreations; and then, toward the end of the period, the emergence of organized sports as we know them today. The traditional village pattern of recreation was one of fair and festival breaking periodically with great zest upon the monotony of the laboring year. These festival occasions were essentially "people's holidays." The whole community was present. There were market booths and a variety of sports and games roundabouts: swings, coconut-shies, dancing on the green, races, wrestling, bear-baiting, cockfighting, feasting, and morris dancing. For example, in the hamlet of Lark Rise in the 1880s, which was in some sense a "survival" of earlier conditions, there were two major festival occasions in the year (Feast Day and Harvest Festival) and two minor ones (Palm Sunday and Christmas), with a few smaller ventures for children, such as May Day (Thompson 1945). Many of the sports and games the children learned at these festivals were practiced in the long summer evenings on the village green. Prior to the nineteenth century many of the children's own singing games and country dances were played by adolescents and adults alike both at the festivals and on the village green. All games of fair and green were played in an informal and unregulated spirit—as compared with today—whether games of a gentle hue (e.g., Poor Sally) or games of a rougher texture (e.g., Shinty).

In her book *From Lark Rise to Candleford,* Flora Thompson lists some seventeen singing games known by the girls of Lark Rise and in addition the following local games: marbles, Peg Tops, skipping rope, Tip It, Hopscotch, dibs, Catchball, Pin-a-sight, Kick an Old Tin, catapults, nesting, Mushrooms, climbing, blowing eggs, spadgering. Otherwise village recreation at Lark Rise appears to have been restricted to sewing parties, casual conversation, the inn, and, as the century advanced, church socials, concerts, and penny readings. Many of the immigrants who arrived in New Zealand between 1840 and 1890 would have had a repertoire of traditional lore perhaps a little more extensive than that outlined above. Most were, as Trevellyan (1942:475) says, if not villagers then "only at one remove from the villager." Others, however, must have had their game stock impoverished by the unpropitious industrial conditions of the "Bleak Age" which preceded emigration, and also by the current religious reaction against all forms of entertainment.

In the first half of the nineteenth century these village patterns were interrupted by a tremendous upgrowth in spectator and professional sports: circuses, minstrel shows, amusement parks, dance halls, concert saloons, beer gardens, and horse racing. People whose work had become less vigorous and whose opportunities for recreation were extremely limited developed the habit of watching professional entertainers and professional sportsmen rather than participating themselves. After the mid-nineteenth century this interest in spectator entertainment was partially succeeded by another phase: an interest in amateur participation in recreation, as opposed to professional participation only. Improved communications, the proliferation of national organizations, the conditions of urban life, and military crises all contributed to the new turn of events. The "New Era" had burst upon England and America in the 1860s and 1870s but was not fully noticeable in New Zealand until the 1880s and 1890s.

These changes were reproduced in New Zealand. In the first years of the colony's life we catch a glimpse of village fair and sports meetings that were akin to their English counterparts of the same period. Both fairs and sports shared the characteristic generality and informality of their English prototypes. The New Zealand fairs, like the traditional English fairs, were people's festivals, but they were unlike the English fairs in that they had the festive and sporting side without the commercial functions. The New Zealand fairs had transformed the traditional English fair into sporting events.

In New Zealand therefore, the "social legatee" of the English fair was not a fair but what came to be called an "Annual Sports Gathering." In most of the early settlements, Anniversary Day became the day for the annual festival. In the South Island, however, New Year's Day, the traditional festival day of the Scots, retained the honor. The first Anniversary Day in Wellington appears to have contained a mixture of traditional entertainments but no country dances. The Scots in the South were the only ones who retained their traditional dancing in the pioneering era. There was, for example, dancing to bagpipes at the first Caledonian festival in Dunedin of 1863. Elsewhere the general rule was ballroom dancing in the evening.

Here is a description of a Wellington Anniversary Day in the early 1840s:

As Anniversary Day drew near we held a two-day's fair and races on Te Aro flat. All the settlement turned out in its best—man, woman, and child. It was quite a family affair. Such fun we had. There were funny calico-coloured booths and a Punch and Judy show, and a queer little grandstand from which we watched the races. Then there was a clown, a Grimaldi we called him. He used to rush about and pretend to kiss the women. Fancy a Grimaldi at Trentham! You might well laugh. Then there was the greasy pig to chase—and what shouts of laughter there were, and wheelbarrow races, and a greasy pole, and sack races in which everybody joined. It was also a part of the day's sport for all the young bucks to try and mount a white Spanish donkey which belonged to my father. But no one ever did, and he appeared to thoroughly enjoy the fun. Afterwards the races were held at Berhampore (Wellington) and we used to drive out to them in bullock drays. Dear me, how we used to bump over the dreadful road, and rattle over the stones and roots of trees.

The Caledonian and other Anniversary Sports Meetings of a later period contained many of the same elements included in the description above. Some typical events at different sports meetings are the Highland fling, hammer-throwing, wrestling, footraces, sack races, quoiting, pole vaulting, caber-tossing, bagpipe music, small-sword exercises, walking, boat-pulling, acrobatics, professional sportsmen, merry-go-rounds, Aunt Sally, horse racing, Catching the Pig, jumping, wood-chopping, sawing, wheelbarrow, Punches, and Poney. Children were present at these meetings—racing, eating, dancing and generally becoming involved in the diverse and novel sights and sounds. At the Caledonian Sports, Dunedin 1871, "with as one cynic said—a zeal worthy of a better cause, a number of lads and lassies took part in an unofficial game of Kiss in the Ring" (*Evening Star*, 1848–1948; Feb 24, 1948, p. 19).

Later, when sports developed along more specialized lines,

these sports gatherings lost their significance in the community. Something of their general and festive nature, however,
was continued in agricultural and pastoral shows, which
during the last thirty years of the century took on the characteristics of the traditional fair and at the same time gave birth
once more to the fair's commercial characteristics. There were
agricultural shows, pastoral shows, poultry and horticultural
shows, ploughing matches, and dog trials, and many ended
with a banquet in the evening. Children were usually present,
with or without permission: "What makes me remember that
show? [the first Masterton show in 1871] I had played the wag
from school and when I went back after the show I got a good
dose of supplejack." The children also played on the grounds
after the show day. With machinery left on the showground,
"We schoolboys used to grind dried cow dung in a corn crusher.
I can recall two boys who had a finger crushed" (Bannister
1940:8). In smaller areas the "general community festival" was
first of all a school or Sunday school picnic, which will be dealt
with in the next chapter.

With respect to particular sports, as opposed to "general"
sports gatherings, there were informal adult games that children could imitate. In Wellington in the 1840s, for example,
"the Scotch boys introduced a game of Shinty, which for a long
time remained a favourite. On Anniversary Days for several
years, besides the now abandoned sports of greasy-pole climbing, greased-pig chasing, there was a royal game of Shinty on
Te Aro Flat." Most of the sports of the 1840s, 1850s, and 1860s
were of an "all-in" and sporadic nature, like the game of Shinty
or the traditional games of the village green. In Wellington,
"football was indulged in the streets (most of them yet unformed), but there were few rules and no umpires." In this
unorganized form, football was played sporadically in several
places throughout New Zealand before the onset of rugby union
in the early 1870s. Several areas had the experience of some
form or other of football, and sometimes of several forms in
different halves. Cricket too was played informally, but it was
more widespread than football.

In addition, most areas had their own special forms of
recreation which were sampled by the children in these years.

In the mining districts there was wrestling, and most of the "styles" of the time were reproduced in the school playgrounds. In the South Island there were the activities that go with ice and snow: curling, skating, and sledging. Elsewhere there were boat races, and children sailed their toy boats in imitation. There were steeplechases and later, in the well-to-do homes, croquet. Lawn tennis arrived in the last twenty years of the century, but again this was mainly for those who could afford the expense of a "green."

It must have been of some satisfaction to the early settlers in New Zealand that the time-honored poaching war between landowners and peasantry was transformed into sport in which all classes, not just the privileged, could share. In England, poaching was "not only the livelihood of outlaws, but the passion of men of all classes" (Trevellyan 1942:22). In New Zealand, hunting became one of the earliest forms of recreation, a means of providing food, and in some cases a necessity for self-protection. There were pig stalking, eeling, pigeon shooting, duck and pheasant shooting, and trout fishing. One informant speaks of his job as a boy in the Taranaki in the 1880s when he was given a rifle with which to shoot animals (pigs or wild horses) he saw while the men were clearing off the scrub. The competitive spirit, in the organized form that we know it today, was apparently often lacking in these early sports, as is shown by comments in the Christchurch press in 1863:

It is a common source of complaint that Christchurch is singularly destitute of healthy and invigorating amusement. . . . The Football Club has languished. We have always held the game to be a very hateful one under any circumstances, and it is only among boys that it can be played without fear of serious consequences. Cricket takes too long, Christy's Minstrels are entertaining but not exercising, a constitutional is unthinkable and the boat club is more given to beer and tobacco than rowing.

In general, that seems to have been the state of affairs before the colony began to take its sports seriously from the 1880s on. We find here a pattern of sport that had many of the features we associate with English village life. One could hardly expect children's sporting recreation to be any different.

The period between 1870 and 1900 was one of increasing activity in organized sports. By the 1870s and 1880s practically all sports of any moment in England were organized into large-scale associations. The effects of this organization were felt in New Zealand, but not fully acted upon until well into the twentieth century. Although cricket had been known from the earliest days, it was not until this later period that, along with football, it gained a firm hold and play became well organized.

The pattern of social recreation in the very early years was much like the pattern of early sports in that it was sporadic and vigorous, and, on the whole, informal. English social functions that survived in the new country were the frolics, feasts, weddings, harvest homes, and Christmas festivals. The nature of much of the settlers' regular social life, however, was dictated by the geography of pioneering. The roughness of the terrain and sparseness of settlement, for example, made social intercourse difficult at first. Again, when and where visits were possible, new social media sprang up, in particular, letter reading, teacupping, and that most universal social affair the soiree. Soirees were held on every available occasion. At school openings or anniversaries children participated in the eating and occasionally in the games. Children sometimes participated also in such activities as the frequent musical and part-singing evenings, visiting the ships, sewing frolics, working bees, making things for bazaars, afternoon teas, observing at the blacksmiths, or at the local store, weddings, harvest homes, and Christmas parties.

There is record of special harvest home picnics and Christmas parties for children. Dancing, which along with feasting was the most important and vigorous of pioneer recreations, also made its demands on children. Many informants, especially those whose parents were well-off, report much time spent in their early teens learning the formal steps from the local dancing master. Sometimes these rituals were something of a penance! In one case dancing was for all ages, seven to seventy, and children directly participated. There was occasionally a place for children at the improvised, and later professional, spectator amusements that sprang up as soon as organized life of any kind was established, that is, at theaters, institutes, concerts, glee clubs, minstrels, readings, drama clubs, bands, and musicians. Some circuses even provided contests for children as part of their program.

We can see that the sporting and social recreations of early New Zealand adults did not provide an abundance of game lore for the children to imitate. Recreation was improvised, informal, and sporadic rather than a regular round of traditional procedures.

Up to this point, our concern in Part Two has been with adult recreation and how that indirectly affected children's activities. Now we shift the focus to the way adults *directly* handed down to children their methods of play.

Not until the later years of the nineteenth century did picnics that were especially for children become an important feature in community recreation. In the earliest days picnics were either small-scale excursions with a few friends (the form of the traditional English picnic) or general community festival picnics—or a combination of both, which was most common. The community picnics consisted of an expedition to some spot of natural beauty and games. As such they contained elements from both the traditional picnic and the traditional fair. It might even be said of these excursion-festive-people's picnics that, as a resort to some remote spot of beauty they were an annual and perhaps nostalgic pilgrimage to the spirit of the village green. They were generally held on one, several, or all of the following occasions: New Year's, Christmas, Boxing Day, Anniversary Day, or the Queen's Birthday.

The expedition type of picnic involved simply a long walk or ride, scenery, food, campfire (kettle and roast potatoes), and a rest. It might be to bush or to beach, by daylight or moonlight, and if on a large scale might well end in the evening with a dance, which would be apt to go on until the dawn of the new day. It is likely that the annual sports which have been spoken of began in some places on these general community picnics. This was definitely the pattern in some districts, and also the pattern in some American states during this period.

The following report of the growth of the annual picnic at Taieri, Otago, provides a good idea of how the general community picnics grew, ultimately catered to children, and then split up into separate picnics, some for adults and some for children.

Donald Reid's estate at Salisbury was typical of the larger holding when life centred 'round the economy of the farm. Crops were hand-sown and harvested, and the wool and grain were processed in the home while a steady trade in farm products was developing with the town. . . . In 1859 Reid, realizing that the single labourers were homesick and lonely, began taking the men annually for an [excursion] picnic amongst the native bush. Later, trees were planted on the hillside and grew up to provide a sheltered place for the annual picnic. At this site, on a long form, Mr. Reid provided bread, rounds of corned beef carved by himself, milk and a small keg of beer. The latter was an important amenity to homesick people. This picnic was the event of the year, the Christmas festivity. There were no other holidays and nothing to do even if you had them. There were no conveyances. Gradually this picnic grew very large until it embraced the whole population at that end of the Taieri plain [Otago]. By 1873 there were some 200 people at every picnic. As the families increased it was called the "School Picnic" simply because there were more children and because they made provision for them. The day generally began with a lolly scramble. It was a joke to start things off. The lollies were thrown out of an enormous cannister containing boiled lollies and conversations, mixed with half a bag of hazel nuts. Up would go the lollies and the gathered folks roared with laughter as the lads and lasses scrambled and dived, the more timid ones skirmishing on the outskirts with little success. The next day some of the boys would comb the grass for residues. They might find a trinket or two, but there was little money about in those days. A man with a big tin which he beat with a stick yelled out each event: "Roll up for the married ladies race!" or "Roll up for the tug-o-war." For the men there was the tug-o-war, tossing the caber pole-vaulting (without a bar), wrestling, (which was a struggle to put the other man off his feet) throwing quoits or horseshoes, obstacle races through horse-collars, Hop Step and Jump and long jump, sack-race. The sack race was one of the most important at Christmas. The men would cheat, put a hole in their sack and generally fool and tumble in order to make the children laugh. The great event of the day was the "married ladies race." For years either Mrs—— or Mrs——, the female race horses of the district, won the earthenware teapot. There were few other prizes. The young people played ring games— Rounders and French Tig. The slightly older couples spent a lot of time on the fringe of the picnic flirting and "whatnotting." For the school age children there were races and Hop Step and Jump, with little prizes. Boys' and girls' races were separate. As the years passed the size of the keg increased. Not that there was ever enough in the early days for more than mild satisfaction. By the 'eighties, however, the keg had a much more central place in the proceedings although still well camouflaged. The local Minister, moved by current prohibition agitation, decided to remove the Sunday school children from the picnic. They were afterwards catered for separately. As the school children and the Sunday school children were the same there was only the one picnic. In the late 'eighties the adult picnic faded out of existence although the Sunday school one continued. When the picnic was lost to the children in this way some of the older people carried on meeting each other in the 'eighties and 'nineties at clan gatherings. Here they played such things as Thread the Needle, Egg and Spoon, Trim the Hat, Whistle While Your Tie Is Done Up etc." (Shaw and Farrant 1949:21)

According to Kempthorne, the women (not the local land-owner) were often the first to arrange these picnics, for whereas the men could meet at the store, public house, or blacksmith's, there was no equivalent meeting place for women. "Picnics were one of the pleasures of the time. There was one given by Mrs. McKeller of Brooksdale, and she invited anyone who could bring some children. Father took the waggon" (Kempthorne 1947:100). In very isolated districts such picnics were often the only social occasions of the year; consequently they tended to be numerous. One informant reports that at Tahataki in South Otago between 1875 and 1880 every year there would be the school picnic, the church picnic, the Early Settler's Picnic, and a picnic put on by the local landowner for his daughter's birth-day. In addition, the children of Tahataki would go off to the picnic of the adjacent school at Purekereki. Attending picnics at adjacent schools seems to have been a widespread practice. Thus the Horoeka logbook for February 10, 1905, records, "Only fourteen children present today owing to a large number of them going to the Pukenhinau School Picnic." A later and wiser(?) teacher at the same school cut his cloth accordingly. On March 11, 1910, the same logbook states: "School closed on account of Pukenhinau picnic as there would be no atten-dance."

Clearly, any occasion might be an excuse for a picnic. It was largely a case of no picnic, no society. And this continued to be so in isolated districts well into the new century. For example, "The school was closed to allow the children to attend a picnic to celebrate the opening of the local creamery" (Horo-eka Logbook, December 4, 1903).

The games at these community picnics seem to have been played mainly by adolescents and to have been ring couple games with a slightly romantic flavor about them. In some cases both adults and children were full participants. In others, children participated only sporadically, but conditions differed from place to place, and it is difficult to generalize. The following examples show details of practices in various districts:

The grown-ups, mainly adolescents, played Rounders, Kiss in the Ring, and The Jolly Miller. The children joined in a little but mainly imitated afterwards in the school grounds. (1875; South Clutha)

Oranges and Lemons, Rounders, Nuts and May, Tug-o-War, Jolly Miller, Green Gravels, and Kiss in the Ring were all played especially by those who had just left school, and the last was the most popular. (1895; Waikouaiti)

Nuts and May, Twos and Threes, Kiss in the Ring, and Bull in the Ring with children and adults playing. The young adults would all be in for Kiss in the Ring. (1900; Naseby)

Kiss in the Ring, Drop the Handkerchief, Twos and Threes were played by all present. (1885; Bay of Plenty)

The teens would play Nuts and May and the adults would join in for Jolly Miller. But children alone played Oranges and Lemons, Green Gravels, Pretty Little Girl of Mine, Ring a Ring a Roses, and Pop Goes the Weasel. (1890; Dunedin)

[The O'Briens] often gave an afternoon party in their paddock where a crowd gathered on horseback and in traps. Then there were games of cricket, Rounders, Prisoner's Base, Teazel, Drop the Handkerchief, and races for sweets until we all sat down to cakes and other luxuries on the grass before retiring home to our evening duties. Some of the boys who attended these feasts can remember their feeling of sadness when the wish to eat more remained but the feeling of fullness prevented their gratifying it. (1880; Motueka)

A potato race and others for all. (1895; Rockville)

Sack races, potato races, Mulberry Bush, Jolly Miller, Oranges and Lemons, Nuts and May, Green Gravels, a case of all in. (1875; Wakefield)

The township school picnic day was an outing long looked for and enjoyed with zest. Plump and busted beauty played Jolly Miller with whiskered manhood under the peach tree, and the dames picked up their skirts for the foot races and ran like wekas. (1880; Waikato)

Stock games were Rounders and Twos and Threes. In spite of the cramping dresses, the ladies were able to put much energy into their games, quite comparable to that which the present generation can do in much more suitable attire. Kiss in the Ring, as I remember, was not often played by the proper young ladies of the time, although I have seen it engaged in. Dancing on the green did not get much vogue on account of the miserable roughness of the green and the type of dancing at that time being too decorous for such activities. (1881; Heriot)

Quoits, cricket, skittles. No singing games. (1870; Takaka)

Games were played in which everybody joined. (1860; Port Chalmers)

In the first decades of this century, when I was a boy in Waimea, not a school tea party (an all-district event) went by without playing Bingo and/or Drop the Handkerchief. These were also the usual games at "hop-sprees" and end-of-picking payouts where there was ginger-pop or better. The nucleus of the same company was present at both. They were also seasonal games amongst children, or at least, a pre-tea-party craze used to set in beforehand and taper off again soon afterwards, perhaps to break out in a fresh place unexpectedly. November was tea-party time, and March and April were the hop-picking months, and at these times there seemed to be an almost intuitive urge towards the games, as if the urge were in the air. (1910; Waimea West)

One way the children's picnics grew out of these general community picnics has already been suggested. The prohibition movement, which grew in force during the 1880s and came to a head in 1893, had a definite effect on the adult community picnic. One informant says, "In the nineties the publican's booth disappeared from the picnic" (1890s Lawrence). But the separation of the children from the adult, or general, picnic was also the result of the increase in picnics and picnickers. "In the eighties, the one picnic in each district seemed to suffice, but in the nineties and onwards, additional opportunities for meeting were made" (Heriot). Another influence on the growth of children's picnics may have been the increased interest in children's welfare that marked the latter half of the nineteenth century. According to G. M. Trevellyan, "this enlarged sympathy with children was one of the chief contributions made by the Victorian English to real civilization" (1942:545). The picture drawn in former chapters makes it apparent that this supposed greater sympathy for children should not be overemphasized.

In some areas church or Sunday school picnics existed from the very beginning. In early Otago, for example, church and school were practically one in many districts. There existed a parochial unity embracing all phases of life, and it was natural that this unity should be expressed in terms of a church or Sunday school picnic. Elsewhere the school rather than the church was the community center. The school picnic was typical of those places where the population was religiously heterogeneous and of insufficient size to support separate and "general" church picnics. In many cases school picnics were clearly general community picnics.

While the very first picnics were often called school or Sunday school picnics, they in fact catered as much or more to adults than to children. "It is somewhat difficult to distinguish what were purely school picnics, and what were not. Such events were made an opportunity for a social gathering, of much wider appeal then merely the entertainment of school children" (Kempthorne 1947:97). This continued to be the case in the more isolated rural areas until a much later date. Thus at Horoeka on February 21, 1903, the school picnic was held: "It being a beautiful day, over one hundred people journied to the Waihi falls. During the afternoon, prizes for merit were presented. . . . A jolly little dance was held in the school in the evening." The change that took place over the years, then, was not so much a change in the name of the picnic but, in the larger areas, a change in the function of the picnic. The school or Sunday school picnics of the 1890s catered more specifically to children.

The picnics specifically for children of the 1890s symbolized the breaking up of the general community picnic festival, just as the football clubs of the 1880s and the amateur athletic clubs of the 1890s represented the breaking up of the general community nature of sports gatherings. Both the organized sports clubs and the children's picnics heralded a new era of specialized recreation and rung out long centuries of communalism in social enjoyment.

The activities and games children learned at the picnics of the 1890s are recalled by our informants:

We met at the school in drays and buggies. The drays were decorated. Then there was a great procession to Moeraki. The band from Oamaru played all day long. There were prizes for elocution and singing. Running, jumping, Hop Step and Jump were for prizes. The races were held along an old railway track. There was no Nuts and May in my day; that came later. (1885; Hampden)

The annual Anglican picnic was held close to town. They provided big basketfuls of sandwiches and mugs of tea for lunch, and buns and tea for the afternoon interval. We would run races all the afternoon, footraces, short and long jumps for girls and boys. Prizes were sixpence for first and threepence for second. If you were very fast you could win a lot in an afternoon. (1880; Oamaru)

All the food was provided. Yeast buns were the treat. We would sit around in a circle to get it so no one could get an extra share. In the evening we would get cake and gingerbread. (1885; Hampden)

There was Twos and Threes, Rounders, Jolly Miller, Drop the Handkerchief, and Jingo Ring. The adults would join in. We went in wagons on Boxing Day and the Prince of Wales' Birthday. (1880; Timaru)

The only time the boys ever played Oranges and Lemons was at picnics. Older folks joined in, but it was principally the children and the teachers who played. (1895; Waikouaiti)

Each youngster got a paper bag with an orange and apple, a few sweets, two buns and a fig or two. There was always a tug-o-war if there was a rope, races, sweet scrambles, and swings. Oranges and Lemons, Nuts and May, Drop the Handkerchief, and Rounders. (1875; Dunedin)

Jolly Miller, Grand Old Duke of York. (1890; Dunedin)

Ring and Ring a Rosie, Merry Ma Tansa, Mulberry Bush. (1875; Dunedin)

Drop the Handkerchief, Farmer in the Dell. (1890; Dunedin)

Jolly Miller, Thread the Needle, races, Drop the Handkerchief, Fill the Gap, Twos and Threes. Throwing conversation lollies and Kiss in the Ring by the adolescents. (1890; Moeraki)

Oranges and Lemons, Nuts and May, Prisoner's Base, Green Gravels. (1895; Granity)

Twos and Threes, Jolly Miller, Jingo Ring, Drop the Handkerchief. These were at sports meetings and New Year. There were few school picnics and only an occasional Sunday school picnic. (1890; Ngakawau)

Twos and Threes, Oranges and Lemons, Nuts and May, Rounders, Jolly Miller, Green Gravels, Mulberry Bush. (1895; Westport)

Drop the Handkerchief, Oranges and Lemons, Nuts and May, Three Dukes, Grand Old Duke of York, Mother Mother. (1875; Nelson)

Jolly Miller, Green Gravels, footraces, jumping, and Kiss in the Ring in which adults joined in. A man would have lollies sewn in little bags to his coat. That was one of the things we thought was just all right. We went to the picnic for this more than anything. Of course he had to be young and vigorous. There was a lolly scramble for the younger children and a small greasy pig for the older ones. (1895; Carterton)

State school picnics did not come into my experience till about 1901. During 1880–1900 church organizations held picnics regularly and sometimes ran short social evenings for children. It was only on those occasions outside their homes that boys and girls played together. (1880; Taranaki)

The other place at which adults took children in hand and taught them games was at home. Often this teaching was quite incidental, taking place on any evening when there was time to spare or at "evenings" among friends. There were also "special occasions" when games were played. On these occasions and at other times the main participants seem to have been the youths, with younger children and adults participating less frequently. There are few records of children's parties and parlor games in the first thirty years of the nineteenth century, but records indicate that the pattern was much the same as in the latter part of the century, although on a less extensive scale. There is mention, for example, of a tea party for children in Dunedin as early as 1851, of school feasts in Wellington during the 1840s, and of school and children's treats in other places.

The improved communications in the last thirty years of the century, and the growth in population, led to a marked increase in parties for children and evenings for adults. "Although the homes, were, on the whole, neither large nor elaborately furnished, there was a large measure of social intercourse, and musical evenings at which social games were held, were a feature of the life of the 'sixties, 'seventies and 'eighties. Charade evenings became very popular during the 'eighties and 'nineties and featured very largely as a popular pastime of that period" (Bowman 1948:193).

The churches, for their part, ran afternoons for the children. An informant recalls the local Presbyterian and Methodist church "bun-rushes," so-called because buns and tea were provided. There was seldom any cake to be had either at home or at the rush (1880; Waikouaiti). In Timaru (1880) children called the same affair a bun fight; in Invercargill it was a tea fight (1870). To the adults it was a "tea meeting" or "soiree." These tea meetings were the early form of what later became the church social with games (and of what in 1950 was the Bible Class dance). But it appears that games did not have a great part in the earliest of these "bun-rushes," for they were more often occasions for eating rather than for playing games. Perhaps they were the childhood equivalent of the banquet, which was a pioneer recreation, second only to dancing in popularity. The children's tea party (or banquet) offered a golden and seldom obtained opportunity for a mild gorge, enlivened by an element of hearty competition for the spoils, as the terms "fight" and "rush" suggest.

For children in well-to-do homes there were private afternoons that might be called, for example, "a book afternoon" or "a song afternoon." "Each child came in fancy dress supposedly representing the title of a book or song or whatever the afternoon was supposed to be. There were games" (1880; Wellington). The following recollections give an idea of the types of games played at afternoon and evening parties:

The O'Briens' loved to entertain children in their beautiful home, and parties with games, music, and dainty suppers gave us a pleasant glimpse of cultured life, and their picture books, magazines, and the *Illustrated London News* were a treat we fully appreciated. (1880; Motueka)

Up till the early nineties we had many large children's parties. Also at evening parties in the late eighties and nineties we played Musical Chairs, Spin the Trencher, Family Coach, Dumb Crambo, Charades, The Priest of the Parish Has Lost His Considering Cap, Russian Scandal, Queen Anne's Dead, General Post, and perhaps once during an evening I See a Ghost. (1885; Nelson)

We did such things as imagining we were having tea out of pieces of broken crockery. We all dressed up, which was a frequent diversion at parties. (1875; Wakefield)

Consequences, Author Artist Poet, Proverbs, Telegrams, making little words out of one big one, word-making, cards such as Beg o' My Neighbour, Snip Snap Snorum Borum Bass, Poker, Vingt-et-un, and Grab, especially Animal Grab. (1900; Palmerston North)

Postman's Knock, Blindman's Buff. (1885; Bay of Plenty)

Blindman's Buff, Hide the Thimble, Forfeits, Musical Chairs, Simon Says. (1890; Moeraki)

Forfeits, Postman's Knock, Tit Tat Toe, Mrs. McKenzie's Dead. (1870; North Taieri)

The Priest of the Parish Has Lost His Considering Cap, Blindman's Buff, Fire Air Water, Noughts and Crosses, shuttlecock, Musical Chairs. (1870s; Dunedin)

Doocking for Apples, Hunt the Slipper, Forfeits, Postman's Knock, Family Coach. (1870; Dunedin)

Blindman's Buff, Hide the Thimble, Postman's Knock, Consequences, Forfeits, Musical Chairs, Family Coach, The Priest of the Parish Has Lost His Considering Cap, Simon Says, and acting. (1880; Nelson)

We had nothing to do in the evenings except play cards with the neighbours. (1880; Takaka)

Spoons, How Many Eggs in the Bush, Winks, Queen Sheba. (1890; Rockville)

Postman's Knock, Consequences, The Priest of the Parish Has Lost His Considering Cap, and pandemonium reigned while they were played. (1895; Westport)

The whole outlook of adults toward recreation, sports, and other pastimes has changed since the period 1870–1920. People thought they were "having a jolly good time if they sat through a couple of hours of sentimental songs and recitations, to be followed by a cup of tea with cakes and a polite farewell at the door" (*Auckland Star,* May 7, 1930, p. 21). In 1913 it was noted: "The modern feverish thirst for excitement and amusements was unknown to the class that worked. . . . Young folks helped their parents in the housework and never felt that lack of picture shows or skating rinks" (1860; *New Zealand Herald* [Auckland], Nov. 13, 1913, p. 10). Another writer recalled that youngsters survived without numerous common amusements simply because they had never heard of them. "We were happy at home; those evenings were never monotonous. We had books at any rate" (Cowan 1948:46).

Perhaps what had been most characteristic of this early era in the history of New Zealand recreation was the lack of differentiation between children and adults. Here the local situation mirrored the relatively undifferentiated relationships of children and adults that dated all the way back to the middle ages. After World War I all this was to change as children became increasingly segregated from adult life and made marginal to the economics of the larger society. Childhood was to be differentiated both in its educational and recreative aspects in a way that it had not been before for masses of children throughout human history.

12 schoolteacher and playground

From 1840 through 1890 there is evidence of increasing adult influence on children's free time. A similar pattern of influence can be found where schools are concerned, but again the influence was more indirect at first. Most teachers looked at the playground negatively or indifferently, but the arrival of gymnastic apparatus, cadet drill, physical training, and playground supervision gradually forced teachers to take a more active approach.

The gymnastic apparatus of swings, Roman rings, ladder, and giant strides is still found in some school playgrounds, particularly in Otago. There is little information about the precise manner in which this apparatus was first introduced into the schools. It can only be assumed that some school committees and teachers, influenced by prevailing world attitudes, sought to introduce the apparatus for the benefit of the children. For example, in his report for 1862, Dr. Hislop, secretary of the Otago education board and inspector of schools, reporting on the Waikouaiti school, wrote of the teacher: "He has received in an eminent degree the affection of his pupils, and he manifests much interest in the exercises of the playground, where he has erected a rotatory and a common swing, which are in constant requisition during play hours." And one informant states: "I should like to mention the remarkable work of Mr. J. Walker in providing teachers and schools with a good type of physical instruction. It was a treat to see him put the West classes . . . through military drill, or in charge of the Normal School gym during an evening meeting, on the trapeze, with the Roman rings or horizontal bars, etc. He did great work persuading the board to supply schools with gymnastic apparatus" (late 1870s; Christchurch). Playground conditions, however, often left something to be desired. "The playground was bare earth with a morsel of gravel 'round the 'giant stride.' In winter it became a quagmire. Boys who fell over and muddied their clothes were allowed to stay out of school while a comrade scrapped off the mud with a pocketknife. Victims willing to roll in the mud and volunteers to scrape them down were seldom wanting" (1910; Marton).

Both sexes used this apparatus, but practices varied from community to community. "We had ladders, horizontal bars, and parallel bars, but those were only used by an enthusiastic few and occasionally for drill" (1875; Papanui). Hislop's swings, mentioned above, were described by one informant: "They were made out of two great rounded heavy timbers and massive bolts, strong enough to hold a cartload of horses. They were placed in the girls' playground and used only by them" (1900; Waikouaiti). Even though they were sturdy they were apparently not reckoned strong enough for the boys! In 1905 Terrace End, Palmerston North, had a similar arrangement: Swings were placed in the girls' playground only. In 1890 at Arthur Street, in Dunedin, the girls were less fortunate: There were giant strides, Roman rings, and a ladder in the sheds, but the girls were not allowed on these until the boys had left the playground at four o'clock, and then they were permitted only ten minutes of play. Elsewhere the girls had no say at all. For example in 1870 at Invercargill:

Talk about physical culture! We had it and no mistake. An open-air gymnasium, trapeze, Roman rings, ladders and all. Its position was the eastern side of the playground. The boys became very expert, but what about the girls? The woman's rights movement was then in its infancy, and girls were not supposed to need physical culture.

In some smaller country schools, however, it was a matter of free-for-all, and first-come-first-served, no matter what the sex. "A swing was the only thing we had to play with" (1875; Tahataki).

The provision of this equipment did not imply that there was any supervision of its use. The strength of the material and in some cases the separation of the playing times of boys and girls was meant apparently to guarantee the children's safety, although in some cases the sexes were neither segregated nor safe. In 1880 at Ravensbourne School, Dunedin, swings were erected for boys and girls, and many brave spirits went over the top each day:

Emily Mullinger was excellent on the swing, and others craved to be her partner. In 1881 the boys' swing was reerected and they were repaired again in 1884, and new ropes were provided in 1886. The swings were the great attraction in the playground, and what a scramble to get possession.

There was, however, no provision for other children's playground activities.

Following the arrival of the gymnastic apparatus came the introduction of cadet drill. Teachers were prepared for the idea of organized extracurricular activities by the setting up of a sprinkling of cadet companies in the closing stages of the Maori wars. These companies flourished in the early 1870s, but by the time they were written into the Education Act of 1877 they were already on the decline: "In 1874 the military authorities began to complain of the waning interest in volunteer matters, and more particularly of the fall in attendance of Cadet Corps" (Leckie 1933:314). Before their revival in the 1890s these companies were not extensive. Most teachers were too occupied with the normal duties of the classroom to take on the responsibility of instructing cadets and to spend time keeping the necessary records. But cadet instruction was the thin end of the wedge. The 1877 act recognized in effect that extracurricular activities were a legitimate part of schooling, that schooling could not be considered as a purely academic concern, that there were wider responsibilities to be taken into account. Military drill in New Zealand, as in most other countries, was therefore the first extension of school function to move into the area of supervised children's activities outside the classroom.

This extension of school function contained the seeds of yet a second extension. The 1877 act also stated that teachers should make provision for physical drill, and in some cases this was done, although not always in a systematic manner, for example, "Mr. Bennett on cold mornings would lead the scholars 'round the ground at a trot in what was called the 'snake run' to warm them up" (1880; Wakefield), and "The headmaster would take us to the top of the hill and spend a morning looking at and pointing out the houses. Exercises he called it" (1870; Nelson). In the majority of cases, however, physical drill appears to have been neglected for military drill. This first venture into the playground was marked by all that sternness of mind customarily associated with Victorian attitudes. It was perhaps no accident that the first officer appointed by the Southland education board combined the joint function of drill instructor and truant officer.

Cadet drill naturally provided opportunities for playful escapade: F. M. Leckie (1933) speaks of "horse play with guns." But the military instructors were apparently amusement themselves. Until these instructors were provided free to the education boards by the government in 1893, they sometimes combined military instruction with the duties of janitor. The Invercargill record, for example, speaks of a Mr. Patrick

Walsh, "formerly a Sergeant of the Royal Irish Fusiliers and of Faugh-a-Ballagh fame." This gentleman was generally armed with a short length of broom handle and on one occasion pursued a school inspector who dared to criticize his methods. He pursued the latter with stick and lurid language. Before his dismissal, however, he had provided "games" for the boys in an even more direct manner:

The call to "Fall in" by that commanding voice of the bewhiskered, tall old Crimean Irish Soldier was something to remember ever. No loyal soldiers got off the mark in quicker style than the boys at drill when ordered "Forward at the double." They bolted to the tall boundary fence on the East. When the charging squad was a few yards off the fence, Pat's voice could be heard far in the rear commanding a halt. But the order would be conveniently mistaken for something else as the boys sprang to the top of the fence, which suffered accordingly. At such a moment the stick was handy to stop some boy from knocking his board mount to pieces.

Other instructors were not so amusing, but instead exerted a severe and disciplinary influence, both outside the school and on the drill ground. Some were even exprofessional strongmen.

In addition to drill, the cadet companies engaged in sham fights and shooting competitions. The shooting competitions involved tests of skill between different schools and were in most places the first interschool organized sports. These tests of skill and the annual visits and long trips they occasioned provided ample opportunity for escapade. In some schools where there were no such military ventures the children reproduced the phenomenon in their own way:

Sham fights of a military nature were organized amongst us, probably in imitation of the military reviews that were for some years held on the Wallacetown plains when the volunteer corps from all over the Southland part of Otago would assemble and carry out sham fights and other military movements. With the boys, flax sticks and flax swords were the weapons used. In these affairs the court martial was not forgotten. Well do I remember an occasion when I was court martialed and sentenced to run the gauntlet along the road between two rows of such soldiers who were commanded to deal out to me as many cuts as they could while I passed. I can say that some prepared for it by obtaining harder weapons than mere flax ones. Needless to relate, I did not loiter on that trip, but by the time I had travelled the lines I had some good furrows and a quite warm feeling under my trousers. (1870s; Waianiwa)

In the period between the turn of the century and World War I adult interest in cadet drill and physical training grew more extensive. At first, imperialistic and Boer War enthusiasm was directed toward the cadets rather than toward the physical training movement. During this time, however, the extension of knowledge and understanding of the values of physical training contributed to the displacement of this first and predominant emphasis. After 1912 a great amount of the earlier cadet enthusiasm was directed into the new physical education scheme of those years. The details of this transition are important to an understanding of the transformation of the teacher from academic pedagogue to playmaster.

With respect to military drill, the most important changes taking place in the first decade of the twentieth century were (1) a greater proportion of the drill was actually done by the teachers themselves and (2) drill was often undertaken with great enthusiasm. It was generally admitted by headmasters and inspectors that the cadet system helped to strengthen the internal discipline of the school which was often very poor in the classes of the adolescent aged pupil teachers. They would have agreed heartily with the Duke of York's well-chosen metaphor, spoken at a cadet corps camp in 1905, that the value of the cadets was that they "enable the teachers to get a better grip of their boy" (1905; Ashburton).

In these cadet companies there were dummy rifles, caps, uniforms, flags for the children, and Saturday morning classes for the teachers (Education Department Files 1912). Public support was extensive, and by the middle of the decade, 1900–1910 military camps, valuable presentations for rifle shooting (one ominously enough from the Colonial Ammunition Company), and articles and photos in the weekly newspapers were a regular feature according to the *Journal of Education*. In 1910, to cap it all, Horatio Herbert Kitchener hero and commander of the British in the Boer War arrived on the scene. In order to convey some inkling of the unabashed jingoism which prevailed in this decade, and which it must have been difficult for teachers to resist even if they had wished to, consider the following report of Colonel Wolfe, officer in command of the Auckland District's Junior Cadets. It is 1912 and he is commenting on a recent Junior Cadet parade:

Honour to whom honour is due. Your cadets were magnificent. I have never seen a finer performance wherever I have been. When one considers the dangers of our Empire at the present time, and the help that can be afforded to the Mother Country by the readiness for war of the Overseas Dominions, the hearts of all true Englishmen, Britishers, Colonials or whatever one may call them, must bound with pride at the spectacle of last Tuesday's Parade. God and King is the watchword and I feel that this is the cry of all true Britons. Let the motto of our junior cadets be "Excelsior," let them realize that they are coming forward as the first fruits of the Empire for defense. The Empire great as it is, is unaware of its latent strength. (*Auckland Herald*, July 1912, p. 24)

Suddenly in 1912 the Junior Cadet movement was swept away. There were a number of reasons behind that move: The compulsory clause in the 1909 defense act meant that the junior cadet system, which was introduced primarily to encourage voluntary enlistment, was rendered superfluous; the same compulsory act meant that there was now a large amount of unprofitable overlapping between the junior cadet system of the primary schools and the new cadet system in the secondary schools; the defense department resented the existence of a military organization independent of itself (the Junior Cadets were placed under the education department by the act of 1901); the new government was bent on economy and not particularly attached to a system that had been an advertisement for previous politicians, in particular, Richard Seddon; the physical culturists and medical authorities saw little physical value for children in the existing system of military drill, and even Lord Baden-Powell criticized the system on behalf of the Boy Scout movement, which he contended was infinitely superior and might wisely be incorporated in the school curriculum in place of the cadets.

From the point of view of this study, the most interesting feature of the "throes" which led to the expulsion of the junior cadet system was the manner in which teachers arose in its defense. Their enthusiasm for their new extracurricular "bull ring" activities was shown in their reaction to a depreciatory statement made by General Godley of the defense department. He had the misfortune to refer to the junior cadet system as a "bogus military organization." Strictly speaking, he was more-or-less correct, but his remarks were not interpreted by the public and by schoolteachers in a logical manner. There was instead an uproar throughout the country. Newspapers protested. Groups of teachers were reported to be up in arms. Godley's remarks were captioned a "Gratuitous Insult," "Teachers take Umbrage," and the like.

Nevertheless, in this first decade of the century not all teachers had taken kindly to their new and extended duties. Earlier there had been echoes in the *Journal of Education* of that more narrowly academic attitude which previously had been the assumed attitude of all teachers. Teachers were voicing the last protests of an older order of education in which the teacher was concerned with little but classroom subjects. Such views contrasted sharply with those of the junior cadet enthusiasts. In 1903 a group of Otago teachers put out a pamphlet inveighing against the new demands of technical education, manual training, physical education, and military drill. Earlier in the same year one teacher expressed himself sardonically along the same lines:

A few years ago no authority outside the Board's Inspectors dared enter a schoolroom and upset the usual arrangements. But we have changed that. Technical Inspectors come round from Wellington in order to give teachers much wise counsel about the "brightening of school work and school life." To this the practical man listens politely, but smiles to himself at the childlike ignorance displayed in regard to the actual difficulties of the schoolmaster's work. Now a very imposing person in the shape of a real live Major is touring our schools in order to show the poor ignorant teacher the futility of his methods of discipline and to indoctrinate him in the principles of military drill; again the schoolmaster listens; again the time-table arrangements are upset in order to introduce this new panacea for all the ills of school life. (*Journal of Education*, March 21, 1903, p. 5)

When the junior cadet system was abolished, the education department quickly channeled current teacher enthusiasm into the new physical education scheme. A new syllabus was issued, itinerant instructors were appointed, and courses were organized for teachers throughout the country. According to an editorial in the *Journal of Education* in February 1915, there was "a general state of enthusiasm for the physical training instructors and the new syllabus amongst teachers."

The groundwork for this new interest had been laid in a number of ways. In Otago the gymnastic apparatus was systematically incorporated in all rural and urban schools after 1900. Teachers were expected to take exercises on this apparatus and were examined for their work with it and for their work with the allied apparatus of wands, dumbbells, and clubs. Informants tell of having to raise the money to buy their own dumbbells or clubs, and of the care lavished on silvering the clubs with aluminum paint in order to make them attractive for the school concert (1905, Waikouaiti; 1908, Palmerston North). In 1902 recommendations were made by the education department's military instructor that the Swedish system of exercises be incorporated in a physical training syllabus for schools. The promised syllabus did not arrive, however, until 1908. Meanwhile, readers of the *Journal of Education* were becoming gradually acquainted with the idea of physical education through occasional articles appearing there. There was a 1901 article entitled "Physical Culture in the Public Schools," taken from the *Ohio Educational Monthly,* and a 1904 article of faith by a Colonel Parker entitled "Physical Exercise," which discussed its immense values. In 1906 the Physical Culture Society of Wellington investigated and reported unfavorably upon the methods of physical training in public schools; other investigators, mainly of "eye-efficiency," (or vision) reported unfavorably on the oppressive conditions of schooling. Then halfway through 1906 Dr. Truby King brought the matter of children's education before the public. He launched a crusade in the press and in lectures against the excessive pressure of school work he alleged existed in New Zealand primary and postprimary schools. Great publicity was given to the fact that several former primary-school scholarship winners, as a result of overstrain, had been sent to the mental hospital at Seacliff. Education boards drew ministerial attention to this state of affairs. King recommended that teachers pay more attention to children's recreation and open-air games. With the influence of medical men like King and the influence of the physical culturists, the public and the teachers of the day were being well prepared for the time when every master would consider it his duty to be on the playground. In 1907 the *Journal of Education* remarked in an editorial, "The mass of the people in this colony are, we believe, rapidly becoming alive to the fact that it is the duty of the state to attend to the physical welfare of the children in our public schools."

While the attention of teachers was being turned toward the playground by the provision of playground apparatus and by the growing importance of cadet drill and physical training, their attention also was drawn by the increasing need to supervise the spontaneous activities of children on the playground. For example, the growing complexity of school organization made its demands. When children were massed together in their hundreds in small urban playgrounds, their play had to be supervised for safety's sake. Although in some cases before 1900 teachers did pay attention to the playground, the general tendency was for teachers to neglect their charges during play hours. Thus Leckie (1933) says:

What strikes one as the weak spot in the school of these early years to 1881 was undoubtedly the lethargic attitude or positive indifference of the masters towards their charges after school hours. This lack of interest was responsible for loose discipline in all directions. It is sad to recall the splendid raw material going to waste year after year, without coaches of any description, or attempts to teach the youngsters cricket, football, boxing or other sports. Letters appear in the local press from time to time referring to this very defect. There were no prefects, or at any rate, one cannot recall them or their office; consequently, some of the boys got into mischief.

Other sources also claim that there was no attempt to provide for the supervision of the children:

There was much brutal sport—ducking, bleeding noses, and black eyes with shirts torn in piggyback fighting. Perhaps the play was reflex of the brutal flogging within the classroom. We were left to follow the teachers' example as we liked best. Later the parents complained about the torn shirts, and I remember we had to stop the mass piggyback fights. (1875; Dunedin)

Like every other school there were countless fights among the boys. . . . One rule was that the playground should never be departed from during lunch hour. This deprived those who took pleasure in playing Fox and Hounds from extending their operations over miles of country within easy distance of the school. Of course the rule was regularly broken. (1870s; Green Island, Dunedin)

School games were entirely unorganized, yet the pupils always had some sports every day in recess and at lunchtime, many of which were invented by the pupils themselves. (1880s; Greendale)

In the late seventies and eighties the playground activities were practically in the hands of the children themselves. There was little in the way of organized games as we knew them in later years. Possibly the lack of younger teachers in a school of this size was responsible. (1885; Papanui)

Of course we had our playground games. These were not organized in the modern sense, for the teacher took little or no interest in them. (1873; Waianiwa)

The master never participated in the playground. There was no such thing as practice after school or interschool matches, though I remember in 1896 a new headmaster tried to get a game of Rounders going. It seemed funny to us that he should be mucking around with our play. Perhaps it was a first symptom of the new age. (1890; Gisborne)

It would seem that playground supervision arrived initially to protect the school property and to protect the children. But the former was probably reckoned the more important at first. As soon as the grounds began to take on any semblance of respectability with grass and flowers, the teacher had to protect the property, and he was responsible for seeing that no damage was done. "At his [the teacher's] insistence the scrub was cleared and a fine terrace raised on two sides of the playground. Woe betide the boy or girl who walked on the turf edging. We can recall his look of annoyance, and shout of 'Now, now—keep off the turf' " (1900; Waianiwa). Attention to the school environment was stimulated by the manual training legislation of George Hogben, and in the first two decades of the century school gardening became something of a fad (the *Journal of Education* gives much space to gardening and nature notes during these years), and not an entirely misplaced fad, considering the wastelands of flax and slush out of which the gardens had to be created. In many areas trophies and shields and other awards were given out for the best-kept school property in the district. A further incentive was added after 1916 when teachers received grades for their "taste and care with respect to the school environment." Children playing in the midst of school properties valued to the extent of five grading marks could hardly be left unsupervised.

By 1900 the school population was large enough for the rougher games of an earlier period to present a positive danger to children crowded within a small playground area, but it was not until 1908 that the *Journal of Education* first mentioned the problem. Health was the concern during these years: "The question of increased area of school grounds is one that must soon be faced by the Education Department. The large number of children already crowded into confined spaces in our urban and suburban schools must ultimately effect their physical welfare." But by 1908 most of the more dangerous games had already disappeared, at least from the playground, supervision of some sort being an established practice.

The teaching staff made use of the cadet organization to help with playground supervision and to protect children and property. "The school cadet . . . wore his uniform with a red sash each day. It was his duty to see that no bread crusts or paper were thrown on the school ground" (early 1900s; Palmerston North). A 1907 article in the *Journal of Education* advocated that cadets be used that way. The aims of supervision as set forth in the article are a fair comment on existing playground conditions:

To ensure increased supervision over the playground, to prevent marking, scribbling and writing about the buildings, to keep the grounds neat and tidy, to promote suitable games, and to see that all, especially young children and new pupils, receive fair treatment, I have been in the habit of electing monitors and monitresses. The elected deal with playground supervision in their own way, only reporting to me when there is a deadlock, or when they are unable to cope with the case. Occasionally I am called in to assist with advice, which is eagerly put into practice. . . . Instead of electing the boys, I have appointed as monitors the sergeants and corporals of the cadets. Each then takes his turn as officer of the day. (*Journal of Education,* October 15, 1907, p. 185)

The first example of rule-making for playground supervision was in the regulation of the 1902 Otago education board, clause 47, which said: "Every member of the staff shall take his turn in the supervision of the playground." In the departmental regulations of 1904 it was stated that inspectors should, among other things, report on the teachers' supervision of the playground during recess. This suggests that the practice had been established for some time and was already an unwritten law in many schools. However, although "supervision in recess" was mentioned in these departmental regulations, details on the nature of this supervision did not appear in most board bylaws until the 1920s and 1930s, as far as can be ascertained.

In the earlier years there were undoubtedly playground accidents and other incidents that brought irate parents to school and led teachers to keep a more careful watch on their charges, but there is little evidence for this. In those times there may have been greater implicit acceptance by parents of the hazards of the playground. The first mention of accidents in the *Journal of Education* came in 1921, when under the heading of "Accidents to Pupils" an overseas article was printed, the editor noting: "This highly interesting article is of some topical interest to teachers in view of recent cases in court." The first mention of the subject in the *Education Gazette* occurred in the early 1930s: "The attention of the Department has been drawn to accidents which occur from time to time on the playgrounds. In some cases parents are inclined to think that these are due to lax supervision. Teachers are therefore urged to supervise with special care whenever the work of play is such as contains possibilities of personal injury" (*Education Gazette,* September 1, 1933, p. 139). There were also several articles on accidents in *National Education* during the 1930s. In fact, the 1930s seem to have been a period of new consciousness of playground dangers. This was also the case in England. Perhaps this accentuated consciousness had something to do with the final excision of ruggedness from the playground that took place in that decade.

Because teachers took an interest in gymnastic apparatus, cadet drill, physical training, and playground supervision, they were drawn closer to the playground, but this did not markedly influence children's play. Gymnastic apparatus introduced new acrobatics to children, and drill and physical training provided new subjects for imitation, but while the new supervision replaced the previous lack of supervision, it was of a negative rather than positive nature, a preventative rather than a stimulant, and on the whole this negative approach remained general until World War I. The main effect of these various influences was indirect rather than direct. They accustomed teachers to the idea that the playground was their concern, but they did not themselves greatly influence teachers' attitudes about the nature of the play that should take place in the playground.

13 *the playmasters and the new philosophy of play*

While the indirect influences described in Chapter 12 were gradually changing the nature of teacher attitudes to the playground, other more direct forces were also in embryo, forces which ultimately had the effect of transforming playground supervision from a negative activity aimed at the prevention of crime and accident to a positive duty leading to the promotion of certain specialized play activities. These new influences, which ultimately became all-important in the teacher's attitude to the playground, were organized sports and the philosophy of play that paralleled it.

During the 1880s, football and cricket clubs had sprung up throughout the country. In 1888 the first Anglo-Welsh football team toured the country. New Zealanders acquitted themselves reasonably well and football grew apace, particularly after the depression years. In 1890 there were seven hundred clubs in the country, and in 1892 the New Zealand Rugby Football Union was formed. Then from 1903 to 1905 several events occurred that were destined to have immense effect on the New Zealander's attitude to sports, particularly to rugby. In 1903 a New Zealand rugby team won all its matches in New South Wales, scoring 400 points to 13. In 1904 a New Zealand team defeated an English touring side, and finally in 1905 the touring New Zealand team won 31 out of 32 of its matches in England, scoring 839 points to 39. For a young colonial country the achievement was dazzling. Politics bowed to sport. The Prime Minister is said to have cabled his country's congratulations. Overnight, as one writer said, "the 1905 tour . . . provided us with a national Myth" (Weller 1949:24). This national event, which had such an immense effect upon the general public, can hardly have failed to influence the schools and their teachers.

Up until the 1890s teachers in most areas appear to have paid little attention to rugby. As early as the 1880s there is record of some interschool rugby matches, but little account of teacher participation. In most cases the game seems to have been spread not by teachers but by the boys.

Later several boys . . . returned from grammar school in Wellington and brought with them a knowledge of the rugby game, and one of them had a football. This was the start of the game in Carterton. . . . The chief difficulty was the ground, for few clear paddocks of the necessary area were free of logs and stumps. Learning to punt, drop kick, and place-kick were about all that could be done at first. (1880s; Carterton)

There is record that primary-school boys in the 1870s and 1880s even formed clubs to seek matches with teams of equivalent merit. In many cases pupil teachers were apparently responsible for bridging the hiatus between the interests of teacher and pupil. In this respect, although themselves the products of educational abstemiousness, these pupil teachers had a broadening effect on the sympathies of the system within which they

worked so hard. In most of the schools in the early years, teachers were in the main mature "dominies" or "masters," not
usually interested in the playground activities of their children. One reminiscer, referring to the relations between
teacher and pupil says, "There was a feeling of detachment,
and each seemed to hold aloof from the other. . . . With the
passing of the years, however, with younger and more ardent
teachers on the staff, the atmosphere changed and a degree of
mutual confidence was engendered" (1875; Papanui). Pupil
teachers of thirteen or fourteen years or more were not always
loath to join in the playground games that they had been playing themselves as pupils a year or so before. Apart from their
natural interest in the games it may have been their only
chance for exercise or their only chance (albeit not always a
successful one) to take it out on some of their unruly age-mate
pupils. Pupil teachers going to new districts took their games
with them and handed them on. Thus:

Mr. McLeod came to the school when I was in the headmaster's
room; he being but little senior to many of the boys, we did not take
him too seriously. . . . Looking back now I am convinced that we
went over the edge at times. He earned our thanks by introducing
rugby football into the school; he played with us and taught us the
game. We seemed to take a special delight in bringing him down,
but being more careful of his clothes and appearance than we were,
he did not give us many chances. He got rid of the ball promptly,
and, as he was the teacher, we could not mix it with him or tackle
him unless he had the ball. (1880s; Waianiwa)

By the late 1890s a new generation of teachers had arrived
—teachers who as boys had themselves played in the sporadic
interschool fixtures of the preceding twenty years and who now
gave their time voluntarily to coaching and organizing school
teams. In the last decade of the old century and the first decade
of the new, there were regular interschool sporting competitions in various centers. In Wellington, for example, there were
primary-school football championships in the 1890s and also

School Cadets and volunteers.

primary-school matches against the Wairarapa. After 1900 there were regular football, cricket, and tennis practices and interschool games in Wellington, and as early as 1907 a Wellington City School Sports' Association was formed.

Informant W. H. Clark, himself a teacher, surveys the changes in rural schools between 1880 and 1920:

Till I was fourteen years of age and had left Taranaki, no teacher ever took the slightest interest in the many games played by boys. Even the few interschool games boys played were organized and arranged by the boys themselves. In the period between 1890 and 1900 only one teacher took an interest in school football or cricket. After that period, adult interest became more general. Any other game was ignored or opposed. As late as 1920, soccer and hockey met with considerable opposition and in some cases were quite barred. Between 1900 and 1910 at Horowhenua an interschool athletics meeting was arranged, and our little grade three school participated. Again in Wellington between 1910 and 1920 our grade four school took part annually in an interschool athletic competition.

Athletics, it is worth noting, had in these years a position of importance paralleling that of the major sports, cricket and football. This was a direct carryover from the importance of athletics in the annual sports meetings of this age and particularly of the preceding age.

The same period saw also the growth of interest in the recreation of girls. After the Boer War, for example, physical education for girls had become an accepted doctrine even if not the unexceptioned practice. This drill was sometimes taken by "drill sergeants," but in some places, women teachers played their part. "The physical education of girls, consisting of poles, clubs, dumbbells etc. are now exclusively done by women," reports the *Journal of Education* in 1908. As a part of the same interest there was at the same time a growing concern for the health and physical welfare of girls. The recommendations of the Physical Culture Society in 1906 are a pointer to the new attitudes and a fair comment on existing conditions: "That teachers receive instructions in the matters of hygiene and dress, and that they be enjoined to direct the attention of the girls particularly to the injurious effect of tight underclothing, and that the boys wherever possible be allowed to exercise without coats and collars."

This new attitude to girls' recreation posed a problem that had not occurred in the case of boys. The boys had football, but what was to be the recreation for older girls? In 1901 in the *Journal* there appeared an article entitled "Games for Children" and in 1903 another entitled "Games for Growing Girls." Both were from overseas sources, and the introduction to the second indicated the contemporary problem: "It is not easy to entertain young girls ranging in ages from 12 to 16 years. The manager of clubs, guilds, associations and Girls' Friendly Societies often seek in vain for some solution to the constantly recurring problem 'How shall we amuse the girls who are too old for childish games?' " The problem was not easily solved, and it was the lack of a solution that largely accounted for the overwhelming success of girls' indoor basketball when it was introduced into Bible classes in the second half of the first decade. In 1906 the Reverend J. C. Jamieson, a Presbyterian youth worker, toured New Zealand introducing basketball to girls' Bible classes. It achieved great popularity, although it was first regarded as somewhat ridiculous by the onlookers. From this source it spread to the primary schools as an outdoor game, and after 1910 it became the first organized sport for girls carried out on an extensive scale. By 1912, for example, fifteen girls' teams were entered for the primary-school basketball competition in Auckland. Associations for primary-school basketball were established in Dunedin and Wellington in 1914.

Thus in the first decade of the twentieth century the pattern of preventive supervision which had replaced the earlier lack of supervision was itself modified by voluntary coaching of a sporadic but often vigorous nature.

But the football-loving community and the football-loving masters did not just proceed in mute silence to the task of turning child players into sportsmen. There were teachers interested not just in taking sport but also in the ideas behind their undertaking. These ideas were at first often expressed as a part of the hostility of some teachers to the prevailing extracurricular activity, military drill. One letter to the *Journal* in 1909, for example, said:

All boys, both in town and country, at this age are eager for games, cricket, football, and the like, and to insist upon the continuance of military drill is, I fear, to make our growing lads thoroughly sick of soldiering. . . . If plenty of training of other kinds is found for our lads, *training on the discipline of the football and cricket field*, they may later on be brought in for the final military training. [Italics added]

The connection made between discipline and sport is worth nothing. It will recur again and again.

One of the first spokesmen of the new outlook was H. A. E.

Milne, principal of the Auckland Teachers' Training College. Under his aegis the first training college female teacher of physical education was appointed to instruct women in 1910. Milne was an advocate of bodily training and physical fitness, and his views read like a local rendering of the "Spartanism" of Granville Stanley Hall. As is evident from his training college report of 1910, however, Milne was ploughing a new furrow: "Tennis was played by every student in the college. Everyone received two separate hours per week, but some looked upon this as a waste of time, and it was difficult to get them to see and feel the need for a break which increased vitality and greater output." He went on—and here is Rousseau, Spencer, Hall:

The longer I live the more I am convinced of the need of active sweating exercises followed by cold baths for young people—it clears them physically and mentally. . . . A student unable to take part in a game is not, in my opinion, suited for school teaching. Playing with your children is the surest help to influencing them that I know, and if the teacher is unable to do this he loses a help he cannot get in any other way. (Baird 1942:24)

This was a comparatively new view in 1910. Today it is commonplace, the wise tip of every headmaster to every young teaching student on the problem of discipline. In some respects Milne's views read like an echo of the English public school attitudes of the previous century. They read also like an echo of the New Zealand reproductions of the English public school. Thus one writer, off to Christ's College, Christchurch, in 1870, wrote: "It was of course a great advance in my educational life . . . giving me a place in the renowned college sports, tops and marbles of course being derided, and great emphasis being placed on cricket, football, and the fives court." This is reminiscent of Stalky's attitude to similar infantile diversions (Kipling, 1968).

Milne's views are important because by 1950 they had become the unquestioned assumption of the majority of teachers. In September 1912 he said in the *Journal of Education:*

As character training is admitted to be our goal, it is interesting to see what effect the play of the school games has on it, and consequently comes the corollary, what are the most suitable games to produce this effect. [Milne assumes the answer and proceeds.] Games undoubtedly have a great effect on character, summed up in the one word, "sportsmanlike." They give it its true initiative, promptitude, courage, unselfishness, and the power of leadership; they promote social growth and in many other ways improve one's powers, but when all is said and done, it is learning to "play the game" and never to hit "below the belt" that constitute the great values.

It was *mens sana in corpore sano* again. But the New Zealand version was destined to be somewhat muddier and definitely more proletarian.

The new outlook received support from other directions. It was an answer for those who felt that the state of children's health was so poor "that scores of children ought to be roaming the hillsides" (*Journal of Education,* May 15, 1912, p. 83). It supplied purpose to physical education and tangibility to play theory. And most important of all, it was easily intelligible to the sports-minded public.

In 1914 the *Journal* published an article entitled "Play as a Factor in Education" by J. S. Tennant (later Professor of Education at Victoria University College), its first on the subject, which put before institute members the latest views on play, chiefly those of Karl Groos. Tennant gave the views a twist that made them particularly relevant to the local ethos. "We must recognize the necessity for teaching our children how to *play,* " he said, and then added, as if the two were equivalent, "We should teach them all the *games* we can." It was an appeal as necessary then as it is in part superfluous today. Physical educationists, for their part, also emphasized games. In 1912 "the official attention was directed to the value of organized games and these weekly found a place in the programme" (Butchers 1930:235). The *Journal* in 1913 records the appeals of a number of teachers for help in organizing their games programs. In 1916 the president of the Educational Institute devoted a great proportion of his presidential address to the question of sports and character. It was the first presidential address in which a place had been given to sports:

Inseparably connected with the health of children are the physical conditions under which they pass their school life. . . . So long as certificates of proficiency are granted almost solely on work done in a few academic subjects, and no official recognition is given to skill in some of the broader activities of school life, the pupil does not realize a material need to excel in such physical exercises as swimming and jumping. . . . In emphasizing the need for manly qualities the war is already making a demand on the schools for their development in the young. . . . In England the President of the Board of Education is asking for the inculcation of a patriotic spirit in school children. I believe it will be through school work in the playground that we shall have to stiffen up the moral fibre. . . . The value of team games for adolescents in developing co-ordination of effort and esprit de corps has long been recognized as of great educational value. . . . As a people we probably owe much of our character development to our love of these games.

Once again it was the alliance of sport and character that was stressed.

It is clear that the carefree, albeit strenuous, approach that had characterized the sports of the old village green was on its way out. Sports, in particular rugby, were beginning to take a place of much greater importance in the national ethos than that to which it would have been entitled as a mere recreation. Perhaps, as Murdoch says, "through Rugby a young country conscious of its weakness found a justification for national pride" (1943:207). The subsequent "All Black" (New Zealand's name for their representative rugby team) victories of 1924 did little to alleviate this tendency to high seriousness in the matter of rugby football. In fact, it may be true that in the years that followed, rugby almost ceased to be a sport and became instead a "religious exercise" (Mulgan 1949:15). Whether or not this was the case, there is no doubt that football and sports in general helped break down the isolationism of the syllabus-bound school in the first decades of the new century: The community ideals of sports influenced both the teachers and the children; the community placed a new and intense value on certain types of recreation; the teachers followed in step; there arose a philosophy of sport and play which was fated to change drastically the teachers approach to the children and to their play, and in turn was fated to change just as drastically the nature of the children's play itself.

14 *an era of change in play*

Between 1890 and 1920, changes were taking place in the general recreative patterns of the community that affected the play of children. By 1900 communications were much improved and the colony was more prosperous. As a result the new energy liberated for recreative purposes manifested itself in an intensification of the recreative forms that had characterized the preceding twenty years. It was the last although frenzied phase of nineteenth-century recreation. Social evenings, school concerts, and picnics flourished with a much greater intensity. Mulgan, speaking of 1900, paints the picture as follows: "Much more than today, people stayed at home and made their own amusements. They gathered round the piano and played card or round games. There may have been a few gramophones. The moving picture was still a curiosity; Hollywood was in the future. Stage plays, however, and musical comedy and vaudeville, came frequently, and for its size New Zealand received a remarkable number of overseas entertainers of all kinds" (1949:6).

During this period also the school and church gradually extended their recreative functions beyond the annual picnic and tea meeting. Functions of a broader social nature were arranged, and the extensive play at parlor and other social games that had gone on in the preceding years made it possible and natural to make use of these games. In this way the training the children had received in their homes and in the playgrounds in those earlier years contributed toward new social forms. The church which had hitherto provided only for occasional bun-rushes now began to hold social evenings at which parlor games were played and supper was served. These parlor games were approved by the church in a way that the relatively sophisticated ballroom dances were not.

The school also broadened its scope in this period and was responsible for such social events as fancy-dress balls and garden parties. At the balls the children played games like Lavender Blue, Highland Fling, and then Grand Old Duke of York, and at the garden parties "the children were all trained by the teachers in the maypole dance. There was also the ribbon dance, in which we did massed drill with coloured scarves" (1910; Temuka). Concerts were popular with the children and parents, though their preparation took a large amount of time and the effort required to train the children was often something of a persecution for the teachers. Boys clad in uniforms and with wooden muskets performed cadet evolutions on the stage. Children acted, recited, and sung. In some cases there were even mock debates by children on such subjects as "Should women enter Parliament." "Very popular entertainments were the magic lantern shows. Serious gentlemen with illustrated travel talks toured the district with horse and trap; some specializing in visiting schools to collect the nimble threepences from the children" (1890s; Otago). Then there were the breakup ceremonies: "What great prize givings we had. Assembled in the quadrangle we listened to speeches from the mayor of the town, the chairman of the Chamber of Commerce, and waited for the announcement 'School is now closed until——, the date generally being lost in a burst of cheering" (Invercargill). School bands made a call on some children's time. Many of these were founded in the 1880s and lapsed and revived sporadically thereafter. They provided their own peculiar opportunities for escapade. Thus in Dunedin of 1888 it was reported that "the drum was punctured by a stone thrown by a larrikin from above the quarry."

Until the death of Victoria, the Queen's Birthday was always a holiday. Subsequently, royal holidays appear to have been somewhat more commonplace. In Queen Victoria's day any holiday was a community holiday and a reason for joint celebration. Later a holiday was everyone's private concern and there was no peculiarly group lore arising out of it. But in Victoria's time—

> Hip hip hooray!
> For the Queen's Birthday
> If you don't give us a holiday
> We'll all run away.
>   (Dunedin 1870; 1890)

> Hip hip hooray,
> For the Queen's Birthday
> On the twenty-fourth of May.
>   (Charleston, 1890)

The inspector's visit and the royal visit of the Duke and Duchess of York (1901) were also occasions for special holidays and provided opportunities for play. And what a boon the Boer War must have been:

In those stirring days when bells and whistles were wont to sound the paean of some fresh victory—Lady Smith relieved, Cronje surrendered, Mafeking relieved—the schools promptly emptied into the streets. Streams of boys and girls making for the Post Office Square swelled the din and excitement of the noisy demonstrations, to which even staid and venerable citizens contributed.

Events held on such holidays in the 1890s included football, rifle shooting, and picnics (Tuapeka).

Guy Fawkes Day was not forgotten. Throughout most of the nineteenth century not many children had much experience with fireworks, and Guy Fawkes in most places meant only a bonfire, as was the case in most English villages at that time.

For weeks beforehand the boys collected material suitable for a royal bonfire on the night of November 5th. Sometimes if the policemen had not been consulted, or if the pile was placed where it was likely to cause damage to adjoining property, the boys found their timber and branches scattered in all directions by the ruthless hand of the law. (1840s; Wellington)

But in the period we are at the moment concerned with, things had changed. In the larger towns Chinese crackers were in vogue (1880; Timaru), and by 1900 they are said to have abounded in the main centers. In the South Island the fireworks were held on New Year's night, the evening after the Caledonian Sports, rather than on November 5. One female informant (not a typical informant) describes the event in Dunedin:

Guy Fawkes Day we celebrated with papier mâché masks. I can remember the hot, painty smell of them yet when you had worn them for a while. We did not as a rule make a guy, though I seem to have a faint recollection of doing so once—and we would certainly not have been allowed to drag one 'round and ask for pennies. We would let off a few crackers, but fireworks were generally associated with New Year's Eve. We always spent the Christmas and New Year fortnight at the seaside or in the country, and my father usually took an assortment of simple fireworks with him for New Year's Eve. (1890; Dunedin)

According to Johannes Anderson the children's Guy Fawkes rhymes of the 1880s were more extensive than those of 1950 (1949:382). This seems to have been generally true, although there are exceptions, as we shall see. One old rhyme not generally used but reported from Dunedin of 1875, a rhyme which was used in Scotland, was used here on New Year's Eve:

Git up good wives and shake your feathers,
Dinna think that we are beggars,
Only bairnies come to play,
Git up and gi us our *hog manay*.

The longest example of a Guy Fawkes rhyme comes from Christchurch of 1920:

Please to remember the fifth of November,
The gunpowder treason and plot.
I see no reason why the gunpowder treason
Should ever be forgot.
Four and twenty barrels lain down below,
Blow old England overflow.
Happy was the night, happy was the day,
See old Guy Fawkes going to his den
With a dark lantern and a candle in his hand.
Get out! Get out! you dirty ole man!
Holla, Holla, boys, make the bells ring.
Holla, Holla, boys, God Save the King.
A pound of cheese to choke him,
A bottle of beer to wash it down,
A jolly good fire to roast him.
Christmas is coming, the pigs are getting fat,
Please put a penny in the old man's hat.
If you haven't got a penny, a hapenny will do
If you haven't got a hapenny, God Bless You.

The informant claims that as children they would never get their money unless they were able to chant masterfully this particular rhyme from beginning to end. Often they would be lined up beside their "Guys" and the money was given to the child able to say his rhyme the best—and that generally meant the loudest. He remembers also the pennies that were thrown down to the crowd of children from the Express Building in Christchurch. This practice, and the following one, is reported also from other centers. Certain adults delighted in heating the pennies on a shovel held over the fire. These were thrown out with the other pennies, much to the consternation of the children who were striving to catch them or pick them up. Generally the children would pick them up irrespective of the burn, or kick them into the gutter to cool in the water. Many carried the scars—burns—of Guy Fawkes for many weeks after. Another trick was to wrap a penny in silver paper so that it would look like a half-crown flying down. And pennies were occasionally dipped in hot lead with similar intent. One Christchurch informant had a trick by which he was always successful in getting many of the pennies thrown down. As the pennies fell he would run forward, jabbing at the bending children with an open safety pin. As they recoiled he would seize the coins.

In most cases the rhymes used in later years were relics only, although at Millerton on the west coast in 1949 I came across a rhyme in a form more complete than usually is the case. "But the second verse isn't important," said my informant, "because by the time you get to it, everybody is outside looking at you, and you feel so embarrassed you don't want to go on." The Millerton rhyme was:

[1st verse]
1 Guy Fawkes Guy, Stick him up high,
2 Stick him on a lamppost and there let him die.
3 Christmas is coming, the goose is getting fat,
4 Please put a penny in the old man's hat
5 If you haven't got a penny, a halfpenny will do,
6 If you haven't got a halfpenny, God bless you.
[2nd verse]
(Repeat 1 and 2 above)
7 A pound of cheese to choke him,
8 A bottle of beer to wash it down,
9 And a jolly good fire to roast him.

Anderson states that the full song was usually sung and by groups of half a dozen, "producing an effective volume of sound, nothing like the tiny piping of the present" (1949:382). The tiny piping was usually little more than lines 1 and 2 above together with

> Penny for the Guy
> A halfpenny will do
> If you haven't got a halfpenny,
> You're a mingy Jew
> ["or nothing will do," or "God bless you"]
> (Forbury)

In some places a little more was said. At North East Valley, Dunedin, there were lines 1, 2, 7, 8, and 9. The following comment in the *Evening Post,* (Wellington, May, 11 1949, is a fairly accurate description of what had happened:

Guy Fawkes Day seems to be another honourable institution that is now on the decline. It seemed so this morning when a few desultory small boys roamed the streets seeking a few pennies to buy the traditional fireworks. "A penny for the guy, Mister?" was about the best that could be heard from most collectors. Gone are the good old songs and chants. . . . Bands of juvenile pirates complete with hideous masks swarmed about the trams at Courtenay Place for a while this morning like beggars in an Eastern Market. They did some brisk business too. A few scooters, carts, and prams were decorated with the conventional stuffed sugar bags and old hats and coats, and these made some attempt at the time-honoured parading that precedes the real Guy Fawkes Festival.

In the old days, however, it is clear that the festival was not always as "pure" as it might have been. Informants report: "We had few fireworks. There was not the money to buy such things. Instead we would get together in mobs and roam about causing mischief" (1890; Gisborne) and "Guy Fawkes Day was a battle royal. Different parts of the village clashed together with flax whips and rotten eggs. Later all would combine to burn the Guy" (1895; Collingwood). In the 1940s the evening had other sidelights: "On these occasions, there were crackers down necks, in hair, and everywhere imaginable. I don't think we ever enjoyed anything more than Guy Fawkes Day. I remember the first time I went to such celebrations, though, I ran home screaming" (1945; Hawkes Bay). Another informant recalls, "One of our special tricks was to tip a sky rocket over just as it was going off—just to see the way it would make a clean sweep of a crowded street" (1935; Wellington).

April Fools' Day cannot be said to have ever been a very significant festival in the New Zealand child's year, yet in a year almost completely devoid of significant festivals, except for Christmas and Easter, it had its importance. In the nineteenth century it was an adult hoax as much as a play activity of children. There was, for example, the well-known press hoax in the 1880s at Dunedin; on April 1 the morning paper described a nonexistent whale that had been washed up at Tomahawk beach. Crowds turned out to see the monster, and those returning elaborated on the immensity of this "fish." For the greater part, however, April Fools' Day has always been the day when children made fools of one another and of the teacher, though an informant claims that the distance between teachers and children in those days was too great for any worthwhile tricks: "The teacher's authority could be so peremptory you were never sure what might happen if you abused the licence" (1895; Gisborne). Others were more successful:

Another thing we remember well was sticking tails on him [the headmaster] on April Fools' Day. Hilarious laughter used to proceed from the class as he strutted 'round the room with his long dust coat on and the tail sticking onto him; but he always had a trick of getting even with the class. In the middle of recitation there would suddenly be a dramatic pause and he would make a frantic rush to the window exclaiming, "Boys and girls, there is a house on fire!" After everyone had jumped up on their seats and were on the tip-top of excitement, he would calmly walk back between the forms and, ordering the class to sit down, resume work with a smile on his face. (1874; Green Island School)

We were not happy till we had fooled somebody before twelve o'clock or whatever the time limit was. Grown-ups for preference, and a teacher if possible. We were not very ingenious. "You dropped your handkerchief" was a favorite gag, or "Somebody wants to see you at the door." (1890; Dunedin)

My observation of April Fool at a later day was that it completely interrupted the normal playground play, at least for the preschool period 8:30 A.M. until 9:00 A.M. At Forbury in 1949 I observed groups of children wandering around arm in arm as if fortifying each other by expressing their hostile tricks and jeers only against those outside the arm-linked group. At North East Valley School, Dunedin, if other children tried to trick you after twelve o'clock you said:

> April Fool's Day is past
> And you're the April Fool at last,
> Four farthings make a penny
> And you're a bigger fool than any.

Or simply "Ya Ha! You're the biggest April Fool." Sentiments could be expressed in terms of playground scribble: "A duck in the pond, a fish in the pool, whoever reads this is a big April Fool" (1941; North East Valley, Dunedin). Other tricks were: We put books on the cupboard so that they would fall on the teacher. (1935; Wadestown)

At one time I used to dread April Fools' Day, as my mother was so good at putting things across me. When we were small our main gags on the way to school were "Look at the monkey over there in the paddock," "So-and-so has a new duck pond. Look at it." (1945; Hawkes Bay)

April Fools' Day is a day on which you try to fool everyone without them knowing it, for example, pin paper on their backs, put a drawing pin on a chair, tell a person to look in his or her letterbox, and so on, everything being silly. (1949; Devonport)

"That boy has got two pairs of glasses on." "You dropped your handkerchief." "There's ice on the baths." (1949; Caversham)

"Eh mister, your tyres are flat." "Eh, you've got your lights on." (1949; Nelson)

Other special occasions of this period had important effects on children's play. Both Inspector's Day and the last day of the term had interesting play manifestations. It is clear from all accounts, for example, that Inspector's Day was a day of great strain both for teaching staff and children.

It was a day of extra tension and general anxiety. The school was polished and our slates washed. There were flowers in the fireplace and the teacher had his best suit on. Intuitively we felt it was an important day. The atmosphere was ceremonial. Fortunately these educational Mussolinis had a knack of expatiating on various subjects, and a good deal of the inspection went by the board. (1890; Gisborne)

It was a nightmare. All maps were turned to the wall, nobody was allowed home for a hot dinner; it was as if our last day had come. (1900; Moeraki)

A whole year's work led up to it; next year's work depended upon it. When the end of the year drew near, all the work was laid out and carried through with the inspector's visit in view. We knew all the signs and portents, and when the day at last came we sat in a sort of solemn hush until the door of the classroom opened to admit the arbiter of our fate. (Invercargill)

As a counterbalance, some women recall that they enjoyed putting on their best frocks for the occasion (1905; Palmerston).

The children reacted to this situation by being numbed

into inaction; relieving their pent-up feelings with a display of fisticuffs, or making use of their unusual liberty to play in an unaccustomed manner. In the first case, the atmosphere of the schoolroom spread over into the playground. Thus—

We were too scared to do much on Inspector's Day. (1875; Dunedin)

The children were more inclined to hang around the school on this day. (1895; Nelson)

We were all too aware of the special occasion to play—everyone was very quiet. (1932; Newtown)

Too scared to play, we sat in the shed. (1934; Clyde Quay)

In some places aggressive play resulted:

Some years ago, for some unexplained reason, many of the fights took place on examination day, when the inspector was making his annual visit. (1890; Carterton)

It was a time-honoured custom upon the occasion of a visit from the inspector always to hold a fight between two boys. And it would be a fight to the finish, too, with red noses and black eyes. Perhaps to play off old scores or to show one's superiority at fisticuffs. The inspector usually took one class at a time, and the remaining classes used to wait in suspense like a panel of jurymen until they were wanted. And of course the suspense was relieved by witnessing or participating in a fight. (1899; Waitara)

The interruption of the normal routine stimulated also other unusual play developments. The most characteristic of these seems to have been that girls and boys played together, although this was not their normal habit:

The only times the girls and boys played together were on certain special occasions such as the inspector's visit and the last day in the year. On these occasions we wore our best clothes. The game we played was Twos and Threes, and we played this in the boys' playground. On Inspector's Day we had a lot of time in the playground because the inspector examined only one class at a time. As well as playing the round game we would take turns at reading to each other from good books, for example, the latest edition of Cole's comic book for children. Another thing about the day was the fact that when the children were all together everybody would say what they thought of each other's ability. It was a frank recognition of one's merits in singing, arithmetic, and other spheres which was never vouchsafed one at any other time in the year. (1900; Waikouaiti)

At this time classes were frequently pushed out into the playground and boys and girls played together even at Kiss in the Ring. (1895; Westport)

At exam time we played Hares and Hounds all 'round the hill and in Pearson's bush. (1870; Ravensbourne)

Just on the very day when quietness was wanted the children seemed to make the greatest hullabaloo, a reaction to so much hushing-up perhaps. They all played Farmer in the Dell very noisily for example. (1948; Caversham)

This was the only day the teacher organized games. On Inspector's Day we played In and Out the Windows, Twos and Threes, Drop the Handkerchief. (1910; Temuka)

But examinations and inspectors had other consequences. Children might try to fortify themselves against an unknown future by resort to superstition:

Shivery grass, will make you pass.
A rusty nail, will make you fail.
(1900, Moutere)

Not a very adequate science, perhaps, but the best a child could contrive facing the odds of the unknown. An inspector sometimes suggested a game to the children, which was not likely to make the children see him in a kindly light: "The inspector made us all sit upright on the gravel. He then made us touch our toes with a jerking forward movement to see who could move the furthest from one sitting position to the next. It was agony on the backside, but he wouldn't let us do it on the grass" (1870; Takaka). Little wonder that eager hearts avidly accepted rumor as gospel truth: "Rumour was always a lying jade, but on this occasion she brought a windfall. April 8th, 1904—school was closed today on account of a report which was afterwards found to be untrue, that Mr. X the inspector had suddenly died" (Papatawa).

The last day at school was also a day for letting off steam and was commemorated in rhyme:

Two more weeks and we shall be
Out of the gates of misery,
No more writing, no more French,
No more sitting on a hard board bench.
No more walking two by two
Like the monkeys in the zoo
No more spelling, No more sums
No more teachers to whack our bums.
(1935; Wellington)

No more spelling, no more books,
No more teachers dirty looks.

No more spelling, no more French,
No more sitting on a hard board bench.

Examples of activities reported as peculiar to that day are: "Terrific flouting of authority," "many fights," "Follow the Leader on bikes over all the area prohibited during the year," "cutting up teacher's strap and general vandalism," "cutting up strap." "On breakup day there was a departure from the established division of the playground into girls' and boys'. This license was given because the recognized game to finish the school year was "Kiss in the Ring" (1860s; Caversham).

In these years, picnics, always of importance, became in some areas a fetish. One teacher, writing in the *Journal of Education* in 1910, says,

---

In Dunedin the "picnic holiday" occupies the whole of February and a large part of March. During this time the various occupations, trades, houses, schools etc. all set apart separate days for a picnic. In all this time the whole of school work is interfered with by irregular attendance. Its worst effect, however, is the unsettling of the pupils' minds and their disinclination to attack work. They have just come back from six weeks holiday and are kept in a simmer of excitement during another six weeks.

The picnic itself retained much the same form as described earlier, with, if anything, a decrease in the number of traditional games played. One informant describes one of these latter-day picnics:

Picnic day was the great event of the year, and it was a tragedy if it was wet. By five A.M. we had the blind up, watching to see if it were fine. We were too excited to do more than play with breakfast and then followed a frantic cleaning of white shoes, with mother saying they should have been done last night, looking out the white hat, worrying whether we should catch the boat or train, and we always did. Arrived at the place of the picnic, we rushed to the hills, as though we did not roam the hills near home every day, till word would flash 'round that the races were starting, and we rushed back to take part. I never won anything. Lollie scrambles, distribution of lime juice—watered down to tastelessness—with everyone sitting in rows so as not to get two lots. Then the rumour that the drink was running out before reaching us, and the relief when it was replenished. Complaints from mother that I had been away when the photographs were taken—I always was away no matter how long I hung around. The occasion may have been organized by the school or the Sunday school (strange the number of previously unknown adherents such Sunday schools had when the picnic day arrived). Sometimes it was just a private affair and the latter had thrills all their own. Fishing for cockerbullies, those small fish having no conceivable use except to be caught by small children at private picnics. Lighting the fire and boiling the billy—this involved the use of about two cords of wood, resulting in it being impossible to get near enough to the fire to boil a kettle until it had nearly died out. The water was always smoked. Toast made by this fire tasted so much better, and if we could roast a few pipis or cockles the meal was perfect, though the shellfish were full of sand. Soft drinks were a feature, and in those days they were in queer-shaped bottles, with a pinched-in neck containing a marble pressed against a rubber washer at the top by gas pressure. Cars were not available to ordinary people, so a long tramp to the nearest suitable place was usually involved with hampers of food, fishing lines, bats, and balls. The end of the day came too soon. Or did it? By the time the sunburned, tired bodies had struggled back to civilization— twice as far on the return journey—and had crept to bed, it was usually voted a long but very good day. And we woke in the morning with a very red back to find sand on our pillows. (1910; Petone)

But this pattern of social evenings, Queen's Birthdays, Inspector's Days, and communal picnic outings was in its last, if climactic, phase. The attempts of some schoolmasters to justify the annual school picnic on the grounds that it increased the children's knowledge of the local geography was a symptom of decay. Reason was no aid to the festive spirit. This order of recreation may be said to have ended with World War I.

The period 1890 to 1920 was also one of heightened activity in children's unorganized games. Taken as a whole, there were slightly fewer traditional games than there were before 1900. Games that were common before 1900 and were also well known up to 1920, but not much thereafter, are: Jolly Miller, Green Gravels, Pretty Little Girl of Mine, Three Dukes (or One Duke, or Two Dukes, or Saucy Duke), Thread the Needle,

Smuggling the Gag (or Gag), Egg cup, Stagknife (or Knifey or Momley Peg), Fly the Garter (Flying the Gap), Shinty, Cat's Cradle, Tipcat (Cat and Dog), Knucklebones, (Jacks, Knuckles, Chuckstones, Hucklebones), Trim the Hat, General Post, Bingo, Honeypots, balls, Lotto, shuttlecock, quoits, Egg and Spoon, croquet, skittles, Botany Bay, Butcher's Bat, Fill the Gap.

Those less generally known during this period are the following. *Otago:* London Bridge, When I Was a Lady, Follow Her to London, Round and Round the Village, Goosey, Touch, Space Ring, Space to Space, Holding, Kit Cat, Scramble, Wiggle Waggle, Hurling; *Canterbury:* Trading, Brewer, Chuck Farthing, Parson's Cat, What Colours the Sky; *Golden Bay:* Jenny Jones, Teazel, Tallyho, Homaiacky, Stealing Grass, King Pin. The games that were no longer played were mainly the rougher ones of the boys' playground, and that in itself was symptomatic. Just as the tenor of community life had quieted, so the tenor of the playground quieted during these years. The increased provision for and consideration of children at home, in parlor, picnic, concert, military drill, and sports left less need for some of the older and rougher forms of outlet. At the same time, teachers through their supervision excised some of the more strenuous pursuits from the play area. The taming of the playground thus proceeded in two directions, one positive, the other negative, both assisting toward the same end. The only other games that seem to have disappeared in this period are some of the more remote games of the earlier period, known by only a few older informants and never generally played in any case. Quite often only the name of the game would be remembered, but no details of it.

With these exceptions, the general picture of the period is one of both heightened and varied activity. In places where there were large numbers of children and sufficient playground space, the new freedom (a more prosperous community, less child labor, better roads, no pioneering exigencies, no Maori threat, little unemployment) resulted in a new abundance in play—particularly for girls, the great majority of whom were as yet untainted by the demands of modern sports. Boys had experienced sports since the 1890s, and in these decades of the twentieth century that sport had its taming effects upon them. Girls, on the other hand, were in no need of taming. Their greatest need was liberation, and this age gave them their first important experience of freedom before the dawn of a new era after 1920. The period also saw the beginning of the very important commercial influence upon children's play, an influence which was to be of major importance as the years passed.

Although some of the rougher games had faded from the school playground, they were still in many cases played elsewhere. At school, however, there was little place for Duck Stones, with its dangerous stone-throwing; Tipcat, with "cats" a danger to eye and window in a crowded area; Buck Buck, with its backbreaking potential, particularly on asphalt; punching forms of Bar the Door; Cap On and Fly the Garter, also a danger on hard grounds and in crowded areas; hoops, Whip Top, and kites, for which there was less space. As we have seen, many of the more strenuous and skill forms also lost their former importance in this period, because the skills they employed were now utilized in football practice (Bull in the Ring, Hares and Hounds, Cockfighting, Paper Chase, French and English, Prisoner's Base). There is reason to believe too that the throwing and hitting skills of cricket decreased the importance of Tipcat, Cunjo, and Egg Cap. But if some of the rougher games left the boys' playground and many waned in importance, this was counterbalanced by the fact that there was now much better provision for the equipment and coaching of football and cricket. There was in many places a new opportunity to play those sports, without there being as yet the sports mania that militated against playing anything else. On the whole, sports was still the preoccupation of individual enthusiasts, not the obsession of a whole people. This allowed variety.

Some of the most common informal games that grew to importance in this period were those connected with scrapbooks, collecting, and "swapping." Scrapbooks and collections became more important, and transfers and scraps were more readily available. Postcards were a craze around the turn of the century, and special albums could be bought in which to put them. The various weeklies (for example, the *Otago Witness*) asked children through their "children's pages" to write about their collections and their hobbies. Children were encouraged to join the "Little Folk's Circle" and the like. "In consequence, the children who were members regarded themselves as a select band in the school. They were more important than the others, both in their eyes and in the eyes of the others" (1900; Waikouaiti). The weeklies in those days were far more concerned with domestic matters than they are today. There were far more hints to the housewife and articles on family matters which children could cut out and put in their scrapbooks. Colored papers and all sorts of pictures were not used so freely in the schools and were not so easily obtainable outside school; consequently they had a far greater value in the children's eyes. Some firms of the period even found a way of employing child labor at a distance. Through the periodicals they advertised for children to sell their "scented sachets" for prizes of such things as cheap brooches and beads. Prick books, "Poppy Shows," and bottles of colored glass were a greater craze than they had been in previous years. Old Judge, Vanity Fair, and Cameo cigarettes already contained cigarette cards which were of interest to children although they were not made especially for children. They starred the actresses of the day. After 1918, however, cigarette cards—animals, scenes, stamps, and so on—as well as pictures of sports stars in boys' magazines, poured on the market. Then with free albums and prizes offered for complete sets, swapping set in as an informal game of some seriousness.

The important thing about these particular informal games was that they were all incidents in the domestication of the playground. They reflected the increasing introduction into the playground of games of a quieter hue. They represented, too, the first steps in the transference of children's play interests from the world of their own play objects to a world of play objects contrived by adults for commercial purposes. The children's play world was in fact on the verge of that vast-scale commercial exploitation which occurred in the years that followed World War I. This commercial influence was also felt in play at home. Some of the activities mentioned above had a major place in home play, a place of far greater importance than in the earlier period before 1890, even when the children played them then, and this shows that the adults of the day were making a greater allowance for children's particular play needs. This fact must have contributed tremendously to the "quietening" of children's play. As adults gave more consideration to children's own requirements, so the gap between the children and the adults would decrease, and so too would the anxiety which naturally arose when that gap was an impossible barrier. Such anxieties normally expressed themselves in terms of very hostile and even brutal actions toward other children or adults. This consideration for children was to proceed at a great pace in the years that followed. Its full effects on the playground will be noted later.

Scrapbooks are an example of the new home play:

I had a good-sized scrapbook which took, I think, years to fill as it was a point of honour not to buy the "scraps" except very occasionally, though they could be purchased in sheets. I collected my scraps instead from crackers, attractive Christmas cards, and coloured advertisements from magazines. (1890; Dunedin)

The scraps mentioned were sold in shops throughout the 1890s but increased in numbers after the turn of the century. Like the transfers, they came mainly from Great Britain and Germany, and if anything the German sheets were the more beautifully printed. Leading up to World War I, and particularly after it, Japanese scraps became more important. They were very good and very cheap. One informant said:

Scrapbooks were foolish things and used exclusively for rainy days. You bought a book especially for the purpose with paper of the "drawing paper" type. Then you bought sheets of highly coloured figures attached slightly to each other. The sheets were about foolscap size. You cut these apart and rearranged them in groups to make pictures. If very imaginative, you might really arrange a picture with them to which you gave a story, but mainly they were arranged more with a view of geometrical design than anything else. Sometimes we cut figures out of cardboard cartons and used these instead, but the need for care in cutting out usually spoiled them by leaving bits of background attached to the figure. Tiring of these, we would do transfers. (1903; Petone)

Johannes C. Anderson (1949) says, "These were the days when coloured almanacs constituted the picture gallery of many people," and, we may suppose, the source of many a scrapbook.

Transfers were known and used well before 1900, but they became more popular around and after that year. An informant from Wakefield mentions having a few in the 1880s, and a report from Dunedin of the 1890s says, "We decorated our possessions, our hands, and even our faces and sometimes our schoolbooks and storybooks, with these, though the latter was discouraged." At Takaka in the first decade: "We would attempt to construct another picture out of the elements of these transfers by putting them all together." And at Wellington:

We bought sheets of these, and having dipped them in hot water put them on the flyleaves of books and tried to make the transfer transfer. For years one double sheet had flowers on top and animals below. The flowers—particularly the red carnation which was first on the left top—usually came out well, but the animals were always minus a foot or an ear or half a body. Many years after I was adult I came across a double sheet of these transfers and found that it was fact and not as I thought that I began on the flowers and was tired when I came to the animals. I cannot account for this, as they would be all made by the same process. Most of our schoolbooks were poorly decorated with these transfers.

At home too there were paints and clay. "Painting in painting books and over pictures in magazines was a great wet-day pastime." Outside on a fine day there was always mud pies and even in some cases mud pigs: "It had to have legs made of sticks so it could stand" (1900; Moeraki). The school itself provided scope for this pastime.

At school there would be a painting period when instead of inkwells set in the desk there would be wells of green watercolour together with paintbrushes. We became expert at filling in our painting folios with all sorts of grasses, especially ones with seeds, as they looked more fairylike. Pencils were not allowed. Our homework books were not complete without a painted spray or posy of forget-me-nots or violets or a small scene in the top left-hand corner of each page. We used mostly to copy Christmas cards. The grasses during our lesson were painted from nature only. Sometimes we were allowed to paint daffodils or violets, etc., from nature. It was marvelous what we did with the wilted-looking flowers that some of us brought with us. (1908; Auckland)

It is reported that "smudgographs" were made surreptitiously during lessons:

A piece of paper was folded. On the upper half of the fold a name was written . . . then while the ink was still wet the paper was folded over and pressed. The result was a symmetrical design often weird and wonderful and sometimes even beautiful. Good white paper would be used, and extra effects could be got by using coloured inks for some of the letters." (1890; Westport)

Another indoor game was beads. It is reported from Petone in the early years of this century:

Some thought these were only girls' games, but most boys came to use them when we had a couple of wet days together, especially in holidays or weekends. Beads were usually bought in little barrels at one penny a barrel. The barrels were very nice little things and would sell well empty now at much more than the one penny. The beads were a mixed lot of all colours but mainly of one size. They were strung in colour designs for necklaces, and the more ambitious made rings and wristlets of beads about four or five wide with designs to suggest perhaps rubies set in gold (yellow) etcetera. The beads were set four or more wide by putting a needle on each end of the cotton, and after threading four on the first needle, the other was brought 'round the four and put through the beads from the other side. This process was repeated till the ring or what have you was long enough.

There have been more recent reports of children making their beads of wattle seed (1949; Aramoho) or hawthorn seeds. "We made seed boxes of wild roses" (1949; Ongarue) and "We threaded hawthorn berries and gum nuts."

Riddles were a popular intellectual game of the day. Elderly informants speak of Cole's *Funny Picture Book* as a source for many of these (1900; Akaroa). Examples are endless:

One of the popular riddles during the Boer War was "Why does Kruger wear red, white, and blue bracers?" Answer: "To keep his trousers up." (Waitara)

"Why is a girl rolling down a hill like a revolving lighthouse?" "Sometimes you see it and sometimes you don't." (1870; Takaka)

"Spell 'hungry horse' in four letters." "M.T.G.G." (1910; Palmerston North)

"A riddle, a riddle a farmer's riddle, Alive at both ends and dead in the middle." "A man ploughing with a team of horses."

"What is it that cannot go up the chimney up nor down the chimney up, but it can go up the chimney down and down the chimney down?" "An umbrella."

"A little lady with a red red head and a white white gown. The longer she stands, the shorter she grows, Come a riddle, come a riddle come all bandy Joes" "A lighted candle."

There were also tricks with words, for example, the story of the hidden rivers: Ohau (Oh how can I cross the great river); Waikanae (Why can I not swim to the shore); Otaki (Oh take yee a boat and gently row); Manawatu (In the manner what you did before); Orona (Oh row away gently, for life in a boat); Horowhenua (is simply a horrow when you are afloat) (1870; Wellington). Then there was the widespread but spurious Latin sentence which begins "Infirtaris, in Mudeelis."

Pin dips were also another popular amusement. "A pin or a bull or a button, To see a rary rary show show show!" (1875; Tahataki). A piece of glass backed by cardboard was covered with a piece of paper that could be flicked up to show the "rary rary show" or had a slit in it through which one could peep. One saw through the glass a variety of colors, pieces of colored paper, flower petals, pictures, and later pieces off cigarette boxes. Sometimes these had been arranged in some pattern, at other times they were kaleidoscopic only, and the perceiver had himself to add the configurations of intelligibility. The price for the view was always a pin "which we did not want anyhow but always accepted," a relic from an age when such things were rare. Pin dips were known also as "poppy shows" (perhaps it was the similar flash of color that gave the same name—"the poppy show"—to the exciting experience of seeing a girl's dress blown upward by the wind; pins were not charged for flowers of this sort). In fact, the pin dip or the prick book may have developed from the poppy show. The poppy show was common before 1900 and the prick book after that date, a fact connected with the ever-increasing stock of picture cards and magazine pictures available to children.

We had a thick, strong book. Between the pages of this we placed old Christmas cards and other pictures. The book was held tightly closed. Your mates then came along, and for the price of a pin they were allowed to jab their pin at the pages. If they struck a page on which there was picture, then they kept the card. In any case they gave up the pin. Some of the cards in those days were very ornate and seemed worth having. One could almost say that you were either a buyer or a seller, as one day you would have quite a number of cards and another day mostly pins. In any case, Mother was always the real loser, what with the pin tin being raided, to say nothing of the Christmas cards. It was quite a craze while it lasted, and plenty of fun. (1910; Auckland)

The progress of coveted pictures from one book to another is said to have been watched with great interest, and the girl who had it for the time being was besieged with requests to be allowed to prick her book.

A related activity was the "fairy garden," which children made on a dish or in some corner of the garden. Fairy gardens apparently had more than one purpose: "You invited the grown-ups to see them or mentioned casually during the evening that you had been making fairy gardens through the day, and were suitably pleased and surprised when three-pences and pennies were found in odd corners of the 'garden' next morning as a reward from the fairies" (1890; Dunedin). These gardens may have developed from the London child's grotto, which was also a constructive activity with financial as well as intrinsic returns. The peep shows of a later day made in a boot box probably developed from fairy gardens, cameras, films, and the like. One looked through a hole at one end of the box and saw therein a miniature landscape with electric light poles (matchsticks). The scene could be colored by light sifting through colored papers over the top of the box. Objects could move as they were pushed backward and forward through slots.

It was natural that in an acquisitive society like our own, collecting of all sorts should be universal in all historical periods. Stamps, with their potential monetary value, were the favorite item to collect. Even adults collected stamps! Before 1900, stamps, birds' eggs (which also had a cash return), seashells, and marbles appeared most frequently in reports of collections. There was report also of collecting other natural objects, but collecting was seldom the craze that it became in the twentieth century when it was actively encouraged by the commercial world.

We would make collections of roadside wild flowers and grasses, and sometimes on arrival at home these were lovingly pressed between paper or in a book, but they never survived for many months and there was no idea of sticking them down or cataloging them. (1900; Lower Moutere)

I collected trademarks for a time and pasted them in an exercise book. Some of them were quite attractive. We had a museum just made out of odd boxes and that was kept in a shed, but then we were promoted to a small glass-fronted cabinet in my brother's bedroom. It contained mostly birds' eggs, shells, bits of coins, and other odds and ends given us by visitors who had travelled and picked up curios. (1890; Dunedin)

Sometimes rather odd collections appear in reports.

We would collect bee stings. This was done at school in the lunch hour. The bee was caught by the wings and then made to sting your wet belt. Unfortunately the stings were often collected elsewhere. (1915; Auckland)

We washed hopefully for specks of gold in the creek that clattered down through the town, and every child collected specimens, stones with bright specks in them, until parents would grow impatient and throw the whole lot out. (1905; Te Aroha)

One of the most universal of all collecting games, it is said, was collecting the "whacks": "How many did you collect last week?"

Sweets did not arrive as frequently as they do today, but they were appreciated no less.

It was great day for the children when a parent who had been to town or a visitor from a distance brought a present of sweets or liquorice. (Waipu)

Both boys and girls of families we were intimate with made toffee, plain and nut. The nuts were the kernels of peach and plum stones saved from the jam-making season. Occasionally acquired pennies were spent on boiled lollies, acid drops, bull's eyes, or very special coconut ice in a block 4" by 1½" by 1", price twopence. (1880s; Wellington)

When the pennies were scarce, substitutes had to be contrived, and there is record of boys and girls sating their constant gnawings with coffee beans and soaked whole wheat. The latter was a school pocket favorite especially in winter: "This stuff strengthened the teeth and jaws in a wonderful manner, and it was better than the plug tobacco resorted to by some of the older fellows" (Invercargill). Sometimes it led to disaster, as, for example, when a half dozen boys of Waikouaiti 1900 ate the new soft wheat from the threshing mill and went down with a color comparable to yellow jaundice; apparently the wheat was not meant to be chewed until it was hard. In the North Island there were chewing-gum substitutes:

A practice which gave pleasure to children but was frowned upon by parents and schoolteachers was the chewing of kauri gum. When the bark of a kauri tree is pierced, the gums rums out in the form of a sticky fluid that gradually hardens when exposed to the air. At this stage the gum presents the appearance of the drippings from a candle. Children eagerly sought the gum while it was still viscous but neither too soft nor too hard and, when necessary, they cut the bark of a tree to secure a supply. Sometimes the gum passed freely from one mouth to another without regard to sanitary considerations. Chewing gum found in the possession of a child at school was promptly confiscated by the teachers, to the great grief of the owner. (Waipu)

Some of the practices of the day, with apples in particular, do not belie the view that "for the child it is still possible to weave an enchantment over eatables" (Stevenson 1946:127): There was a little rhyme with an apple pip that I was taught by my grandmother:

> Apple pip, apple pip, fly over my head,
> Bring me another apple before I go to bed.
> (1911; Blenheim)

And when we] had a cake or sweets or something nice to give someone else we would put both hands behind our back and say:

> Navy Navy Nick Nack
> Whit hand will ye tak
> Tak the right or tak the wrang
> And I'll begile ye if I can.
> (1890; Amberley)

After the turn of the century the numbers of sweets in the shops increased. Here, derived from several accounts, are some of the sweets to be found in city shops around 1910.

Certainly lollies were food, but the amount of amusement we derived from them was much greater than their food value. A youngster with a few pennies to spend would call a conference, shop windows would be looked over and the merits of various items debated, and the money spent in a series of shopping expeditions —not all at once. Liquorice straps and cinnamon bars might be selected for the first course—costing together a halfpenny. They would be eaten first, as your palate might change its mind thereafter. Next there might be all-day suckers, raspberry eye-openers, shock absorbers, changing-balls, Dutch cheese, sherbert suckers, and sherbet boxes (with a little ring inside), aniseed balls, blackballs, peppermint walkingsticks, honeycomb bars, hokey-pokey, green sticks, raspberry sticks, treacle sticks, hundreds and thousands (beloved by Scottish boys), and another semisoft stick, pink outside and black hard core. There were also flat sourish transparent discs, which in addition to being very edible could be used to secure windows with cracked glass.

Another fine biscuity sweet came in tins with a picture on the lid of a boy on a cycle. They were wafer-thin flakes about the area of half a crown, and they had a wonderful taste but they were dear —threepence a tin—and were seldom bought.

Then came the Tobler craze. Toblers were chocolate bars with a picture with each cake. When you got a full set you were entitled to a box of chocolates. Thousands saved them, but few got the complete set as there were a few pictures which seemed almost unprocurable.

And conversation lollies! No need for a shy young lover to worry about being tongue-tied when he could pick out a pink, heart-shaped lollie carrying the message "I love you." With each would-be lover armed with a bag of these sweets the romance could run its full course from the first dawn of love, through the whole courtship, engagement, and marriage up to the birth of the first child, with scarcely a word spoken. Quarrels were soon made up when the boy could pick out a lollie with the words "I'm sorry I made you cry" and the girl could reply with some reconciling phrase such as "You and who else?"

Chuddy—now called "chewing gum"—was then in the zenith of its popularity. There was no monotonous repetition of peppermint flavour but a wonderful array of wild rose, lilac, violet, jasmine, honeysuckle, and thousands—well, dozens—of others. The base was wax rather than gum, and the flavours were a little pronounced, but there was no gainsaying their personality.

The list was endless—mulford violets and roses, sen-sen, gobstoppers, raspberry drops, and lime drops. Of all the list of hundreds of varieties, chocolates, jubes, and liquorice all sorts alone seem to survive. Will the others come back again, or are they the victims of standardization? I know that if I could advertise a party to the old-time boys with the inducement of a few of these old-time sweets I could collect a big nostalgic group to talk of the good old days as they licked at an all-day sucker. On our way home from school we used to buy a little wooden box filled with sherbet, which was a sweet powder with a slightly lemon tang in which was imbedded a ring with a little coloured stone, such as a ruby or sapphire or emerald. All for one penny. We would proudly wear the ring and, I must confess, "show off" if we had a larger stone than someone else.

Every home tended to have its own unique games. Some were of trifling significance, others had a more important place in the family group. A few are worth mentioning:

On Saturday night we sought permission to "line up our tea." We selected what we thought we could eat and lined it from our plate across the table in the order in which it was to be eaten, for example, sandwiches, scones, biscuits, cake, jelly, etcetera. We thoroughly enjoyed this but were not often given permission.

One game we played on Saturday morning was to hide each other's clothes all 'round the rooms of the house, then we had to march 'round and 'round the rooms till we found the first garment required, then the second, etc., calling out "Where is my vest?" "Where is my blouse?" till all were found.

Our father told us a story every Sunday evening for about fifteen years. I think the modern child misses this. Although stories still have a great appeal they usually have them read.

Perhaps one of the most important developments in this period were those which took place in girls' games. There is evidence, for example, that those peculiar games of girls, which we may call "leader games," became important in these years. In these leader games one player went out in front of the others to "lead" them. She gave them instructions as to what they were to do. And they competed among themselves to see who could become the leader. The leader, it might be said in passing, was usually a very partial referee at best. Games of this nature had at this time such names as Giant Steps, Steps and Stairs, and Calling Names. Their growth was itself an indication that the girls of the day were enjoying a greater freedom in their playgrounds.

The period was also notable for the variety in girls' play. In those places where girls were segregated from boys, freer in dress and footwear, and unchallenged by sports, there was often a quite remarkable variety in their play. The following accounts give an idea of the girls' games played in different schools of the period:

Most of the singing games were played 'round the centre pole of the shelter shed. Sometimes, however, they were played outside. They included Green Gravels, Duke a Riding, Surrender the Tower, Jenny a Weeping, Rushes and Reeds Are Bending, My Fair Young Lady, Draw a Bucket of Water, Merry-Go-Rounds, Mother Mother the Pot Boils Over. Other games were Hopscotch, skipping with rhymes, Pounds Shillings and Pence, How Many Eggs in the Bush, Tig, Rounders, penny catches. Knucklebones was on the way out. We played it mostly at home. There was no basketball. Others were Sheep Sheep, Wiggle Waggle, and Solomon Says. (1905–11; Onehunga, a large urban school)

This school was for most of this time a two-teacher one and about half the children came from two Maori pas in the district. Probably on account of the Maori element the games played in that school were more diverse, skilled, and cooperative than those of any school I have observed since. I remember two essentially Maori games, Cat's Cradle and Homai, but the others were all traditional English games I think. These other included: Fill the Gap, I Wrote a Letter, Twos and Threes, Green Gravels, Fox and Goose, Oranges and Lemons, Puss in the Corner, Slip the Button, Rotten Eggs, Hide and Seek, Drop the Handkerchief, Here Comes Two Nuns, Colours, Bells, marbles, hoops, Kick the Tin, Black Hole of Calcutta, Stones, Butcher's Bats, skipping with a few rhymes, Knucklebones with stones, Mother Mother the Pot Boils Over, Honeypots. (1912–20; Ohau)

Games included Walls, Hopscotch, Knucklebones, Kick the Tin, Butcher's Bat, trains, Drop the Handkerchief, Teazel, hoops, stilts,

Prisoner's Base, Rats and Rabbits and Rips, quoits, marbles, Consequences, Poisoned Stag, Bar the Door, Ghost in the Garden, Who's That Going Round My Stone Wall, Skin the Snake, Poor Old Tom, Poor Sally Is Aweeping, Hands on Hands, Stacks on the Mill, Steps, Giant Strides, Statues, Eggs in the Nest, Elements, walking on Hands, Rounders, Tinker Tailor, Bites, or Knifey. (1910–20; Rakaia, country school, mid-Canterbury)

There are games recorded in this period for which there is no record before 1900 though they may well have existed under other names. *West Coast:* Dunk and Davey, Spang Weazling; *Wellington:* Who Goes Round My Stone Wall, Beg o' My Neighbor, Bellahonie, Run a Mile, On and Off the Bridge, Here Come Two Nuns, Colours, Isaac and Rebecca, Scrag, Diabolo, Bumble Puppy, Homai, Fives; *Auckland:* My Fair Young Lady, Rushes and Reeds, Surrender the Tower, Walls, Ball Hopscotch, ball games, Solomon Says; *Hawkes Bay:* Wolf Wolf Go Home, Homai; *Canterbury:* Poor Old Tom, Rats and Rabbits and Rips, Steps, Skin the Snake, Steal a Peg, Toodle-em-Buck, The Gag; *Golden Bay:* Who's That Walking Round My House Tonight, I've Come to See Poor Mary Jane, Steps and Stairs, Creeping, Branding, O'Leary; *Otago:* Sir Roger de Coverley, Who's That Knocking at My Door.

When we look back and regard earlier centuries as being rife with folkgames, we may well be mistaking the immediate past (1900 to 1920) for all of olden times. During those two decades there was a novel confluence of picnics, games produced by the existence of school playgrounds, the effects of a new commercial concern with children, and a new concern with their organized sports and recreation. It may have been the best of all times for children in terms of the variety of games and other recreational possibilities. Perhaps at least it was superior to the rural isolation of the immediately prior period and the television isolation of the time yet to come.

15 *the organization of games*

The "new philosophy" of the playground influenced children in various ways. Educational legislation was affected by the new attitude toward sports. Both teachers and the community came to give overwhelming importance to organized sports in schools, and this emphasis was both abetted and counteracted by movements in physical education and minor games and by the way in which organized sports were affected by changes in school organization. The detailed attention given to organized games contributed more than any other factor to the desuetude of the traditional and unorganized games.

With respect to legislation, in the changing attitudes of teachers there was a steady movement away from the narrow but scholarly nineteenth-century criteria of education, toward an attitude approximating the sports-loving outlook of the ordinary New Zealander. In the period from World War I onward this sports-loving attitude became firmly embedded in the structure of the educational system by official but pliant enactment. Various regulations compulsorily fastened the teachers' interest in the playground, but they did not determine the last jot and title of what the teachers should do when there. Consequently the sports-loving attitudes of the ordinary teacher and citizen permeated the regulations, giving their own particular substance to the regulations' content, even if not changing their original form.

Organized games were first mentioned officially in the physical education syllabus of 1912, but as has been shown they were already taking place regularly in the main centers well before that date. At refresher courses in physical education, which were held throughout the country in the years after 1912, physical education specialists drew the attention of other teachers to the recreative value of organized games. Therefore it was natural that when the Teacher Evaluation and Grading Regulations of 1916 came along they should think of playground activities in terms of these games. The grading regulations themselves contained no mention of games, but they did contain a clause giving special grading marks for attention to the environment. This clause referred specifically to school grounds and to work in the community, but it was interpreted generally to refer as well to organized games. The increased attention teachers gave to organized games after the issue of these regulations was very noticeable.

Inspectors' reports of 1917 stressed the wholehearted manner in which teachers were undertaking this new branch of school activity. The Wanganui board report of 1917 says, for example,

---

Organized games now form an important feature of the playground activities of pupils, and there are few teachers who fail to give adequate attention to playground duty. During the coming year we hope the Physical Instructors and the Medical Officer will formulate some simple system of testing the effects of drill and games, so that we may have more reliable data than we have at present on which to base a conclusion.

This report indicated a difficulty: How were teachers to be graded on their work in organized games? One method proposed was for the physical education specialists to assist the inspectors. In 1919, therefore, the physical instructors were asked to make reports on the physical instruction carried out by teachers so that these reports could be used by the inspectors when grading the teachers. "Organized games" was one of the most important categories under which the instructors were asked to report. These new responsibilities of the physical instructors implied that not only the teachers but also the inspectors were interpreting the new regulations to mean that children should be coached in the major sports. During the 1920s a writer in the *Education Gazette* explained the new official attitude:

Increasing attention is being paid everywhere to games as a part of school life, and Inspectors now take official cognizance of the teacher's work in connection with their organization and superintendence. The new progress card provides specifically for the entry every year of the teacher's estimate of each pupil's activities in this respect. Consequently the theoretical importance long attached to games has begun to take intensely practical shape. . . . Versatile skill in games . . . will not be overlooked in grading. (Butchers 1930:495)

It is clear from the same article that the "official" as well as the teachers' attitude was also the popular, or public, attitude: "These inter-school contests in seasonal games, in athletics and in swimming have rapidly become a feature of primary school life throughout the country in the conduct of which parents have heartily co-operated with the teaching staffs." The fear was expressed, however, that this sporting movement might take an undesirable direction: "It is emphasized that the use of grounds and apparatus must not be unduly appropriated by representative teams alone." This was an accurate comment on what was actually happening. Teachers' enthusiasm for the new order was indicated further

by their requests of 1921 "that the Minister of Education
. . . give official recognition to sport by setting aside one half
day a week for the sole purpose of physical recreation, the
syllabus to be re-arranged accordingly" (*Journal of Education,* February 1, 1921).

But officialdom, having cooperated with the teachers in
their tendentious interpretation of the 1916 regulations and
thus, more or less, led them into the playground with the use
of the grading incentive, was content to leave teachers there
with less specific attention to their grading rewards—or at
least so it seemed to many teachers. But the fault lay as much
in the teachers' interpretation of the regulations as, strictly
speaking, in any deficiency on the department's part. In 1921,
for example, the special grading marks given for work in "the
environment" were assimilated into other categories. There
followed complaints from many teachers that their work with
organized games was no longer being adequately recognized,
and the press gave publicity to their protests. At a meeting of
teachers, the director of education earnestly claimed that it
was not so: "The Department was heart and soul in favour of
school sport," he said, and teachers "were still graded for
their work but under different categories." The teachers at
the meeting did not appear to be oversatisfied with the director's assurances, and their unrest was not quickly allayed. A
further protest along the same lines appeared in *National Education* as late as 1930. But grading or no grading, there was
clearly complete unanimity in all quarters about the worth-
whileness of school sport. The new "ideal" itself was never
questioned.

Meanwhile, other changes had been taking place in the
same period. Girls came in for their share of increased attention. Basketball grew rapidly, particularly in such organizations as the Y.W.C.A., and a New Zealand Basketball
Association was formed in 1923. The rules were standardized
in 1928, and the sport flourished after that date. To give some
idea of its increase among adults, and children, there were in
1930 only eight adult basketball associations in the North Island, but in 1948 there were twenty-two. Since there had previously been no organized game for girls in the winter, and since

there was now a demand for one, it was natural that such a suitable game should make rapid progress. One informant speaks of the change in attitude:

The attitude of older people was bit scoffing. I remember hearing people say that it was a silly game with so much waving of arms in it, and I know that my own parents thought in the years 1917, 1918, and 1919 that girls ought to be interested in something better than a game like that. By the time I went to Training College in 1923 the attitude had changed. (Dunedin)

Women's hockey was also played in the early 1920s, but the large space required for hockey as compared with basketball did not allow hockey to develop as extensively. Basketball was so appropriate to the Victorian legacy of quarter-acres and tennis courts.

As the 1920s proceeded, sports for boys and girls increased in importance. Community attitudes toward sports continued to have a greater influence on the new approach to children's play than did the ideals emanating from play theorists, physical educationists, and medical authorities. Consequently the worldwide postwar boom in sports expressed itself at the primary level, particularly for boys in highly competitive and glorified matches between representative school teams. Teachers and community took a live but narrowly directed interest in children's play. Previously children had been left to make their own way in the playground, but in these years adults intervened on behalf of sports. They began to influence children to think about their play in a definite manner, to think of their play as a means to the development of skills in sports. They may not have done this consciously, but it was implicit in their coaching, in the cups and trophies they awarded, and in their own adult enthusiasm for sports—not an enthusiasm, let it be noted, for the traditional game remnants of some bygone age. Even the schoolboy literature of the time moved toward the same end:

Any historian of the remote future relying exclusively on old volumes of boys' magazines for his knowledge of the British way of life in the early twentieth century, notably the 1920's and the 1930's will record that the country was the battleground of an unending civil war between a small vigorous race known as Sportsmen and a larger, sluggish and corrupt race known as Slackers. (Turner, 1948:247)

So severe, in fact, was the sports competition between schools which adults and teachers encouraged that in some cases it did more than just influence children's play, it threatened to upset the normal balance of education itself. Already in the early 1920s there was a reaction in the secondary schools against the "gladiatorial combats" of rugby and cricket. In the primary schools the same reaction did not gain force until the 1930s, although some misgivings were felt much earlier. The reaction in primary schools came later, since games there became organized after those in secondary schools. In addition, matches between primary-school boys did not have the spectacular quality and community-wide interest that those between secondary-school boys did. Nevertheless, the tendency in the primary schools was the same as that in the secondary schools.

As early as 1912 an inspector in Wellington reported:

A real danger exists in allowing these games to take up too much of the school time, and to occupy the minds of the scholars to the exclusion of school work. We are constrained to give this warning, as there are signs that in some city schools, football, an excellent game in its proper place, has lately been engaging too much of the attention of many of our boys.

By the 1920s this state of affairs had developed further. In the late 1920s we read of grand-scale interschool and interprovincial primary-school sports tournaments. Athletic tournaments between Hutt and Wellington were held up until 1929. Tennis and swimming cups were awarded in the mid-1920s, and tournaments and carnivals held until the early 1930s. Rugby continued its tournaments up to World War II. Rugby tournaments were held in the Wellington province, for example, including representative teams from Wairarapa, Taranaki, Wanganui, Manawatu, Hutt Valley, Horowhenua, Rangitikei, and Wellington. The movement reached its peak in 1929–30, when with the first issues of the special classroom supplements by *National Education* notes on sports took an equal place alongside the other subjects of the curriculum. It was a vast contrast to the place of such things in the same journal prior to World War I.

In the early 1930s the Primary School Headmasters' Association in Wellington became concerned about this trend and about the growing competitiveness in school sports.* In an effort to put an end to it, they communicated with all the primary-school sports associations, asking them to abandon the practice of awarding trophies. The same concern was felt by some of these associations themselves. The minutes of the Wellington Basketball Association, for example, refer in a deprecating manner to the roughness of play (1927), undesirable barracking (1930), and the poor spirit and rude remarks of some of the contestants (1931). In 1931 one member of the association "spoke to the effect that basketball was becoming too serious a matter in our schools—much of the joy of the game was being lost in the efforts to win. In some schools the shield loomed too large and filled the children's minds to the exclusion of the fun of playing matches with other schools." Another member suggested that the shield should be dispensed with and that "the game for the game's sake" spirit should be encouraged. In Dunedin at the same time, similar trouble was being experienced:

*The material that follows is taken from the minutes of the Wellington Primary School Sports Association (1940): Basketball (1927); Soccer (1921). The records available go back only to the dates given. As far as is known, this information is consistent with conditions in the other main centers.

Good basketball was being played in the schools then, but over-keenness led to bad feeling between schools in certain areas. There was enough of it in evidence to produce an antitrophy bias. The antitournament emphasis developed from the same spirit, partly because the semifinal and final games produced much barracking and too much excitement over the winning of the tournament.

In the end the headmasters gained their wish. In Wellington, girls' basketball tournaments ceased in 1934, swimming carnivals waned, and athletics faded except in one school district. Even the cricketers modified their use of the "Bradman Bat."* Games for points were abolished. No records were kept and publicity was avoided. The demands of sports' associations for Saturday play by schoolboys were firmly resisted. Schools felt they could maintain standards adequately without outside help. The school that had allowed itself to be so influenced by the community in the guidance of its play activities had suffered an "overdose." There were higher educational ideals and values for play than the grossly competitive forms of sports that had grown up in the previous decade. In the 1930s the schools in effect drew in upon themselves and resisted the temptation to any further extremes of "sport mongering." In 1935 the Annual New Zealand Headmasters' Conference capped the reaction by observing that team spirit had been very much overdone, representative matches were an evil, and interschool competition was giving the wrong kind of recommendation to physical achievement.

This reaction did not mean, however, that organized sports did not continue in the schools. The major games—rugby, cricket, basketball, and hockey—continued as before, with the modifications mentioned above, although swimming and athletics suffered the loss of a tournament incentive. Furthermore, the major sports were as impatient as ever with competition from alternative and rival sports such as baseball and association football. Each major code sought to maintain and extend

*Don Bradman was Australia's most famous cricketer at that time.

its hegemony. In fact, toward the end of the 1930s what might be termed the "normal" course of development resumed, although without the earlier harshly competitive note. Athletic and swimming carnivals were revived, and there was renewed attention to publicity. In 1939/40 a Wellington Primary School Sports Association was formed to coordinate the functions of all the separate sports bodies. Meanwhile the children continued to receive additional sporting stimulus in their reading. In these years, *"Champions"* and *"Triumphs"* had a large sale throughout the country. "In the Champion, just before World War II, sport grew from a fetish to a frenzy" (Turner 1948:254).

The war years 1939–45 themselves brought few important changes in attitude. In some areas organized competition decreased because there were difficulties in coaching the teams and fears that an invasion might catch the sportsmen widely scattered. But even in these areas schools continued organized games with one another. In most cases there was no interruption. Sports went on as fervently as before, being what might be termed the only really regular "religious" exercise in a secular curriculum. In Wellington in 1942 a member of the clergy brought before the Primary School Sports Association the "abhorrent" proposal that "all organized inter-school sport should be suspended for the duration of the war." The minutes report that a lively debate followed. In this debate the words "morale" and "character" appeared frequently in conjunction with the word "sport." For example, "Miss — deprecated any proposal to abandon inter-school competitions which were the most effective aid to character building the teacher possessed. The effect of such a move on school and community morale would be deplorable." Mr. — stated that if the proposal was accepted "the standards of sport would deteriorate rapidly." The Honorable Secretary said, "Morale must be maintained and the abandonment of school sport would be a serious blow at morale. Women had stepped forward to do men's work in many other community activities—they would do the same for the children's sport."

In other directions also sports continued to be treated with the same stern seriousness. "Strenuous and sustained campaigns" were waged by the executive of the Sports Association "against the alarming manner in which the city parks and reserved grounds had been taken over by the military authorities." It was apparent that the "serious loss of playing grounds by the schools" was of as much, if not more, importance to the "play masters" of sport than the requirements of the military authorities.

In the same year the minutes of the Wellington Primary School Sports Association report that the world of business was also interfering with children's sports. Boys were being prevented from playing on teams because of pressure applied by their news-agent employers. Members of the Sports Association interviewed the employers, and fortunately these men saw reason in a way that the army authorities did not. The minutes report: "These gentlemen gave ready co-operation and it was agreed that boys should not be required at the earliest until 4:30 P.M. with the exception of those on long and arduous rounds."

In 1945 Saturday morning coaching in cricket and football, which had been so strenuously resisted in the 1930s, was approved by the Sports Association. The difficulties of coaching children with the restricted male staffs available in wartime led to a fear that standards would drop. It now seemed that "standards in sports" as in the 1930s, were the ultimate arbiter, in matters of children's sport, of the school's relationship to the rest of the community. Schools were still perceived largely in terms of their ability to produce good sports teams.

Since World War I, changes had been occurring in physical education which had partly contributed to, and partly counteracted, the importance of organized games. In 1921 the new physical education syllabus introduced minor recreative games, including singing games for infants. It might have been thought that this attention to minor games would have offset an excessive attention to major sports, but this was not the case. The minor games made little headway. The games were not explained in detail in the syllabus, and only one of the references given was generally available in New Zealand (Bancroft 1909). For almost twenty years thereafter, physical education progressed very slowly at best. First, there was the long and fruitless controversy over Renfrew White's postural system of physical education for children, then came the debilitating effects of the depression. The national games won this round by default.

The year 1939 witnessed the appointment of a new director of physical education, Philip Smithells. It was the beginning of a new outlook in physical education, based on the enlightened English Syllabus of 1933. In the early 1940s, for example, a new importance was given to Swedish gymnastics work with benches, stools, and the like. As the 1940s progressed, however, it became clear that the greatest effect of the movement, largely in spite of the intentions of its protagonists, was the emphasis it placed upon the importance of training children in fundamental skills that contribute to the efficiency of the larger-scale movements involved in sports. Teachers tended to give maximum attention to the ball-handling skills. This training occurred particularly in group work, which was perhaps the most characteristic and most successful phase of the new approach to physical training. Naturally an emphasis of this nature assisted rather than countered the importance of the major organized games. It freshened and cleaned up the tributaries but did not in any way counter the direction of the mainstream. Notwithstanding this implicit contribution to the "main philosophy," the new movement in physical education displayed quite heterodox tendencies, which were not without precedent in the 1921 syllabus. It revived again—but this time with new force—the attention to minor games, and assisted by a growing understanding of the broader educational ideals involved in physical education, the movement gained much support for this revival.

During the 1940s there was in the primary schools a new and in some cases very practical emphasis upon the importance of organized games for *all* children, not just for representative team players. Those who were too young or too infirm to find a place in the school representative teams should not therefore be deprived of the enjoyment of organized games. Most teachers concurred with this viewpoint. The difficulty arose only when steps were taken to implement the belief. At this point the "importance of organized sport" usually reasserted itself. For example, if all the "sportsmen" and the "sportswomen" on the school staff quit the school on sports afternoon to travel with the school's representative teams, as they usually did, who then was left to take the minors for minor games? Who but the aged, the decrepit, and those who had a constitutional indifference, if not repugnance, for all vigorous forms of physical activity?

Out of this situation arose heresy. In Wellington during the war years, with a shortage of male teachers to accentuate the difficulty, heresy certainly arose. For example, it was suggested before the Primary School Sports Association in 1942 that "house games," that is, games within each separate school, replace interschool games. The request was based on fears of invasion, the shortage of men teachers for coaching purposes, and the more positive attitude toward the games of minors. The proposal, however, was strenuously opposed on the grounds that "standards would drop." In 1944 the matter came up once again and was supported by several headmasters because it provided for greater pupil participation and better use of staff." It was believed that under the system of interschool sports the school was upset every Wednesday afternoon, when teachers left with children to take part in interschool sports. There was nothing worthwhile the remaining teachers could do, recreatively speaking, with those children left behind. (This position was the same as that of the preceding twenty years.) Once again the proposal was opposed on the grounds that standards would drop. One speaker urged: "The healthy and desirable competitive sporting element encouraged by inter-school competitions could be lost if inter-house games obtained." The house system alone provided little incentive to the children, and while it attempted to make mass participation possible it neglected standards of play. The result of this argument was that three schools, including one headmaster who in 1942 had regarded the house system as unworkable but now tergiversated, broke away from the Wellington scheme of interschool competition.

In 1946 a more heretical and perhaps even more hairbrained scheme was proposed. A serious attempt was made to assimilate minor games into the system of interschool organized sports competitions. A member of the Sports Association suggested that there should be interschool minor games competitions. Originally this motion had added the clause "even if necessary by the curtailment of the advantages now given to school teams playing in inter-school games." The proposer maintained that interschool games catered to only around 20 percent of the children and that these were already naturally gifted physically. The meeting accepted this proposal and moved that schools try out the arrangement. It is significant, however, that the above clause was deleted from the motion. The Sports Association was not prepared to take action on this proposal; it was prepared only to entertain the "idea" of an even greater extension of interschool competitive sports, if it did not interfere with existing arrangements.

It was clear that the growth of the minor games movement was to be tolerated only as long as it did not interfere with the existing hegemonies of the major sports. Nevertheless, the movement itself, and the fact that most city schools now made some provision for organized games for the younger children, was evidence of a broadening attitude.* The same expansion of vision can be seen in the greater tolerance that existed in both primary and postprimary schools toward alternative major sports—baseball, hockey, and soccer.

After World War II the regular interschool sports competitions proceeded apace. Quadrangular football tournaments were resumed and swimming and athletic tournaments were reinstituted. National councils for some primary-school sports were proposed. And in 1949 the three apostate Wellington schools that had adopted the house system in 1942 returned to the interschool fold. It appears that standards *had* dropped.

In 1936 the hope was expressed that with the increased number of decapitated schools,** "the highly organized competitive sport of the primary school will give way to something

---

*It would be wrong to overemphasize the strength of this minor-games movement. There was no chance for its success without the continued enthusiasm and stimulus of physical education specialists. In a number of schools, for example, I observed that the minor-games afternoons were being used for little more than coaching in football and other major sports skills. Standard-one boys in one Dunedin school spent the games period practicing passing rushes with a football.

**Schools with the top standards, five and six, removed.

more childish and informal" (Beeby 1936:129). Actually nothing of the sort occurred. Where previously the senior teams were drafted from standards five and six with an occasional player from standard four, now the players were drawn from standards three and four with the occasional player from standard two. The system of interschool sports, which meant chiefly rugby and cricket, extended downward in the school. Even where decapitation did not exist, more scope was given to the standards three and four children to play organized teams against the standard three and four children from the decapitated schools.

Nevertheless, some new decapitated schools introduced a more enlightened concept of organized games than had existed previously. Here and there physical educationists sought to give some point to the minor games of some decapitated schools by providing annual field days. These field days catered to all the children from standard one to standard four. Children from groups of decapitated schools (usually about six) were brought together for a day of folk dancing, community singing, a few races, and many minor games in tabloid form, and this annual festive occasion provided an objective for the minor games afternoons of the rest of the year. In one area a number of schools even replaced their erstwhile annual athletic championships with this new picnic day of minor games and folk dances. Furthermore, there was even a movement to reintroduce some of the old traditional games on these annual occasions.

The annual field days are worth noting, but they were an exception to the general practice in which the dominance of a few major sports held sway in the minds of all, young and old alike. The major sports defined the content of regulations, determined the relationship of the school to outside sporting bodies, directed the momentum of physical education, delimited the role of alternative games, and, in fact, defined the most acceptable meaning of the term "play" itself.

16 *modes of modern recreation*

Although the importance attached to organized games had a major impact on children's games, it is doubtful whether that influence matched in importance the influence arising from the nature of modern recreation as a whole, and the changed physical environment in which children played in the twentieth century.

In modern civilization there is an ever-increasing mesh of roadways, telegraph poles, and crowded living quarters which present their own particular threat to children's games. For example, telegraph wires lie like prison bars across a kite's flight path. The *Education Gazette* of November 1, 1934, reported:

The Canterbury Education Board has received from the Public Works Department a letter regarding a child's kite which was found entangled in the 66,000-volt transmission lines near Temuka. The Public Works Department was put to some trouble and expense in removing the kite which, with its wet string trailing to the ground, constituted not only a menace to the power supply, but to human life. Children should be warned of the danger of flying kites in the vicinity of electric wires.

And automobile-infested roads permit little progress to the hoop or the whip top, or other traditional plays. On September 1, 1936 the *Education Gazette* reported on a conference of road safety: The Minister of Transport said, "Attention should be drawn to the dangers of the following practices . . . (a) Playing games on the footpath or highway . . . (b) Chasing one another or throwing balls . . . (c) Playing tricks with moving vehicles, e.g., touching them with sticks." Other modern-day conditions play a part in the changing pattern of children's games. Bitumen surfaces and asphalt playgrounds are too fast for marbles and too impregnable for Stagknife, and they present an emotional barrier to games that require soft earth, dirt, and grass.

These factors must not be exaggerated, however. There are still ample space and suitable conditions for most of the old games, even in the more crowded parts of New Zealand.

Even the larger towns cover with their suburbs so many square miles of ground that a European would smile at hearing them spoken of as thickly populated urban areas. There are very few spots in towns where trees, flower gardens and grass are not close at hand, and even orchards and fields not far away. (Reeves 1934: 363)

If traditional games are to thrive, urban conditions may be a handicap, but they are not a complete barrier. It is quite possible for traditional games to proliferate under urban conditions, as is evidenced in Norman Douglas's *London Street Games* (1916) and by observations in London's play streets in the 1950s. Something other than mere external difficulty is necessary to wither the game-making spirit when it is directed along the lines of traditional play.

A more important factor contributing to the change in games is the very nature of modern entertainment and recreation itself. Modern recreation is antipathetic to the older and self-motivating types of recreation, including the traditional games. Recreations yesterday were few and far between and in many cases involved active effort of some sort on the part of participants. Today the mode of recreation is different. Entertainment is commercialized. For the greater part, less individual effort is required on the part of the audience, except that it should consume and discriminate. Organizations compete for public attention, then reward the attending public with a round of entertainment (think particularly of television and the movies) which is stimulating, ever-changing, and often sensational. Even in the case of those recreations in which adults themselves actively participate there is an emphasis on stimulation and change. "One of the most striking characteristics of this era . . . is the unparalleled rapidity with which millions of men and women have turned their attention, their talk and their emotional interest upon a series of tremendous trifles" (Daiken 1947:30). The child's world is assailed by similar emphases.* On the one hand, organizations compete for children's attention; on the other hand, they subject that attention to an ever-changing round of 'fads and fancies,' ranging from a new record album which one "simply must have," to the reincarnation of Batman at the local movie theater. Most modern recreative agencies, therefore, *reward* children for attention and attendance, and the message children get is that

---

*Consider for example, the adult crazes: Diabolo (1907), Ping-Pong (1913), Mah-Jongg (1923), crosswords (1924), miniature golf (1930), contract bridge (1931).

entertainment or recreation that does not give such rewards may be neither recreating nor entertaining.

When life is full of an ever-changing variety of stimulating sensations of the above nature, unrewarded perseverance at the old traditional games may seem pointless. Knucklebones, Stagknife, marbles, and other games all require patience and practice to acquire the skill that alone makes them worthwhile. There is today no less intrinsic reward for the application of this patience and practice than there was yesterday. In comparison with the extrinsic rewards that exist in connection with all modern recreative agencies, however, there is in the old games, in effect, no reward at all. In other words, modern entertainment and recreation have the same influence on traditional games that modern sports do. Both teach the child to participate only for adult-recognized culture rewards. There are stimulating rewards for being entertained, just as there are prestige rewards for devoting one's time to sports. Sports and modern entertainment bring in their train adult interest and encouragement. Traditional games whose only incentive is the enjoyment of playing them cannot compete with these other influences. That any such games still persist is testament to the intrinsic importance and meaningfulness of those games to the players.

Let us look at some of the ways modern recreation exerts its influence. Children are implicitly discouraged from constructing their own play objects by the existence of a variety of attractive commercial play objects within easy reach. In the twenty years preceding 1950 there has been an enormous extension and vast-scale commercialization of the "children's market"—evidence of the fact that children's play interests, once ignored, are now regarded as a paying concern. Chain stores began to appear in New Zealand at the end of the 1920s and from the very beginning starred large numbers of cheap toys. Toy-buyers report that since World War II, toys have become one of the greatest concerns of these stores. Adults have justified and assisted this commercial interest in children's toys simply by buying the toys for children and by giving children more money to spend (Morris 1946). For example, it is the custom today for children to have money spent on toys for them and to get amounts of pocket money that their fathers just did not have. Children in the 1890s might, at the most, collect a few shillings with their Guy Fawkes guy. Any child who takes it seriously today is more likely to collect at least several pounds. Thus, children who can so easily buy toys do not have the incentive to spend the time their predecessors did on making play objects. They have little incentive even to be interested in such comparatively unattractive homemade objects.

Pocket money, however, does not buy only toys. It also opens the way into many modern recreative worlds, which leaves little time or desire for traditional play objects or games. One Wellington investigation reported that the children spent their pocket money on sweets, comics, soda, the movies, concerts, and skating (Morris, 1946). Children's time is absorbed as well in listening to radio, attending movies, and reading (particularly comics) in a way that it never was previously. Many also attend extra lessons in gym, art, music, woodwork, and dancing.

It is possible that with the greater amounts of free time children have today, some of them actually have less time to devote to self-initiated ends than did some of their forbears. Innumerable children's organizations also compete for youngsters' allegiance and time, and it is at these places that children nowadays are learning to play games. Practically all the complex games played by children today are organized by adults, whether at clubs (e.g., Scouts) or on the school playing fields, and the fact that most of the groups, places, and times for the playing of games are under adult direction does not lead to the maintenance and proliferation of traditional games. The neighborhood group is the only continuous children's group left free to develop a play life of its own, but it is not usually so constituted as to lead to development of complex organized games. It should also be mentioned that in many homes by 1950 the increasing consideration given by adults to their children meant that those children spent more of their leisure hours with adults, by the television set, at the movies, or, more important, going for trips with them in the family car. This fact suggests that all these modern activities may have left not only less time for the old forms of play but also less psychic need for those particular forms.

Picnics and parties, by 1950, do not counteract these other tendencies. They are less important than they once were, and children reveal that they became acquainted with fewer traditional games through these agencies than was once the case. For example, twenty-two children in the Caversham Model Class, Dunedin, each of whom had been to at least one picnic, had played the following games at picnics: Oranges and Lemons, races, Tag, Hide and Seek, catches with basketball (Taieri Wrestling Club); running, cricket, soccer, sack races (Wharfies picnic); races, skipping, singing, cricket, running (Railways picnic); Ring a Ring a Roses, Oranges and Lemons, Farmer in the Dell, Draw a Pail of Water (Sunday school picnic). Children questioned at other schools demonstrated likewise that most of the games they had played at picnics were skill games. Where there were still a few traditional games, these were played mainly at the Sunday school picnics where some of the old practices persist in an unbroken line from the nineteenth century. In a similar manner the parties of 1950 provide little coaching in the old games. The same Caversham children had played the following games at parties: Musical Statues, Noughts and Crosses with chairs, Charades, Postman's Knock, Tail on the Donkey, Blindman's Buff, Oranges and Lemons, Hide and Seek, Hunt the Thimble, Winks.

Modern modes of recreation have also affected the old game "seasons." In the earlier period the seasonal boundaries within any one school were relatively rigid. But this could continue only as long as the play group was the arbiter of its own play destiny, as was the case when its play objects were chiefly of its own manufacture and its play pitches of its own contrivance. Today children's play groups are subject to the recurrent and unpredictable stimulation of novel play objects entering the toy market. Because adults have taken a commercial interest in the children's play world, they have subjected that world to laws other than the narrowly conservative group laws that previously dominated it. In addition, the old seasons have been further upset by the fickleness of supply and demand in the economy of the modern world. Again the new sports seasons have not only ridden roughshod across the traditional boundaries, they have deprived those boundaries of their erstwhile and paramount importance. The boundaries of the minor seasons which continue to exist are consequently treated with greater carelessness by the participants. Deviators are regarded more tolerantly, because these minor seasons are now matters of trifling concern. The shift in attitude has been not from intolerance to tolerance but rather in the direction of intolerance. It would be rash to conclude, for example, that the tolerance which exists toward deviators from the minor codes also exists toward those who do not play the major sports. Yesterday there was a play world of many and varied seasons whose laws were constituted and often harshly maintained by the children themselves. Today the two major seasons are maintained not just by the children concerned but also by the whole society in which they live. The attitude toward those who deviate from the major seasons of today may not be as harsh as it was toward those who deviated from the minor seasons of yesterday, but the pervasive force of the major seasons today is much greater. It is much more difficult to escape their total influence. Yesterday the seasonal variations were initiated by children and ran their course more or less directly in accordance with laws of the children's nature. They arose spontaneously from the unorganized resources of children. Now the children's pattern of seasonal variation is responsive to many other influences which arise from outside the children's group. Seasonal variation, the play group's hunger for novelty, has become another matter for adult organization.

These observations suggest that the important place given to organized sports early defines for children the "true" meaning of play. There are playing fields, coaching practices, and "first fifteen" honors for the conformers. The prestige of sports and the structure of urban civilization do not foster the older pursuits. In fact, the modern mode of recreation actually discourages them.

Another way to approach this change is by listing the games that are still played as compared with those that used to be played. They are listed in Chapters 5 and 14. It will be seen that there is much less variety in 1950 than in 1900.

Games that were common before 1900 and are still played in 1950, although not as much, in many cases, (the following games played as much or more today are in italics). Horses, *Trains, Circuses, Houses, Schools, Shops, dressing-up,* sledges, stilts, kites, hoops, shanghais, darts, bows and arrows, pea-shooters, whips, transfers, peep shows, *dolls, daisy chains, Tinker-Tailor Grass,* Oranges and Lemons, Nuts and May, Kiss in the Ring, Ring a Ring a Roses, Drop the Handkerchief, Draw a Bucket of Water (or a pail), Poor Sally (or Jenny or Alice) Is Aweeping, In and Out the Windows, Mother Mother the Pot Boils Over, Ghost in the Garden, Mulberry Bush, Rotten Eggs, Moonlight, *Tig* or Tag, *Puss in the Corner,* Twos and Threes, *Tiggy Tiggy Touchwood, Hide and Seek,* French and English, *Bar the Door,* (or Red Rover or King Sene, etc.), Kick the Tin (or boot), Tom Tiddler, Sheep Sheep, No Man Standing, Hen and Chickens (Fox and Goose, Sheep and Wolf), Rounders, *Hopscotch, skipping,* marbles, Leapfrog, Bull in the Ring, Follow the Leader, Sacks on the Mill, Cockfighting, King-o-the-Castle, Paper Chase, Hares and Hounds (Fox and Hounds), *football, cricket,* tops, Hop Step and Jump, jumps, skipping stones, races, throwing stones, Ducks and Drakes, Soldiers (or Zonkers), bird-nesting, fishing, rabbiting, *swimming, swinging,* Prisoner's Base, Pitch and Toss, Eggs in the Basket, Musical Chairs, *Hide the Thimble* (or key), *Blind Man's Buff, I Spy,* Hunt the Slipper, Forfeits, Consequences, Simon Says, *Draught, cards, Noughts and Crosses,* Postman's Knock, Charades, Priest of the Parish, Fire Air Water, Mineral Animal Vegetable, Word-making, *Snakes and Ladders,* Whispers, Family Coach, *Statues, Giant Strides.*

Games less generally known before 1900 but still played in 1950 are the following. *Otago: Tip the Finger,* Tip Tap, *Twopenny Catches; Canterbury:* Bedlams, Odd Man, Prisoners, Trading, Pat Ball, Do as I Do, Spin the Teacher; *Taranaki: Steps and Strides,* Tailing the Donkey, Telegrams.

From this summary it appears up until around 1920 children had a greater variety of games available to them than did children since that time. What we do not know, however, is whether we are actually seeing a greater variety of game *names,* rather than actual games. Settlers coming from many different places brought with them the game names used in their particular area. Therefore, part of the change can be attributed to the trend toward common names, for example, when Bar the Door substitutes for most other versions. Still, the greater variety is impressive. From the beginning of compulsory public schooling until after World War I, most children apparently had active acquaintance with larger range of folk games than was the case in later years.

17 *the playground today (1950): sophistication and mechanization*

Several characteristics of the modern playground (1950) can be isolated. The first thing to note is the playground's sophistication. Nearly all the play activities that were of moment in the naive world of the nineteenth century have slipped down the age scale. If played at all, they are the games of children who are younger than those who formerly played them, and consequently are often played with less skill. This may not be because modern children are not as skillful but only because those older children who once devoted themselves to the development of these games are now spending their time in other more sophisticated pursuits. The various influences and incentives noted in the previous chapters are largely responsible for this. In his *London Street Games,* Norman Douglas sums up the matter in an amusing fashion:

"Marbles are going down in the school, that's certain," says Mr. Perkins. "Marbles are going out of fashion, because they're getting unpopular . . . marbles are not stimulating enough for modern life. It's the same with religions, don't you see? Now take Nonconformity. . . ." (1916:62)

The same trend is noted in children's literature: "With the progressive sophistication of the modern child, what once suited the sixteen year old is now outgrown at fourteen or earlier" (Trease 1948:18).

One can see evidence of this state of affairs by looking at several different types of games. The imitative plays no longer have the place they had with the older children in yesterday's playground. Horses, for example, is seldom seen outside the infant playground, and when it is played there it is generally a part of Cowboys and Indians rather than an imitation of horses as such. The game of Schools, however, retains its rebellious note. The teacher is mostly excessively strict and the children excessively naughty. Several schools have rhymes that exhibit this element:

> Four and four are twenty-four,
> Kick the teacher out the door.
> If she squeals, bring her in,
> Hang her on a safety pin.

When asked, "What's the date?" the children reply:

> Thirty days has September
> All the rest I can't remember,
> The calendar is hanging on the wall
> Why bother me with this at all?

Most of the other imitative games are still played at home, although unusual ones like ploughing contests and "Salvation Armies" have naturally gone. But there are substitutes that reflect modern conditions well. Older girls in some schools report playing at home Social Security, Post Offices, Libraries, Offices, Hairdressers, and Printing Presses. Boys mention Chamber of Horrors, Magic Show, Torture Chambers, Hall of Death, Frankenstein and Dracula, and Inventing Factories. One imitative game that greatly increased its importance in the modern world is Dentists. Since the appearance of school dental clinics and dental nurses this became a regular feature of children's play. The game generally features a preoccupation with filling up cavities or holes in wood, trees, plasticene, or school desktops. Sometimes the players introduce their fake solutions into one another's mouths. There is a tendency to refer to the game dentist (and the real school dentist) in an exaggerated manner. They say, "Here's for the butcher ship" or "I'm off to the horror house" or, when receiving their card, "Here's my grave number."

One make-believe game that has increased in importance in the modern playground is Cowboys and Indians. Such pack games depend primarily on the group's having some common idea around which the dramatized conflict can center, and sixty years ago there were fewer such ideas available than there are today. There is far less mention of these games in earlier years when the stimulus to such group ideas was to be found only in the literature that a few had read. The predicament of the time is shown in the following account:

We used to dramatize some of the adventure stories of R. M. Ballantyne if I remember rightly and possibly Ellis's "Deerfoot" series and others. I don't quite remember how we did it —we must have "doubled" the various parts—except that we would be shipwrecked among the gooseberry bushes in the orchard, which became Coral Islands growing all sorts of food supplies. We used to get the cousins into this sometimes but if they hadn't read the particular books we wanted to do they would be rather bored at having to enact characters they did not know anything about and I think we were happier playing this sort of thing by ourselves.

When an event of such moment as the Kelly affair occurred, there were ample common ideas, for "Kelly Gangs" flourished throughout New Zealand in the 1880s and 1890s. In the second decade of this century the escape of a criminal by the name of Powelka again fused the boys of the country together in imaginative "Powelka" games. These games had about them a flavor of Hares and Hounds or the matter of the police hunting Powelka. Most of the reports of "pack" games in the early days, however, apply to the gang play of older boys and have consequently a "realistic" and often an antisocial rather than imaginative note. The movies and the radio (and, later, television) have done more to provide boys with common ideas for pack games than have any other agencies. Those influences alone account for the immense importance that these games assumed in the lives of primary school boys. In addition, the world wars, the comics, boys' magazines, and even social study projects (usually the Romans) had their influence.

On the whole, by 1950 play objects are more sophisticated and commercialized than they were previously. The construction of the play objects mentioned earlier still continues, though to a lesser degree (e.g., stilts, shanghais), but it is the work of the boys in the upper primary school. In spite of the arguments advanced in Chapter 16, however, modern conditions have, in many respects, released rather than attentuated the creative spirit. Think, for example, of the comparative ease with which modern boys and girls can obtain hobby materials: science kits, model airplanes, art materials, meccano, and carpenter's tools, and so on. Even the greater accessibility of such items as trolley wheels and used tires helps. They all play their part in novel and unorganized constructive play. In fact, in those homes where the parents are wise and the children well equipped with toys that lend themselves to creative activity, the children's imaginative play conditions are probably superior to those of their predecessors.

Other play objects that are characteristic of the modern playground are the trick and paper play objects. In the days of slates there was less scope for these types of play, but along with the commercial toys, and the scrapbooks, collections, and cigarette cards, these play objects have had an essential part in the domestication of the playground. They have helped to deploy children's interests from solely physical outlets to a variety of symbolic concerns. Civilization is saved, for example, when instead of trying to torture a classmate a child says, "Guess what happened to Bailey?" "What?" "This," and the child pulls out the fold in a piece of paper on which Bailey has been drawn with his neck in a noose. When the fold is pulled out his neck suddenly appears as stretched several inches in length—a nice little game known as Hanging Bailey. Another popular paper game is Fortune-telling. In this game a piece of paper is folded into four triangular pieces composed of eight turned-down corners. Four of these corners bear a color and four bear a number, and underneath the last four corners the fortunes are written. The owner holds the paper up in his fingers and asks someone to choose a color, whereupon the owner squeezes up the flap with that color. The other player must then choose a number, and the fortune is revealed. "They say a number, up goes the paper, and lo—your girl's name is Lou, or you win £5,000." Sometimes the fortunes told are comic, sometimes they are complimentary. In one school the game was stopped because the teachers discovered that obscene futures lurked beneath the folded flaps. It is a play object that can be easily produced during school hours, hence perhaps some of its great popularity. Another widespread play object is one in which a boy secretly shows another child a chopped-off finger he had supposedly found on the road. (Sometimes it is said to be his own finger which his father has cut off.) The finger is kept in a small tin. It lies on cotton and is covered with blood. In reality there is a hole in the bottom of the tin through which the owner pushes his finger amply splashed with red ink or cochineal. Sometimes a piece of string is tied around the base of the finger to give it a "drawn" look. Other well-known and typically modern play objects are the tram-ticket-butt-cinematographs, the matchbox cameras, the treacle-tin telephones and the tractor cotton-reels made out of candle and elastic.

Collecting is still an important pastime and, as earlier, the collection of stamps has a greater importance than nearly all the other items put together. Cigarette cards are no longer available, and their place has not been taken by the cards contained in cereals packages. In the 1920s and 1930s cigarette cards were a major part of school life. The bronze-colored Myrtle Grove, the very scarce brown-colored Victoria Crosses, and the All Blacks were cigarette cards of greatest importance, but there were innumerable others, for example, Wills Badges, Pirates and Highwaymen, Happy Family Series, Bonzo Dogs, Proverbs, Birds, and Animals. In the 1940s "pictures" began to play a more prominent part in children's collections. Boys tended to collect pictures that reflected their interests—football players, cricketers, sportsmen, and racehorses; girls collected pictures of the great female exhibitioners of the age, the film stars, and the royal family.

Today children in most schools know and play only a few singing games, and these are played more often by the infants than by the older children. Ring a Ring a Roses, Nuts and May, Oranges and Lemons, and Wash the Dishes are the only universals, with Farmer in the Dell, and Poor Sally Is Aweeping following a close second. Most of the others have gone. Singing games introduced through the infant syllabuses of the 1920s are sometimes played in the schools. Farmer in the Dell and, to a lesser extent, the Alley Alley Ooh have carried over into children's spontaneous play. More recently, Punchinello, introduced by the physical education specialists, has had widespread success. Here and there other remnants and new games have appeared. The widespread use of singing-game books (and other books of games) from the 1920s onward, however, means that many "odd" singing and other games may appear from time to time in different schools. These books arose directly out of the folk-song recording work of Cecil Sharp in the first two decades of the twentieth century.

The great variety of skill games has also disappeared. There are still pockets of tradition here and there, in which some of the old individual skill games continue—Whip Top, Knucklebones, Stagknife, Big and Wee—but with a few exceptions all the older, unorganized team skill games have gone. Most children, for example, still know games like Bull in the Ring, Leapfrog, French and English, Follow the Leader, Sacks on the Mill, Cockfighting, King of the Castle, Paper Chase, kites, hoops, stilts, and Hop Step and Jump, but play them only infrequently or only under the guidance of adults in physical drill or at club meetings. One new minor game, which has been introduced by physical education specialists and has taken on spontaneously almost everywhere, is Longball, which contains elements of Ball Tag and Bar the Door. These are two of the older games that have persisted with great success into the modern era. Longball is played mainly by children of standards three and four, who also play the two latter games. Hence, probably, its success. Prisoner's Base, a revival rather than a new game, has also taken on spontaneously in some schools.

The general trend in skill games is reflected in the fact that fate has overcome tops and marbles. Tops faded much earlier than marbles. One report claims that in Petone as early as 1910 the games seemed to fade. As flax became less accessible and streets more populated, Whip Top naturally departed from the scene. Today where tops is played it tends to be played by the younger boys of standards one and two, but there are exceptions. Marbles has maintained a stronger hold, though it too has tended to be played by children in the lower rather than the upper school. World War II seriously affected marble-playing. Many children grew up without any knowledge of the game. Now that supplies have arrived again, there are flickers of interest here and there, but it is difficult to say whether the few boys seen playing the game will ever develop it on a grand scale once more. Can a broken tradition of this sort be reestablished? Elsewhere the tradition has continued unbroken (with "chippies" throughout the war), and strong seasons still flourish. Of 25 Wellington and Hutt city schools in 1949, 7 reported a big season and 2 reported a small sprinkling for tops. In the same 25 schools, for marbles, 10 reported a big season and 5 reported a small sprinkling. Yet every elderly informant reported playing both tops and marbles in one fashion or other, and also reported the occurrence of large school seasons in these games.

It is natural in a country as ethnically and educationally homogeneous as New Zealand to expect that this demise in games would be much the same throughout the country. But there are many exceptions to this general rule that are worth noting. Wherever older games have persisted it is because the locality concerned has been isolated and has had a tradition of its own at variance from that typical everywhere else. Private schools, for example, with their social and religious selectiveness, have stood slightly apart from the main traditions of play and have in a few cases preserved "relics" of an earlier order. For the greater part, however, their games have been virtually the same as those played in the state schools. The one fairly general exception is Knucklebones, which is still more widely played in private schools than in public schools. In the nineteenth century in England, Knucklebones was a game played at most private and grammar schools and . . . a regular middle-class amusement. . . . The possession of a set of bones implied that the owner belonged to a family who were able to afford legs of mutton, or lamb. Such a respectable game was reproduced in the private schools of New Zealand. As the years passed, however, conditions in England changed. Nowadays it is restricted to the poorer districts of large towns especially in the North and to the country children. It is fairly easy in sheep rearing rural districts to obtain a nice set of bones. Such changing conditions had little effect on the New Zealand private schools. The original reason for playing Knucklebones remained. The tradition of the New Zealand private school had its source in the English private schools of the nineteenth century, not in those of the twentieth, and so in Knucklebones, as in so many other things, New Zealand private schools tended to copy a homeland of some "twenty years before . . . an idealized and never existent land seen through the mists of the softening years" (Campbell 1941:51).

Other places in which "relics" have sometimes been preserved are small and isolated rural areas. For example, the children in such areas often know more of the old parlor games. Occasionally conditions are such that the old games are actually developed to a new level of skill. This is the case at Alexandra in Central Otago, where Egg Pie thrives among secondary as well as primary pupils. It is true also of the game of Sevens as played by the pupils at Lawrence, Central Otago. Even the more isolated provinces and cities preserve more of the older, traditional games than elsewhere. Dunedin, for example, has a greater variety of traditional games than Wellington. But an additional factor to be considered is that in Otago the older tradition of play was well developed and very strong, and that there is also an attachment to tradition unparalleled elsewhere in the country.

The most interesting example of an older and well-developed tradition of play being preserved by the isolation of the area is that provided by schools on the West Coast of the South Island, particularly in the isolated and mining districts of Stockton, Millerton, Denniston, and Granity (Muir 1949:27). The first three of these are located on mountaintops and are particularly inaccessible. Until the later 1930s (post-depression), communications and facilities were poor and entertainments were provided largely by the people themselves. Moreover, many of the recreations were shared by all and had a note of the village green, or rather village mud-patch, about them. The preservation and intensification of these recreations was guaranteed by the homogeneity of a relatively static nature of the local population. Practically every member of the community and every schoolchild was—and still is—connected in some way with the mines. Newcomers to any of the mining communities did not change this pattern, they were apt to come either from other mines on the West Coast or from British mines, where traditional recreations flourished long after they were dead in New Zealand. In many cases groups of families from the British Isles came out in blocs; original British mining villages were in a sense transplanted. Other miners came from Australian mines.

One of the traditional games of the "mud-patches" in those years was handball, a game like Fives, said to have been the main game among the miners of Burnett's Face, Denniston, around about 1900. Later, about 1910, Lazy Stick came into prominence. These and other games were played on weekends or on long summer nights. And every hotel in every mining district had its quoits pitch and its local champions. (Quoits performed the function in these mining districts that Ninepins performed everywhere else before the advent of billards.)

Through the years (and even today, to a lesser extent) children were accustomed to observing these games played by the young men and the coal mine apprentice bin boys outside the pub or outside the library and recreation clubs. It was natural that the children would copy and perpetuate many of these games in their own play. Thus games like Monkey on the Bridge, Duck Stones, Fly the Garter, Run Sheepie Run, Shinty, Sinio, and Gag or No Gag, which faded elsewhere soon after 1900, continued to be played in these mining areas into the 1930s. In the depression of the 1930s most of these games had their last intense flutter before extinction. They were played by the adolescents and younger men during the period in which they were out of work; the older men stood around and watched. The games played during the depression by men at Stockton and Millerton included Rounders, Monkey on the Bridge, cricket, Fly the Garter, kicking footballs, Mark and Collar, and Bar the Door with tackling. After 1935, when these districts became more subject to outside influences, many of these games faded. Even during the depression, however, the roots of this demise were present in the marked decrease in the size of the population. The drop in the Millerton school from a five- to a two-teacher school during those years must have caused a break in the group play traditions of the school.

But even today remnants of these and other traditional games, which must have existed beforehand, still exist in these mining villages. For example, in Denniston we find iron hoops, Big and Wee, Strike the Crayfish (known as Spang Weazling in the 1920s), Cat and Bat (Tipcat), Leapfrog, Hideygo (Hide and Seek; the only other record I have of Hide and Seek under this name comes from the mining district of Glen Massey, Waikato, 1918, which was opened up in 1914 and included among its population miners who had moved up from Denniston and other southern mining towns), Black Peter (Bar the Door), hoops, quoits, and skittles (these are still in existence at some of the hotels). The traditional West Coast quoits have thick iron rims with an inward slope. These are cast toward an iron pin which rises out of a carefully tended patch of viscous mud. The players get points accordingly as they encircle or come near to the pin. It is not the cleanest of sports. Other games are Humpty Dumpty (known as Dunk and Davey in the 1920s), Kick the Tin, and Hot Rice.

At Millerton we find Sheep Sheep, Jack of All Sorts, Cripple Jack, Pancakes, Cauliflowers, Cabbages, and Guy Fawkes rhymes more extensive than is usual elsewhere. Most of these games were played at Millerton until several years ago, when the arrival of a new and sports-minded teacher led to their rapid demise. This teacher concentrated instead on football and basketball and their related skills. At Stockton we find Mark and Collar, King-a-sene, Hot Rice, Circle Hopscotch, Leapfrog. And at Granity a teacher reported that some of the boys still knew Fly the Garter under the name of Fly, but that Monkey on the Bridge was no longer known. In all these areas, and in fact throughout the West Coast, marbles still exists in a more advanced state than elsewhere.

There is another reason for the retention of older game forms in these areas. Not only were the children's play groups isolated, constant, and spurred by adult example, but also children shared more freely in other adult recreations than elsewhere in New Zealand. There was a continuity between child and adult groups in practically everything, not only in games. In the years before the depression the scattered Buller mining districts of this area were relatively well linked by contests at cards and athletics, by recurrent dances, concerts, male-voice choirs and even operettas. Today, also, the children take part in adult activities. At Stockton in 1949, for example, most of the children are said to attend the three weekly film showings with adults on Saturdays, Sundays, and Wednesdays. The children attend the same gymnasium classes, boxing classes, and community center choirs. They travel with the adult football teams. Every Buller soccer and rugby club has a school team that travels with it by bus on the weekends. The boys at the Stockton school, for example, play on the boys' rugby team on the Saturday, and then on the Sunday they play on the boys' soccer team. The effect of all this organized play can be observed in the playground. The boys will not play an informal game of rugby or soccer without a referee and whistle, a function which is usually discharged by one of the bin boys off duty. If no referee is available, kicks alone must suffice. Children are present also at the adult card evenings (usually Forty-Fives the "Irish poker" of the West Coast).

Here, then, are districts that are isolated, with strong ethnic groups, group constancy, and continuity between the child and the adult community. These elements have preserved and developed traditional games in a way not general, although paralleled many times in the British Isles (Marsden 1932).

Finally it should be mentioned that the meeting of Maori and European cultures has also provided an environment of a special nature, in which the spontaneous games of the Maori children gave way to the games of the European. There were, however, some important exceptions. Hand games, Knucklebones, stilts, Whip Top, and string games were traditional Maori games that survived the meeting of the two cultures. Yet all these games had their counterparts in the European traditions of play. This fact suggests that the existence of the parallel games in the European tradition acted as a "permissive" factor on the same games of Maori children, so that the Maori children were implicitly encouraged to continue with these games in preference to others, because these games were intelligible to the European tradition of play. Missionaries and others, who are said to have done such damage to Maori pastimes, may have looked more leniently on Maori pastimes that were recognized as pastimes of "civilized" and not just "heathen" children.

It is now time to return to our main theme—that the older games have generally disappeared or slipped down the age-scale, and that their place has been taken by plays of a more sophisticated nature. Another evidence of the sophistication of the modern playground has been its increase in verbal slickness. Just as there has been a greater place for commercial and contrived play objects, that is, for symbolic objects, so there has been a greater place for verbal symbols and verbal play. The influence of the multiple modern media of information and communication is obvious at this point. It seems likely that modern children use many more "smart" sayings, "smart" answers, teasing rhymes and sayings than their predecessors. As the actual physical violence of the playground has decreased, the number of formalized verbal insults and forms of assertiveness have increased.

It seems likely, for example, that slang knowledge has

increased. Children are occasionally heard attempting to out-slang one another in vigorous verbal contests in which are used such terms as up the shoot, going eyes out, bullswool, go jump in the lake, that's a tall one, go and take a running jump at yourself, shivery dick, shiver me timbers, nincompoop, phoo and phooey, you're telling I, got it on the brain, like smoke in a wheelbarrow, sheila, crow, bud, frig it, grub, holy moses, blast it, mole balls to you, shut your face, I'll bounce you, go hang yourself, nerts to you, go bite your back, have a roll, fluff off, scram, ants in your pants, rag bag, a poke in the snout, a kick in the chops, you're bats, dronk, drongo, dill, drip, dippy, ya big lug, greetings gruesome, who's dented your beak.

Some of the partly-verbal teasing tricks of today are:

Tap a finger on their head and say "head"; tap on left eye and say "chicken"; tap on right eye and say "rooster"; pull nose and say "pullit."

"Oh, look, there's a spider on you. That made you look."

"Do you like lollies? Go up stairs and kiss your dollies."

Give them a push and grab them back. "Just saved you."

Extend your hand. Say "Smell the cheese," and then as they stoop to smell, slide your other fist along your hand into their face.

"See my finger" (hold it up), "See my thumb" (hold it up), Watch my fist (hold it up), "Here it comes"—and punch them.

"Do you know the latest out?" "No. What?" "Your shirt."

Teasing expressions include the following: "Go and play trains in a wheelbarrow"; "Go and tell your mother she wants you"; In reply to "Shut up" say, "I wasn't shut up, I was brought up"; If they forget something say, "Put your head out and see if you're awake"; "You can't knock a flea off a piece of sticky paper." Though it is probable that some rhymes were known earlier but not reported, there are also more teasing rhymes today than there were: Sticks and Stones and Giddy Gout seem to be almost as important as they were before.

Another example of the verbalism of the modern school is to be found in the great number of obscene rhymes known to children today. These rhymes are no worse than those of the nineteenth century, but in intermediate, consolidated, and secondary schools, where a large number of children are brought together from many districts, there is a pooling of all the rhymes, so that a child's potential repertoire is enormously increased. Since children are uprooted from their respective localities before they have any moral independence, it is natural that the lowest common denominator of interests takes on an importance it could not have in the isolated locality where other interests have over a long period of time developed alongside this rhyming interest. It is merely another example of the old saying that what men have in common is seldom what is most interesting about them.

There is evidence that where marbles is still played the verbal element in the game has increased while actual physical skills have decreased, meaning that intellectual alertness has a greater place in the game than previously. The verbal elements consist of terms like "Nuts," which when shouted by one player interrupt the course of the game and prevents the other players from taking some special advantage. For example, if a player shouts "Nuts" when another player is about to clear the track before his marble, then that player is prevented from doing so, unless he has been quick enough to cry "Clears" first. It is difficult to decide whether there are more or fewer terms today than there were, because it is impossible to make an accurate survey of the pre-1900 marble-players. Furthermore, informants tend to remember only the latter stages of their marble-playing, when the rules were more definite and the terms limited. Nevertheless, despite the fact that few informants could give me a number of terms which could compare with the number in use among practicing marble-players in certain areas today, particularly Dunedin and the West Coast, a few informants were able to contribute almost as great a variety of action terms as those in use today. We are then left with two possibilities. Either a large number of my pre-1900 informants have forgotten the variety of their own day, or even before 1900 there was a great variety from place to place in the number of action-terms in use. My two most comprehensive reports on marble terms come from the same area—one from Taranaki (1880–90) and the other from the same district, Waitara (1895–1905). There probably was a strong tradition in that district with respect to the use of certain terms, a tradition that may not have existed so strongly in other districts. A comparison between the terms of one of these informants and a school today reveals a rough equivalence in the number used. Here are some terms from Taranaki around 1880–90: firsts, lay-up, stakes, tips, sticking-taw, nothings, anythings, fade-it, knuckledown stiff, dubs, finking, slips, spanning, placing; and from Dunedin School in 1949: knee high, manyies, tracks, screws, nuts, sleets, kills, forces, dig, dubs, cheats.

Another major characteristic of modern children's play is the way it reflects the urban and mechanized world (1950) in which the children live. The older types of motile objects, for example, the stilts, sledges, and hoops, have largely been replaced by the faster-moving automobile tires, trolleys, and bicycles. From World War I onward there is increasing reference to play on bicycles, including games such as Follow the Leader, Snail Races, races, stunts, dirt-track races, and bicycle polo. Trolleys too came into importance about this time, although they were known much earlier. The trolley was a postwar vehicle that was preceded by the billy cart or dobbin. In Wellington of 1910,

---

Billy carts were absolutely essential for a boy. Originally this was a box—butterbox or slightly larger—set on an axle and with, preferably, a pair of high wheels off a discarded pram, about an 18-to-20-inch diameter, and having long shafts. They were used for every purpose—getting messages, especially groceries, collecting wood off the beach, collecting manure, getting large sods of grass for the fowls, carrying smaller children, or for running races. I never got one large enough for me—I was keen on wood collecting after a storm and a butterbox was so small. One time an uncle bought some timber and built a decent-sized body for a good pair of wheels I had. I dashed off and got a good load of wood, but alas, the combined weight of body and load was too much for the wheels which collapsed. Later, small iron wheels only about three inches in diameter were used, but these were made into trolleys having a board out from the front of the box (from the bottom) and another pair of wheels attached to the front of this. It was then dragged by a rope. The reason for this was that the wheels were able to stand up to any amount of weight, but if you had shafts, the back would keep hitting on the ground when the shafts were elevated slightly.

It is likely that there were more trolleys made and used by boys in the 1920s and 1930s than is the case today. By the 1940s more boys of the trolley-making age had a bicycle of their own. Trolley races and races with sail yachts (a trolley with a sack sail blown along by the wind) were among the games played.

The shooters too have changed. There are more mechanical guns, toy guns, cap guns, and water pistols. One home made toy gun that has become more common, however, has been the elastic gun. In some schools quite complicated guns with triggers are made which release the taut elastic when the trigger is pulled. The parachute is made out of a handkerchief and four pieces of string, and a stone is a modern projectile. So too is the propeller. In the 1930s model airplanes were almost as common as the kites and whips they were helping to replace.

Children's pranks also reflect the times. There are more reports in the modern era of posting dummy parcels and making false telephone calls. In one trick, for example, the children ring up the local greengrocer and say "Is your shop on the tramline?" "Yes." "Well, shift it because there's a tram coming."

Still although the mechanization of the play world is on its way by 1950, the large-scale accessibility of mechanized and later electric and electronic toys, puzzles, and games accessible to masses of children, will not occur until after that date. By the 1980s, along with toys that are modeled after television characters, they will be the most salient aspects of the modern child's play world.

18 *the playground today (1950): speed, freedom, and domestication*

The sophistication of the modern playground (1950) is also seen in the fact that it is a faster-moving place in which to play than the playground of earlier days. Just as there is much more movement and speed in the modern world than there was in the relatively leisurely world of the nineteenth-century, modern playgrounds show constant movement. In nineteenth-century playgrounds there was comparatively little movement in the girls' section, and what movement there was in the boys' section was interspersed with many important seasons concerned with more static pursuits, for example, marbles, Stag-knife, tops, buttons, Knucklebones.

The increased "rate of play" on modern playgrounds is reflected in many games. The most common play object of today is the ball, which is to the twentieth-century playground what the knife was to that of the nineteenth. In its various shapes and sizes the ball has replaced practically all the other play objects in the school playground. The swiftness and motility of the ball as contrasted with stagknives, pocketknives, knuckle-bones, marbles, buttons, bells, caps, and tipcats is an index of the increase in playground speed. Ball-bouncing games have come into their own on the asphalt playgrounds of modern schools and are played in many schools throughout the country. There is no evidence of such games before 1900, but a number of instances between 1900 and 1920 are recorded. The games were known as Fives, Tens, Sevens, and Walls and have been recorded more often since under the names O'Leary or Sevens. Before 1920 there is only one report of the game being played with a rhyme, and this was a rhyme more often used in skipping.

Balls are used extensively in other modern games such as Echo, Rotten Egg, Pig in the Middle, Queenie, Ball Tag, Donkey, Ball Hopscotch. In Echo, which is widely known throughout Southland and in other individual schools elsewhere in the country,

---

the children divided into two sides and each side stood on one side of the play shed, unseen by the other. A ball was thrown by one member of one side over the play shed to the other side. The one catching it ran 'round the shed and attempted to hit one member of the other side before a nearby fence was reached. If anyone was hit, that person went on the other side. The side which was largest when the bell ran won. (Kapuka)

When the catching team catch they're supposed to cry "Echo"; then the other side knows they must run. If the catching team misses the catch, they throw the ball back. I have seen the game played at Takaka without the intervening shed. Rotten Egg, a game known also as Base and Donkey, is similar to the old game of Egg Cap but without the caps. The ball is thrown in the air and a player's name is called. If the ball is caught it is thrown up again. If it is missed, that player cries "Stop" or "Base" as soon as he catches the ball, takes a prearranged number of steps toward one of the other players, and attempts to ball-tag him. If that player is hit, then he is the rotten egg and may fall out, or he may be the *D* of donkey. The game is widely known.

The many variations of organized sports also use balls. Rugby variations include Comp (Nelson), a game in which several players kick in turn at a goalpost, receiving points for the type of kicks they succeed with. Kicks (Karori) is another rugby variation, in which two teams of players kick into opposite ends of the playground. If the opposing team fails to catch the ball, that team loses a point. In a third rugby variation, Mark (Rangataua, Auckland), the player who catches the ball and "marks" it (in the rugby sense) has a kick. Otherwise it is a game of rough and tumble. In Scrag (North East Valley) and Kick and Collar (Moutere), two more variations, everybody goes after the player who has the ball, who attempts to dispose of it as quickly as possible. Cricket variations are Tippeny Runs, French Cricket, Nonstop Cricket, Country Cricket, Peg Ball, and Hot Rice. All these aim to speed up the normal game, and in this sense they are a commentary of the main weaknesses of cricket from the point of view of primary-school children. Tippeny Runs is perhaps the most widespread of these games. Next comes French Cricket. At Waterloo (Hutt Valley) I observed the boys playing a speedy version of French Cricket which allowed them to bat in the normal way, instead of by holding the bat in front of their legs as in French Cricket. The bowler had to bowl through the batsman's legs or within a foot of each side of the batsman to get him out. Otherwise the rules were the same as those of French Cricket. In Hot Rice (Millerton; but known as Hit and Out in Stockton) the players aim to hit the player with the ball (cricket or tennis racquet as bat) anywhere on the body. As soon as the batter is hit he must drop the bat, and the successful thrower picks it up. As soon as the bat is in the new batsman's hand the ball may be thrown at him. The variants mentioned above are adult-invented games that have been passed on to the children.

Other sports also have their variants. In basketball there are the games known as Defense, Sides, and Goals. In hockey there is Shinty, Stick Hockey, Hand Hockey, and Handkerchief

Hockey. In Rounders there is Danish Rounders, Dutch Rivelea Kat, and Hand Rounders. In tennis there is Hand Tennis. And in Longball there are the variations Shortball and Flyball.

The increased speed of the modern playground is reflected also in the greater numbers of tagging games that are played today: Seat Tag, Ups and Downs, Toes Off the Counter, Tiki Tiki Touchwood, Wet and Dry, Colors, Tree Tag, Broken Barley, Keys or Pads, Sardines, I Saw You, Opossum, I Spy, Witch's Tag, Policeman, Beware the Bear, Sharky, Wolfie, Whales in the Ocean, Who Steps in the Dark, Bush Taggy, Burglars, Ghosts, Murder, Bogies, Kikeri, Odd Man Out, Running Waters, Point to the Bell, Penny Under the Chair, Shadow Tag, Black Peter, Tip Tap, Donkey Tag, Snakes, Poisonous Ball, Stone Tag, Pebbles and Stones. Of these games, Tip the Finger is worth more complete treatment. Some versions come with a rhyme:

> Draw a snake down your back
> This is the way it went,
> North, South, East West
> Who tipped your finger?

The players stand behind the It player, who stands with his back to them and finger outstretched behind his back. The players then chant the rhyme, and one of the players tips It's finger. It turns around and tries to guess who did it. Before being told by the players whether he has guessed correctly, It tells the player he picks what that player must do as a penalty. If It has guessed wrong, he must carry out the penalty himself while the other players go and hide. The game then turns into Hide and Seek, and the first player caught becomes It for the next game. The game is known by many names, for example, Tip the Finger (1948, Brooklyn; 1935, Island Bay; 1949, Ratapiko, Taranaki), Draw the Snake (Golden Bay area), Round and Round the Mulberry Bush (1930 Collingwood, Dannevirke), Round and Round the Merry-go-round (1948, Stockton; 1910, Palmerston North), Here We Go Round the Merry-go-round and Tip the Finger (1905, Onehunga), This Is the Way the World Goes Round and Somebody Must Tig (Otago area), This Is the Way the Windmill Goes Round and Whose Is the One to Touch It? (1930; Christchurch), Who Tipped Your Finger Last (1944; Marton), Crown (1949; Rapatiko).

The increased number of tagging games can be attributed in part to the lighter clothing and shoes of children today and the encouragement which children are given to play actively. For the greater part these games are played and developed only by the children in the lower half of the primary school, the only children who are still left relatively free to play and yet are old enough to develop games of some formal complexity.

Increased playground movement is also related to the greater suppleness of modern players, a suppleness manifested in the never-ending acrobatic and handstanding games of girls. Girls in one school claimed those were their favorite games. Asked why they played such games more than the boys did, they said, "Because we haven't as many games as the boys, and ours aren't so exciting." It is clear that the new physical education work in schools played a great part in encouraging girls to develop along these lines.

This brings us to another major, if related, characteristic of modern play, namely, that girls today have more freedom for outdoor play. This has its consequences in terms of their games, and one of these consequences is that their games reflect the increase in the rate of play with which we have been dealing. After all, the ball-bouncing games and the counting-out rhymes are mainly the property of the girls, but their other major rhyming interest reflects the same change.

In the nineteenth century the majority of girls' game rhymes were found in the relatively static singing games. Today the most important rhymes for girls are those which they use in their active skipping plays (jump rope). There are approximately fifty skipping rhymes in use today, of which I have record, whereas before 1900 there were only two or three of these rhymes, and in some places none at all. The rhymes seem to have a variety of origins. Some derived from former singing rhymes, some from old counting-out rhymes (Ickle Ockle), some from hand games (Peter and Paul), and some from the other miscellaneous rhymes of childhood. Some are a mixture of many rhymes adjusted to fit in with the rhythmic nature of the skipping movements. Their diffusion has obviously been aided by the fact that from the turn of the century onward they have been widely recorded in books and magazines. In later years they often appeared in the children's own magazines and annuals. Thus even literature has had an effect on the play of modern children.

Girls' Hopscotch also reflects the trend of the times. The popular avenue diagram of earlier days has almost completely disappeared, but its place has been taken by a diagram shaped like an airplane, a natural development. In addition, a new variety of Hopscotch has arisen; Ball Hopscotch. Rectangular and spiral diagrams, however, continue.

There have been other interesting developments in girls' games. For example, girls have tended to develop their own versions of Bar the Door, versions that pay greater attention to colors, names, and guessing than the orthodox boys' versions. In Colors, for example, the runners at the end of the ground pick colors and the He player in the middle calls out the name of a color at random. The player who has chosen the color that is called then runs across and tries to avoid the He in the center. Other games of a similar nature are Vegetables, Fruits, Initials, In, and Please Jack May We Cross Your Golden River Jack.

Girls have developed certain older games into what is virtually a new species of game. These are perhaps most appropriately called *leader games,* because the aim of every player in the game is to become the leader. These games have a triangular rather than the usual dual formation. In the usual dual form, two or more players compete against each other to see who is the best at a certain skill. This happens in games like marbles, running, tops, and chasing. In these triangular-leader games, on the other hand, the players compete against each other not just to win, but to become the leader or referee who is in charge of the game and directs its course. It does not take a great deal of psychological insight to see what is happening in these games. Here, in effect, is the commentary of young girls on the nature of female social role.

There are several types of leader games. In the commanding types (as in most others) one player, the leader, stands in front of the other players and gives commands. They stand away from her in a group and compete against one another as she commands. Usually the leader stands at one end of prearranged space (often up on the seat at one end of a school shed and the group of players stand in a line at the other end of the space). The aim of each of the players is to move up to the leader. The first player to get to the leader becomes leader herself, but the players can move only when the leader tells them to. Names for other games of this kind are Letters, Mother May I, Steps and Strides, Giant Strides, Statues, Creeping Up, Creepy, Peep Behind the Curtain, The Giant and His Treasure, Giant's Treasure, Queenie, Alla Balla, Johnny in the Inkpot, Busy Bee, Jack of All Sorts, I Sent My Son, Trades, and New York. Girls' acrobatics have a tendency to follow the leader formation. At several Dunedin schools, I found girls playing games of standing on their hands. The leader told the girls when to go up on their hands and she judged who was the winner. The winner—the girl who stayed up the longest—then became the leader. And of course girls' games of skipping, Mothers, and Schools fall naturally into some sort of leader formation.

These examples of girls' play today suggest strongly that the freedom of girls in the modern playground has had an important result for childlore: The girls of today are the chief preservers and initiators of that lore. They are more free than boys from the influences and incentives of organized sports and consequently have more time and are more willing to develop folk-game pursuits. Here, then, is another historical reversal. In the nineteenth century it was the boys who had the greatest number of traditional game pursuits. Today it is the girls.

The fact that in most enlightened schools the boys and girls are free to play in the same playgrounds has had important consequences. In this way the freedom of the girls led to another major characteristic of the playground of today: It is a less aggressive and less turbulent place in which to play. It has become *domesticated*. There is neither the roughness nor the fighting that there used to be. This is reflected both in the games the children play and in the remarks of countless teachers. The reasons for this state of quietude, other than that already suggested, are no doubt innumerable. It is certainly a reflex of a quieter and more ordered condition of general community life. Since around 1940, New Zealand has known a state of economic well-being for all classes never previously experienced in that country. In the home more attention is given to children and their needs, and more satisfactions and security than ever before. As a part of the "new education," the schools have increasingly become places where children learn how to live together, which is one of the greatest factors in decreasing hostility between human beings. Previously schools made little or no attempt to teach children the techniques of dealing with one another, or if they did so, they did it inadvertently with strap or can. At times the teachers even egged the injured child on to stand up for himself and fight the aggressor—the "eye for an eye" philosophy. Teachers now tend to have a better understanding of how to deal with such situations.

More and more children have passed through secondary school and presumably become subject to the civilizing influences of further education. As adults with a wider range of interests, they are likely to have more humane and more understanding attitudes toward their own children, and this in turn would have an effect on the "peacefulness" of their children's play. In addition, there has been greater opportunity for primary- and secondary-school children to express hostile and aggressive feelings through organized sports and to be rewarded for effective but controlled aggression along these lines. In this respect it is clear that the organized sports of post–World War I have served a purpose within the school curriculum that was once served by cadet drill. Irrespective of their respective importance in the outside community, both these extracurricular concerns have enabled teachers "to get a better grip of their boy." They have been of immense assistance in solving the problems of internal discipline—always a problem of some magnitude. "Organized" sports, therefore, must be seen in the perspective of the teacher's immediate and pressing experience of "disorganized" boyhood. It must always be granted that although organized sports have exerted a narrowing effect on children's play, they have at the same time exerted a taming influence.

From 1890 onward the adults of this society moved toward ever greater control and influence over children's leisure time. While there may be nostalgic regret at the loss of the variety of traditional games and some of the wide-ranging and even brutal autonomy of the nineteenth century, there is also recognition that there are in the twentieth century better opportunities in schooling, a kindlier community, and a more symbolic attitude toward life's masteries.

3 a personal epilogue

19 *the control of children in the home, 1950-1980*

The data base for this book ended with my collections of material from schools and informants in 1950. Shortly thereafter I proceeded to the United States on a Smith-Mundt Fellowship and a Fulbright Travel Grant. Although I returned to New Zealand in 1955, I once again left for the States in 1957, where I have remained ever since, apart from occasional brief visits to New Zealand. In my absence there has been no further concerted study of the New Zealand playground of the kind recorded here. The personal speculations that follow are therefore different from the generalizations in the rest of this work. They are offered more as an indication of what we need to know, of inquiries that need to be undertaken, and as an insight into the potential importance of these childhood matters which are still thought in so many intellectual domains to be of trivial importance. They also reflect my many years of scholarly existence in the United States at Bowling Green State University in Ohio (1957–67), at Columbia University, Teachers College, in New York City (1967–77); and at the University of Pennsylvania in Philadelphia (1977 to the present). My speculations on worldwide events can hardly escape having a distinctly American flavor.

Looking over this history thirty years after it was first drafted in 1950, one sees that some of the forces described have been accentuated and that others have changed direction. There is in 1980 much more organization of every aspect of children's lives than existed thirty years ago. Control of children's leisure activities has spread from the school, through television, into the home. If we could say that in the nineteenth century children were brought under partial public control through the school, and in the first fifty years of this century through further control of their schooltime and after-schooltime leisure activities, we can now say that that control has extended also into their own homes. One can view this as a parameter of control set in motion by the forces of industrialization and modern socialized society, whereby parochial forms of control are gradually replaced by national, and perhaps international, forms.

This organization of children's lives is part and parcel of a move in the modern state toward a monopoly over violence. Norbert Elias (1978), who has reviewed the history of sports since the Greeks, believes it is a history of the development of ever more internal psychological controls in the citizen body. Although there may be some truth to this, as a generalization it falters on the barbarity of Roman entertainments, the violence of feudal contests, and the rioting at modern games of soccer.*

In New Zealand there has been a relationship between the increased organization of children's sports and the decreased violence on the playground. While the teachers were brought

*I am grateful to Peter McIntosh, Director of the School of Physical Education, University of Otago, New Zealand (1974–78), for these emendations of the Elias thesis.

onto the playground in order to prevent accidents, protect the environment, and martial cadets, they developed an enthusiasm for being there and participating in sports. Even though they were not the only forces at work, those teachers who had themselves been former pupils and players must have contributed to the domestication of children's play. Given the often barbaric quality of much of nineteenth-century play, described in Part One, this domestication cannot be viewed as an entirely unfortunate development. It is important to keep this in mind as a counterbalance to the nostalgia that most of us still feel for what seems on the surface to have been a historically freer and more spontaneous period of traditional play.

Those brought up in the freer, more pioneering play circumstances of the nineteenth and earlier twentieth century often feel a certain resentment against the movement toward more organized play, for organized play has been regarded as a threat to child spontaneity and freedom. Norman Douglas (1916:155) puts it aptly and amusingly: Not that I'm saying anything against

---

CRICKET in particular. You can do many things with a bat. But there are many more things you can't do. And all these other things are bound to be left outside your reach in the long run, you get taken up by cricket. Because you see, you don't take up cricket . . . you think you do, but you don't; you get taken up. You think you are going to do what you please with a bat, but the fact is that the bat does what it pleases with you; you think it's your servant, but in reality it's a master who drives you along the way he means to go —or rather the only way he can go (that is hitting a ball). It's perfectly true you can play well or badly; but, play as you like, you can't help your faculty for inventing something outside bats and balls getting rustier all the time. And it's true that cricket saves you the trouble of inventing those other games; that's just its drawback, I say. No getting out of the rut! With the bat in your hand you can only do what it allows you to do. Which is a good deal; but not half as much if your hands were empty.

This nostalgia for an earlier and freer time is a strong note in many interpretations of childhood since Rousseau. In New Zealand the nineteenth-century playground was a diversified one, but we have seen also that it was a rugged and often cruel place. If there was a neglect of children at play, there often was at the same time a punitive control over them in home and school. Their freedom itself was a product of neglect rather than forethought, though it was a neglect probably beneficial to producing the type of physical skill and autonomy needed in a rural economy. Their pastimes reflected rural opportunities and were at the same time a survival of games once the preserve of adults in medieval and earlier times.

Since Douglas's time, concern about the spontaneity of children has changed to apprehensiveness about the organizing and manipulative effects of television upon children. Children today are sometimes pictured as a generation of passive watchers transfixed before the "boob tube." However, just as organized sport was a medium for straddling parochialism, television may well be the first medium for international, "global village" influence. As such, it comes in for the same types of criticism earlier leveled at the sports. By contrast, in the years that have intervened since the nineteenth century more homes and schools have become places in which children are permitted and encouraged to be imaginative in creative ways. There is clearly an increased role for improvisation and individuality in creative play and the arts that never existed in most homes in earlier years. In some places there is also opportunity for greater diversity through play and game innovation, even in physical education programs, that is, there are "lessons" in which children are encouraged to invent games. Thus we have the paradox that some of the freedom once found only through neglect and out of doors has now moved indoors and has actually been "organized" into programs for children.

But in either case, whether the organization of the play life is a product of the television or of the creative dramatics teacher, it is something managed directly by adults. Fewer play spaces belong solely to children. Edmund Gosse in *Father and Son* (1907) speaks of the time when, escaping from the intensity of his father's supervision, he lived for a few brief weeks a

"glorious life among the wild boys on the margin of the sea."
Nowadays, through various types of playgrounds, architects
and educators have sometimes attempted to arrange nostalgically for this earlier type of freedom to take place. But here
again the opportunity is organized for the children, not discovered by accident in the interstices of adult culture.

There is reason, indeed, for the hypothesis that the preadolescent gang age child psychologists wrote about in the first
part of the twentieth century has been substantially transformed into an adult apprenticeship to organized sports. In the
United States, as in New Zealand, because the schoolmasters
protested the competitiveness of these games in the 1930s, control of organized sports passed, sometimes partially and sometimes completely, out of their hands into those of the sports
bodies themselves. In the years since World War II, these sports
bodies or associations have flourished as the major vehicle for
the preadolescent's activities in New Zealand, Australia, and
the United States (Martens 1978; Watson 1978). In many places
there are even rules that provide equal play opportunity for the
less competent children. In 1978 in Connecticut a parent
brought a suit against a local Little League group because they
did not honor that provision. What this seems to imply is that
many parents now see these children's sports organizations as
making an essential contribution to the socialization task of
the home. Having once served the school, these sports now also
serve the home. As Watson has shown, lower-class parents
quite explicitly see sports as fulfilling a collectivizing social
function. Middle-class parents, however, tend to see them as a
foil for their children's ambition. In either case, the family
accepts the fact that it is in alliance with an outside agency
other than school and church in the socialization of its male
preadolescent child. There is also at least a beginning of pressure for sports bodies to show the same sporting concern over
the female preadolescent child.

While most of the controversy over these sports still
focuses on whether they are too competitive, give coaches too
much control over children, are physically dangerous, exploit-
ive, and so on, perhaps a more important issue is whether as
a culture we have fundamentally shifted our socialization ar-

rangements. The organization of sports discussed throughout this work was focused largely on adolescents and only more recently on preadolescents. Yet all the surveys of adolescent and college-level recreation today show an increasing degree of diversity, a pursuit of informality, and a flight from hyper-organization in sports at those age levels, as compared with earlier years. It is therefore possible for one to learn coopera-tive team values at an earlier age, the adolescent age being given over more to the development of a superstructure of personal choice and diversification necessary in today's infor-mation cultures. Other trends in today's play suggest that this may be the case. However we read the situation, it seems that boys today probably do not get as much of a political education of the physical kind that came through many years of outdoor play in the rough street games of yesteryear. Their lives are more solitary and more symbolic. Whether this is what makes some parents seek more desperately for team game organiza-tions for their boys we do not know. At least we can say that an immense change in childhood development has taken place.

The other great change that has been coming over the past twenty-five years, in addition to the control of children through the organization of their leisure, a change mirrored both in the omnipresence of television as well as in "creative" programs for children, is the change from a manual way of life to a symbolic one. Social organization is now increasingly the organization of people through information rather than through physical discipline. The modern state is an informa-tion culture controlling its citizens through the airways. Tele-vision is a critical part of that control system. On the other hand, the maintenance of these ever-complex, ever-growing information systems requires that children receive training in diversity and flexibility of perspectives far greater than that ever required in the fairly simple and routine manual worlds of the nineteenth century. It is now necessary to pro-duce generations of children who can be innovative, not in killing birds with catapults but in ideas for use in mass media, advertising, selling, bureaucratizing, computing, edu-cating, and so on. To this end there is increasing emphasis on creative programs in schools and increasing emphasis on the arts in child development, because these have their basis in the child's own self-representations and uniqueness, and increasing emphasis even on teaching children directly how to play imaginatively.

The older view that we need only leave children alone and their spontaneity will do the rest no longer holds. Children can be spontaneous, but only in the limited, traditional ways of the world which were already given. Play is instinctive only in small part. It can be almost extinguished, and in some work cultures it is not only neglected but negated. Where people must struggle hard for survival and need the contributions of the children in that struggle, there is little time for play. Thus in some Indian silk-weaving cultures, Turkish carpet cultures, African herding cultures, and in Dickens's England the work ethic makes good sense. There is no scope for the diversity introduced by imaginative children; all hands are needed at the wheel. Where play is encouraged, current research indicates that it produces diversity and increases creativity. It makes people more flexible and more capable of innovation. Play is the training program destined to produce more innovative people. It is not surprising, therefore, that some of today's educators feel that innovativeness can be encouraged by participating in play with children and demonstrating for them what it is like to be imaginative and diversified (Singer and Singer 1978; Sutton-Smith and Sutton-Smith 1974).

This is a far cry from a Rousseau-like nostalgia for the village green. We might say that if the organization of sports in the first fifty years of this century was focused among other things upon domestication of violence, the organization of play in the next fifty years might well be focused upon the development of the capacity for imaginative innovation. A world civilization like ours can survive only by producing infinitely more people with such capacities. This would mean that although control over the lives of children had steadily increased, there would have been a switch in the direction of afforded freedom. The physical license of the nineteenth century helped produce a child individually autonomous in his management of the physical environment. What may be occurring now is an attempt to produce children who are capable of innovation in things that are social and symbolic, so appropriate to their much more complex social environment.

But these are all speculations, a part of the author's belief that children's play and games may help to illustrate some important lines in contemporary history. In fact, of course, children's play may either exemplify or defeat that social-science wish. We may be safer to move once again to a description of what children are actually doing. There at least we continue to find a tribute to vividness, whether or not we really understand the larger cultural purposes that may be subserved.

With respect to sophistication, the earlier remarks (1950) do not seem to need modification. Everything continues to slip down the age levels, although this progress in infant acceleration is now often more measurable through the toys that the children will play with than through their games. In some sense, as families have become smaller and homes more prosperous, group play in the streets has decreased and imaginative play in the homes has increased. Toys have a role in children's lives far exceeding that of earlier years. In a sense, toys are the second educational curriculum, one with which the modern child may spend as much time as his parent spent in childhood street play. The toys themselves are organized by the manufacturers into a layer-cake curriculum of increasing complexity and mechanical ingenuity. While some argue that Western toys are merely an exercise in disposable consumerism in which the children parallel the excesses of their parents, others contend that they are an exercise in model manipulation, rivaling the parents' concern with washing machines, automobiles, food processors, mechanical toothbrushes, and the like. The argument is that as the child with the shanghai may become an adult hunter, the child with the mechanical doll may become an adult computer accountant. Whatever the interpretation, children at younger and younger ages are given increasingly complex machine-based toys to deal with, including dolls that suck, urinate, and defecate. Even the habit of playing with toy guns, where it is still permitted, seems to have slipped down the age level, and it is the four- through seven-year-olds who tote the plastic machine guns and pistols.

Verbal sophistication continues apace. Television clowns and humorists are available in most homes from the earliest years, providing children with alternate ways of viewing adult behavior. Such playful folks enter the home in comedy and variety show and suggest alternatives that may not be available from more serious parents. As a result, there is a noticeable increase in children's capacity for parody, for mimicking the antics of these comedians, and for making nonsense out of the ever-present commercial jingles and presentations. Children were always "monkeys" in the old-fashioned sense, but there are now more models for them to share in such physical satire. In many tribal cultures all citizens share this capacity for mimicry and representation, but in Western society it has tended to be confined to those who had training as actors. There is some possibility that the availability of flexible television models, and the increased emphasis on natural movement, mime, and improvisation in schools, is bringing back generations of people with more access to fluid bodily movement as a way of expressing the feeling and the meaning of their lives.

A more important form of sophistication related to our increasingly information culture may be the constant practice that many modern children get in games of chance and strategy. There is evidence that games of strategy first arose in civilization at the same time as the institution of social classes and warfare. The rapid modern extension of games of strategy and chance to almost all children suggests that a whole culture is being trained in such ways of thinking, rather than just a military or aristocratic elite, as was traditionally the case. Not only do children get abundant practice at these games from the board, card, and strategy games that they buy in the store, but increasingly such games are introduced in the classroom. Strategy and chance games are invented as ways of teaching children the prosaic subject matters of history, geography, economics, and politics. Organizations exist to promote what has been termed "game simulation." School subjects in these circumstances are taught increasingly in a context of interpersonal bargaining and manipulation which brings some of the motives and ethics of the "smoke-filled back room" into the classroom. Whether one likes it or not, the alphabets of strategic power are being more widely experienced than ever before, even if not exactly in a way that Machiavelli might well have admired. Having made such a statement, one must immediately raise the caution that we are talking about play, not actuality. Every university and every school and every game is after all only an ivory tower. Each deals with the way things might be, not with the way they necessarily will be. Each trains its students in possible worlds, giving them a repertoire of possible adjustments, which they must then engage with actual living. Which of their potential alphabets will pay off cannot be decided by a school or by an exercise in game simulation. Still the point is made that the modern playground trains in sophistication of a strategic sort. But modern children are probably less expert in battle of a physical sort, having had fewer fights and less regular training along these lines. Here again, however, one must proceed with caution, because the present vogue of karate and various other Eastern forms of combat may well slip down the age levels and reintroduce children to such physical arts, although in a more specialized way.

There is little need to mention the increase in mechanical ingenuity and the mechanical toys or actual machines available for children's play (whether bicycles or skateboards with engines or hand calculators or electronic video games on television). Here the changes continue along the same lines as earlier. We may also expect the emergence of human doll figures of increasing informational contrivance parallel to the understanding of which children are capable. Dolls with genitals have already made a minor appearance on the toy-market scene, and human figures replete with all the plastic internal organs have been available for over a decade. The Barbie doll with breasts is the largest selling doll item on the American market. In the future we will probably see a more systematically elaborated step-by-step sequence of figure complexity.

While physical education has become more widespread, physical activity through voluntary play seems to have markedly decreased. More children spend less time in the streets and more time at their television sets. On the other hand, the general improvement in physical health through adequate diet and vitamin intake partly counters this downward trend in gross physical activity. Further countering the trend is the increasing opportunity for specialized training programs in such activities as dance, tennis, skiing, skating, and horseback riding, which have become accessible to the middle class, once having been available only to the wealthy.

All the surveys of recreation change in Europe and America show a shift toward a greater heterogeneity of interests in the adult population. In a comparison of the game preferences of children at Island Bay and Karori schools, Wellington, in 1949, with children in the same schools in 1967, I found a marked decrease in the hegemony of cricket and rugby. Although there was no shift in the total responses of the children, there was a marked shift toward a greater variety of play and games being mentioned than in the 1949 group. If this trend continues, children may become more differentiated in their physical competences. There may be less general activity in the playground, but the same playgrounds may harbor many more pockets of children who have a specialized skill potential in one of many diverse forms of recreation from canoe-rowing to gymnastics.

One clear trend over the years has been for girls to become more active in games, and as they have become more active to participate increasingly in games that were once the preserve of the boys. Although this trend is steady from the 1890s, the greatest shift appears to have occurred after World War I. At the time of this writing we are witnessing another upsurge, as women once again claim a more equally active role in the life and the sports of the Western world. Although prior to 1950 there was no great shift on the part of boys or men toward greater acceptance of the traditionally nurturant and sociable roles of women, there are some signs that such a shift is now occurring, even if on a small scale. One sign of this is the availability for boys of so-called action dolls, which although usually dressed as soldiers or spacemen or scouts nevertheless introduce a boy to the possibility of nurturing and of dressing and undressing doll figures. In earlier years all a seven-year-old could take to bed was his football, boxing gloves, or Scout knife. Now he can take his "action figure." Given the increasing acceptance of the notion that husbands should be nurturant and play with their children, rather than merely feed them or fight for them, this change is perhaps not surprising.

Violence, which has gone from many playgrounds, at least in its older form of fighting pits, is now under attack even in its symbolic forms. Parental groups raise protests about toy guns and about violence on television. There is a continuing and widespread antagonism to "competitiveness" in sports, as well as efforts on the part of some to evolve a newer form of physical education and new "game movements" that stress the more collaborative sides of human behavior. At present these are just trends and are promoted by only a minority of people, but since they are consistent with the long-term trends toward quietude in the playground, they are worth noting.

Our own historical surveys of the play scene in the United States between 1890 and 1960 found changes in game preference very much like those mentioned here (Sutton-Smith and Rosenberg 1961). Both New Zealand and the United States have in common a decrease in status games (Kings, Queens, Priests, Dukes), particularly formal singing, funeral, kissing, and dialogue games (with ritualized verbal routines), and an increase in skipping or jump rope games from 1900 onward. Chasing play continues, but with increasing informality and without the elaborate forms whose place has now been largely taken by organized sports. Physical skills are much more often aided by the use of kinds of sporting equipment (skates, skateboards, bicycles). The traditional varieties of marbles, tops, hoops, and so on, although not totally extinct, are seldom thriving forms of folk play. A full contrast with the situation in the British Isles cannot yet be made because the final Opie volume on singing games is not complete. The record to date, however, makes it look as if much more of the older lore has been preserved there than in the United States and New Zealand. A study is yet to be made of the comparative change in the three countries.

Still, we may safely conclude that in England and the United States, as in New Zealand from 1950 to 1980, recent trends toward greater sophistication, greater domestication, and greater mechanization in play are consistent with those noted from 1840 to 1950. But some of the changes in male sex-role play and the changes toward more general competence in mimicry and toward less general outdoor physical activity and competitiveness, but more symbolic play, may be regarded as novel and more characteristic of the period since the 1950s than of the period before that. These latter changes herald important shifts in the character of our civilization, implying the possibility of new levels and new kinds of creativity in children. These changes may be potentially of greater significance than the domestication of violence which is so well charted in this account between 1900 and 1950.

Most of the foregoing remarks refer to mainstream New Zealand (or American) children. The picture may be entirely different if one looks to new immigrant groups. In New Zealand, as in the United States, the life circumstances of such groups is often nearer to the conditions described in either Part One or Part Two of this book. Such groups are often destined to live in all three eras at once. In the home they may have massive nineteenth-century parental neglect (both parents working), and yet also may be the real victims of television passivity. With few models for alternative activities (reading, visits, creative activity), it is either television or the gang life of the streets. These children sometimes behave in school like the children described in Chapter 3 and must be managed by teachers seldom trained to deal with such a mixture of history and ethnic background. Many teachers will readily aver that the domestication of the playground discussed in Part Two has yet to come in their direction. The longer view is that these tributaries of violence are in fact undergoing such a domestication, but with some of the same perturbation that characterized the lives of those immigrants who were their predecessors in an earlier century—not, of course, that historical precedent is any guarantor of parallel forms of development. We seek here, at least, to take note of these current exceptions to the historical parameters we have drawn.

By way of a codicil, while I have attempted to make my interpretations in this work relevant to the historical phenomena that I have reviewed, the reader needs to be warned that this is a personal epilogue and it is quite possible that my own personality has brought to these interpretations an unwarranted optimistic slant. It is also possible to interpret the same historical material pessimistically and to see it as demonstrating a gradual marginalization of children's function in modern culture. Throughout most of human history the young have lived in the midst of human affairs. In our own century, however, they have been pushed to one side so that childhood and adolescence have become the names for a kind of pet zoo. In this view children no less than animals have been pushed to the margins of our society. Childhood has become a zoo. In defense of this attitude all that has been said here about schools, playgrounds, organized sports, and television could be read as examples of the "zooification" of children. In addition child psychology and child sociology, both of which are largely concerned with the "socialization" or control of children (and seldom ever with their creativity), can be interpreted in the same way. Antithetically, but equally pessimistically, the idealization of childhood in children's literature, child art, and children's play, as well as in the cognitive view that children's thinking is preoperational or primitive, can be regarded as justifications for treating children as especially innocent and requiring control. Like the noble savages of the eighteenth century and the idealized women of the nineteenth, children in this conservative view are seen as irrational, emotional, and rhythmic, justifying colonization, exploitation, or indoctrination at as early an age as possible in the basics of our civilization. In these terms society must hasten children's acquisition of the formalized logic and manners that will enable them to master the ever more complex computers and diplomacies of tomorrow. If this pessimistic view of modern children's position in society is correct, then one might conclude that we are fast approaching the aged phase of modern society where tradition counts for much more than innovation.

Mine has been a more optimistic view though I would stress that it is very difficult for adults of Western society to look at children and know what they are about. A number of thinkers from Freud onwards have pointed out that our own adult thinking may be purchased at the price of forgetting our childhood years. Our concept of childhood is often a product of our own forgetfulness. And although on my optimistic view the recent historical record seems to be one of increasing kindness toward children parallel to our increasing acceptance of our own childishness, we clearly have a long way to go in this regard. Hatred or ambivalence toward children has been more typical and is still the more powerful force if the pessimistic view is correct. Perhaps as the years pass and we play alongside children more, playing with them as well as teaching them how to play, we may discover our own infantile selves in a new way that is not harmful for children and indeed is regenerative for us. To be able to play with children, as well as to be able to play as adults, is perhaps to contain all our ages and all our stages in the same person. We may hope that this is one way in which the struggle for creative personal growth can be facilitated. At the least the present record of children's play makes the point that children no less than adults live in order to live vividly, and that their play—and I would add their art—is the center of such vividness. It seems absurd to me to contrive any future playground or any school or any society in which the pursuit of such vividness is not a major focus of that construction.

You can do many things with a bat.

appendix 1:
sources of information

This Appendix lists the names of people and schools that contributed to this research. The name of each informant is followed by the place and the date to which his or her report refers. If the report was written, the date is followed by the abbreviation "R" (Report); if oral, by the abbreviation "I" (Interview). Among the persons interviewed were some who did not wish to have their names recorded; their contributions (giving place and time they described) are labeled as "Anon." (Anonymous). The names of the schools visited are followed by the abbreviation "SV" (School Visit), and the names of the schools mentioned by children but not visited by the investigator are followed by the abbreviation "SR" (School Report).

In order to show the geographical distribution of the reports, the sources are listed according to provinces. The list proceeds from north to south: North Auckland, Auckland, Taranaki, Hawkes Bay, Wellington, Wairarapa, Nelson, Marlborough, Westland, Canterbury, Otago, and Southland. Under each province, personal sources are given first, then the schools, if any. If the informants are all from different localities, there is a single list of personal sources, with the recorded names alphabetically arranged and the anonymous contributors mentioned last. If there are cities or townships from which two or more contributions were received, the local groups of informants are listed first, under their respective localities, and all other informants are listed together under "Other Towns."

School logbooks which were used are also noted. In general, nineteenth-century logbooks contained little information outside school opening and closing dates, numbers of absentees, and so on. Occasionally, however, a school principal expressed himself more fully.

The *school jubilee journals* used also vary in value. In some districts a practice was made of inviting reminiscences on older times, and some of these were quite useful. Most, however, contain factual materials about buildings, pupils, and teachers.

PEOPLE AND SCHOOLS

North Auckland Province

Mr. W. G. Johnston, North Auckland, 1910–20 (R)
Mr. D. A. McPherson, Whangarei, 1896–1900 (R)
Mr. C. Spanahake, North Auckland, 1940–50 (R)
Mr. I Sparks, Matamata, 1920–30 (R)

Auckland Province

AUCKLAND CITY

Mrs. W. D. Dodd, 1910–15 (R)
Mrs. I. Moore, 1905–15 (R)
Mr. Oates, 1915–20 (I)
Mrs. James Onehunga, 1905–10 (R)
Mrs. Shand, 1900–1905 (I)
Anon., 1935 (I)

OTHER TOWNS

Mr. Anderson, Ohatu, 1920 (I)
Mrs. J. Beever, Glenn Massey, 1912–25 (R)
Mr. J. Ching, Te Mawhai, 1930 (I)
Mr. J. Delahunty, Thames, 1890–95 (I)
Mr. Gillies, Maroa, 1949 (I)

Mr. Holyoke, Bay of Plenty, 1910–15 (I)
Mrs. E. D. McIntosh, Bay of Plenty (R)
Mr. B. Palmer, Paroa, 1949 (I)
Mr. P. Wilson, Tauranga, 1933–38 (I)
Anon., Hamilton, 1935 (I)
Anon., Paerata, 1930–35 (I)

SCHOOLS
Diocesan Girls' High (SR)
Intermediate Normal (SV)
Papakura Normal (SV)
Papatoetoe (SR)
St. Cuthbert's Girls' College (SR)

Taranaki Province

NEW PLYMOUTH
Mr. W. H. Clark, New Plymouth, 1880–90 (R)
Mrs. E. Vivian, Weston, 1885–95 (R)

WAITARA
Mr. N. M. Chappell, 1899–1905 (R)
Miss I. K. Wylie, 1902–9 (R)

OTHER TOWNS
Mrs. M. Blampied, Mangopeetu, King Country, 1900–1910 (R)

Hawkes Bay Province

Mr. F. L. Combs, Gisborne, 1890–95 (I)
Mr. E. S. Harrison, Hastings, 1925–30 (R)
Mrs. A. M. Isdale, Putoka, 1920–24 (R)
Mr. McGregor, Waikatea, 1910–20 (I)
Mr. T. McKenzie, Waingahe, 1930–40 (I)
Mrs. H. Shaw, Napier, 1949 (R)
Mr. Turley, Otane, 1920–30 (I)
Mrs. Verrier-Jones, Napier, 1949 (R)
Anon., Napier, 1890–1900 (I)

SCHOOLS
Napier Girls' High (SR)

Wellington Province

PALMERSTON NORTH, MANAWATU
Mrs. G. C. Birch, 1932–37 (R)
Mr. A. E. Campbell, 1915–20 (I)
Mrs. Lewis, Terrace End, 1910–20 (I)
Mr. J. K. McKay, 1920–40 (R)

Mrs. Murray, 1914–20 (I)
Mr. J. Penketh, 1920–40 (R)
Mr. Philpott, 1930–35 (I)
Mrs. E. J. Sutton-Smith, 1905–10 (I)
Mr. H. Wollerman, 1895–1900 (I)

WANGANUI

Mr. Pirdie, 1930–36 (I)
Mrs. D. Singleton, Wanganui, 1900–1910 (R)

WELLINGTON CITY

Mr. N. Aitken, 1890–1900 (I)
Mr. P. Anderson, 1949 (I)
Professor C. L. Bailey, 1915 (I)
Mrs. B. Barcus, 1890–1900 (R)
Mr. J. Barnard, Johnsonville, 1949 (I)
Miss Burgess, 1949 (I)
Mr. W. Burgess, 1949 (I)
Mr. W. J. Clark, 1910–20 (R)
Miss H. Crump, Lower Hutt, 1935–40 (I)
Miss B. Dibble, Island Bay, 1935–40 (I)
Mrs. Aileen Findlay, 1920–25 (R)
Mr. A. E. Gell, 1905–15 (I)
Mrs. E. Gillon, 1882–92 (I)
Mr. E. B. Goddard, Petone, 1904–13 (R)
Mrs. P. Hattaway, 1920–25 (I)
Mr. D. Hempleman, 1935 (I)
Mrs. Innes, Wainui-o-mata, 1910–20 (I)
Miss Muriel Kim, 1948 (R)
Mr. E. McDonald, Mount Cook, 1880 (R)
Mr. P. Mitchell, 1949 (I)
Mr. B. Piper, Eastern Hutt, 1935–40 (I)
Mrs. J. C. Reid, 1918–25 (R)
Mr. Rendall, Eastbourne, 1930–35 (I)
Mrs. Rome, 1890–1900 (I)
Mrs. W. Sutton, Kaiwarra, 1905–10 (I)
Mrs. D. Tooby, Karori, 1930–35 (I)
Mr. William Toomuth, 1870–80 (R)

SCHOOLS

Clifton Terrace (SR)
Island Bay (SV)
Karori (SV)
Mount Cook (SR)
Northland (SR)

Wairarapa Province

Mr. Barnes, Epokongiro, 1905–10 (I)
Mrs. Catherine Gregory, Kohinui, 1900 (R)
Mr. Jonsen, Carterton, 1895–1900 (R)
Mr. D. H. Leitch, Ratapiko, 1949 (R)
Mrs. Manchester, 1949 (I)
Mrs. T. Muir, Carterton, 1930–35 (I)
Mrs. J. Ponga, Masterton, 1925–30 (R)
Mr. D. O'Connor, 1920–25 (I)
Miss Oswin, South Featherston, 1903–5 (I)
Mr. Roydhouse, 1900–1905 (I)
Anon., Aohunga, 1949 (I)
Anon., Ratapiko, 1900 (I)
Anon., Ratapiko, 1930 (I)

SCHOOLS

Aohunga (SV)
Eketahuna (SR)
Horoeka (SV) (and logbook)
Kohinui (SR)
Makuri (logbook)
Mangitainoka (SV)
Ngaturi (logbook)
Pongaroa (SV)
Rangapiko (SR)
Rangataua (SR)
Waione (logbook)
Woodville (SR)

Nelson Province

BRIGHTWATER

Mr. Bryant, 1920–25 (R)
Mrs. M. Cameron, 1920–25 (R)

COLLINGWOOD

Mr. Page, Sr., 1890–95 (I)
Mr. Wigsell, 1895–1900 (I)
Mrs. Wigsell, 1900–1905 (I)

NELSON

Mrs. A. M. Anderson, 1894–96 (R)
Mrs. C. M. Blackett, 1886–90 (R)
Mr. Goodyear, 1895–1900 (I)
Mrs. Goodyear, 1895–1900 (I)
Mr. Hasse, 1890–1900 (I)

Mrs. H. S. Newbury, 1946 (R)
Mr. Shand, 1875–80 (I)
Mr. A. B. Thompson, 1910–15 (I)
Mrs. Win, 1935–40 (I)

ONEKAKA

Miss M. Peterson, 1949 (R)
Miss Z. Thomas, 1949 (R)

ROCKVILLE

Mr. Berry, Sr., Rockville, 1895–1900 (I)
Mr. Berry, Jr., 1920–25 (I)
Mrs. Jamieson, 1894–1902 (I)

TAKAKA

Mrs. Hasse, 1900–1908 (I)
Mr. Kirk, 1885–1900 (I)
Mr. Lewis, 1900 (I)
Mr. Page, Jr., 1910–20 (I)

OTHER TOWNS

Mrs. E. R. Edwards, Lower Moutere, 1900 (R)
Mrs. E. Hodgson, Richmond, 1885–95 (I)
Mr. Isdell, Stillwater, 1885–95 (I)
Mr. L. R. Palmer, Waimate West, 1920 (I)
Mr. K. L. Sigglelow, Upper Moutere, 1930 (I)
Mr. L. Whatman, Waimea, 1925–30 (I)
Mrs. M. Woodley, Lower Moutere, 1900 (R)

SCHOOLS

Aorere (SR)
Bainham (SR)
Barrytown (SR)
Brightwater (SR)
Collingwood (SV)
Kotinga (SR)
Manganakau (SR)
Motupipi (SR)
Nelson Central (SV)
Onekaka (SR)
Pakawau (SR)
Stoke (SR)
Takaka (SV)
Takaka Convent (SR)
Tarakahe (SR)
Upper Moutere (SV)
Upper Takaka (SR)

Marlborough Province

Mrs. A. A. Barton, Blenheim, 1911–19 (R)

Westland Province

DENNISTON

Miss Innes, Denniston, 1930–40 (I)
Mr. T. Muir, 1930–35 (I)
Mr. Shand, 1910–20 (I)

GRANITY

Mr. Kean, 1900–1905 (I)
Mr. Murry, 1895–1900 (I)
Mr. Prosser, 1930–35 (I)
Mr. D. G. Rogers, 1930–34 (R)
Mrs. Watson, 1895–1900 (I)

WESTPORT

Mr. James Merton, 1895–1900 (R)
Mrs. Murry, 1895–1900 (I)
Miss Strachan, 1920–25 (I)

OTHER TOWNS

Mrs. G. Bleach, Ross, 1920–25 (R)
Mrs. P. Dennahie, West Coast, 1910–20 (I)
Mr. James, Murchison, 1890–95 (I)
Mr. Murry, Seddonville, 1890–1900 (I)
Mr. I Orman, Millerton, 1928–36 (I)
Anon., West Coast, 1930–35 (I)
Anon., 1920–25 (I)

SCHOOLS

Awatura (SR)
Barrytown (SR)
Denniston (SV)
Dobsen (SV)
Granity (SV)
Granity Convent (SV)
Greymouth (SR)
Greymouth Main (SR)
Harihari (SR)
Hokitika (SV)
Hokitika Convent (SV)
Kahatahi (SR)
Kaiata (SV)
Kaihinu (SR)
Kanieri (SR)

Kumara (SR)
Lake Rotama (SR)
Lower Koiterangi (SR)
Millerton (SR)
Paenga (SR)
Ross (SR)
Ruatapu (SR)
Seddonville (SV)
Sheffield (SR)
Stockton (SV)
Upper Koiterangi (SR)
Westport South (SR)
Woodstock (SR)

Canterbury Province

CHRISTCHURCH

Mr. R. de B. Adamson, Papanui, 1903–4 (R)
Mrs. J. R. Allison, 1920–25 (R)
Mr. J. Auten, Shirley, (I)
Mr. L. Cleveland, 1920–25 (I)
Mr. Maffey, Sumner, 1905–10 (I)
Miss I. Norwood, 1948 (R)
Miss B. Odell, 1928–34 (I)
Miss F. Owens, 1893–95 (R)
Mr. G. Parkin, 1919–20 (I)
Miss Rackham, Beckenham, 1935–40 (I)
Mr. E. Riach, 1904–5 (R)
Mr. Thomson, 1925–30 (I)
Mr. G. Van Haast, 1887–90 (R)
Mrs. S. A. Watkins, 1870–75 (R)
Mrs. P. Wilson, Akaroa, 1890–1900 (R)
Anon., 1875–80 (I)
Anon., 1930 (I)

TIMARU

Mr. G. V. Gussell, Adair, 1895–1900 (R)
Mr. D. Hilary, 1935–40 (I)
Mr. Malthus, 1880–90 (I)

WAIMATE

Mr. Dewar, 1914–18 (I)
Mr. McKenzie, 1890–1900 (I)

OTHER TOWNS

Mr. R. de B. Adamson, Heathcote Valley, 1899–1901 (R)
Miss Bowen, Ashburton, 1935–40 (I)

Mr. W. H. Cartwright, South Canterbury, 1900–1910 (R)
Mrs. H. Chapman, Elmwood, 1913–22 (R)
Mrs. McCatchy, Oxford, 1950 (R)
Mrs. Page, Rakaia, 1910–20 (I)
Mrs. P. S. Phillips, Ashburton, 1949 (R)
Mrs. S. Rockell, Amberley, North Canterbury, 1890–1900 (R)
Anon., Akaroa, 1880–90 (I)
Anon., Kaikoura, 1925–30 (I)

SCHOOLS

Oxford (SR)
Christchurch Normal (SV)

Otago Province

DUNEDIN

Mr. C. R. Allen, 1870–80 (R)
Mr. James Begg, 1880–90 (R)
Mr. Chapman-Cohen, Forbury, 1915–25 (I)
Mr. Crawford, 1930–35 (I)
Mrs. Gubbins, 1880–90 (I)
Mr. Harrison, 1930–35 (I)
Mr. Hudson, 1930–35 (I)
Mrs. Hutchison, 1890–95 (I)
Mr. A. Lee, 1900–1905 (I)
Mr. Luke, Anderson's Bay, 1900–1915 (I)
Mr. A. McDavidson, 1920–48 (I)
Mr. McGeorge, 1880–85 (I)
Mrs. D. Malloch, 1900–1905 (I)
Mrs. T. Muir, 1905–14 (I)
Mrs. T. Murray, 1910–20 (I)
Mr. Nind, 1900–5 (I)
Mr. Robertson, 1890–95 (I)
Mr. Shand, 1900–1910 (I)
Mrs. M. Stronach, 1877 (R)
Professor Tennant, 1875–80 (I)
Miss V. Turton, 1870–80 (I)
Mr. Tyrell, 1905–10 (I)
Miss A. Woodhouse, 1890–96 (R)
Anon., 1925–30 (I)
Anon., 1865–90 (I)
Anon., 1870–80 (I)
Anon., Kaitangata, 1927–28 (I)
Anon., 1925–30 (I)
Anon., 1935 (I)
Anon., 1905 (I)

Anon., Maori Hill, 1920–30 (I)
Anon., 1890–95 (I)
Anon., Mornington, 1948 (I)
Anon., Kensington, 1947 (I)
Anon., Tainui, 1935–40 (I)

HAMPDEN

Mr. McCarrow, 1880–85 (I)
Mrs. McCarrow, 1885–90 (I)

WAIKOUAITI

Miss D. Black, 1880–90 (I)
Mrs. Brown, 1880–85 (I)
Mr. J. Brown, Sr., 1870–75 (I)
Mr. J. Brown, Jr., 1915–20 (I)
Mrs. Henderson, 1890–1900 (I)
Mr. D. Malloch, 1885–90 (I)
Mrs. M. Racham, 1900 (I)
Mr. E. J. Sutton-Smith, 1890–1910 (I)
Mr. Templeton, 1895–1900 (I)
Mrs. Templeton, 1895–1900 (I)

OTHER TOWNS

Mr. Bathgate, Outram, 1927
Dr. J. Brugh, South Clutha, 1875–80 (I)
Mrs. W. H. Cormack, North Otago, 1900–1910 (R)
Miss Fisher, Alexandra, 1930 (I)
Mr. R. Gray, Lawrence, 1880–85 (I)
Mrs. Henderson, Catlin, 1895–1900 (I)
Mrs. Johnstone, Tahataki, 1877–85 (I)
Mr. Marton, Milton, 1910–15 (I)
Mr. G. O. Matheson, Palmerston South, 1896–1900 (I)
Mr. Patterson, Heriot, 1920–30 (I)
Mrs. E. Percy, Alexandra, 1910–20 (R)
Mrs. Reid, Salisbury, Taieri, 1860–70 (I)
Mr. C. W. Ross, Queenstown, Central Otago, 1880 (R)
Mr. Searl, Oamaru, 1905–10 (I)
Anon., Alexandra, 1930 (I)
Anon., Caversham, 1949 (I)
Anon., Clinton, 1940 (I)
Anon., Karitane, 1925 (I)
Anon., Karitane, 1951 (I)
Anon., Lauder, 1915 (I)
Anon., Taieri, 1870–80 (I)
Anon., Taieri, 1930–35 (I)

Anon., Tapanui, 1880–85 (I)
Anon., Weddeburn, 1845 (I)

SCHOOLS

Caversham (SV)
Forbury (SV)
Hampden (SV)
MacAndrew Intermediate (SV)
North East Valley (SV)
Ngapara (SR)
St. Clair (SV)
Waikouaiti (SV)

Southland Province

Mr. William Grieve, 1870 (R)
Mr. George McDonald, 1870 (R)

OTHER TOWNS

Mrs. C. Duthrie, Waikari, 1925–30 (R)
Miss Ford, Wyndam, 1940–45 (I)
Mr. Hamilton, Southland, 1948 (R)
Mrs. E. M. Laing, Riverdale, 1900 (R)
Mr. McGibbon, 1920–30 (R)
Mrs. P. McKenzie, 1880–90 (R)
Mr. Phillips, Tuatapere, 1923–24 (I)
Mrs. E. Scott, 1895–1900 (R)
Mr. Young, Isles Bank, 1945 (I)
Anon., Lumsden, 1948 (I)
Anon., Isles Bank, 1945 (I)
Anon., Southland, 1914–18 (I)
Anon., Invercargill, 1925–30 (I)
Anon., Invercargill, 1930 (I)
Anon., Ranfurly, 1948 (I)
Anon., Stirling, 1930–35 (I)
Anon., Gore, 1930–35 (I)

SCHOOL JUBILEE CELEBRATION BOOKLETS

The following booklets were, for the most part, published and written by the schools mentioned in their titles. The only dates given are, in general, those that are part of the title. The later date indicates the year of publication.

Albany Street School, 1874–1924 (Palmerston North, Manawatu)

Anderson's Bay School, Seventieth Anniversary, 1858–1928 (Dunedin, Otago)

Auckland Grammar School, 1869–1929 (Auckland City)

Balclutha Public School, Souvenir Booklet, 1863–1931 (Southland)

Blenheim Borough School, 1859–1937 (Marlborough)

Carterton District High School, 1861–1937 (Wairarapa)

Caversham School Sixty-fifth Anniversary Celebrations, 1861–1926 (Wairarapa)

Cheltenham School District Jubilee, *These Fifty Years,* 1886–1936 (Manawatu)

College Street School, Palmerston North, 1893–1943 (Manawatu)

Dannevirke North School, 1872–1936 (Hawkes Bay)

Dannevirke South School, 1900–1950 (Hawkes Bay)

The Elsthorpe School, Golden Jubilee, 1898–1948 (Hawkes Bay)

Gladstone School, Diamond Jubilee, 1898–1936 (Wairarapa)

Grovetown School, *The Early History of the School of the Big Bush* (dates not given) (Marlborough)

Hampstead School, Ashburton East, Jubilee Magazine, 1886–1936 (Canterbury)

Invercargill Middle School Jubilee, 1873–1923 (Southland)

Kaitangata School, Sixty-first Anniversary, 1866–1927 (Otago)

Karamu School, 1889–1939 (Waikato, Auckland)

Kopuaranga School, 1885–1935 (Wairarapa)

MacCandrew Road School, 1883–1933 (Dunedin City)

Manakau School, 1888–1948 (Horowhenua, Wellington)

Manawaru Public School Jubilee, 1900–1950 (Waikato, Auckland)

Mangapiko Te Awamutu, 1879–1939 (Auckland)

Mangatainoka School, 1889–1949 (Wairarapa)

Manuku School Jubilee, 1883–1933 (Auckland)

Mosgiel District High School, Diamond Jubilee, 1871–1931 (Otago)

Newtown School, Jubilee Souvenir, 1879–1934 (Wellington City)

North West Valley School, 1851–1932 (Dunedin)

Oamaru South School, 1877–1929 (Otago)

Ohakune District High School, *A Mountain and a School,* 1896–1940 (Wellington)

Ohaupo District High School, Waikato, 1869–1939 (Auckland)

Otaua School, Golden Jubilee, 1895–1941 (Hokianga, Auckland)

Opawa School, Seventy-seventh Jubilee Celebration, 1872–1949 (Christchurch)

Otaki School, 1886–1946 (Wellington)

Otepopo Reunion, 1864–1929 (Otago)

Owaka District High School, 1875–1935 (Otago)

Paekakariki School, 1886–1946 (Wellington)

Papakura, 1877–1937 (Auckland)

Papatawa School, 1887–1937 (Hawkes Bay)

Paraparaumu, Jubilee Souvenir of School, 1889–1940 (Wellington)
Park High Street School, 1864–1924 (Dunedin)
Paterangi School, 1876–1936 (Waipu, Auckland)
Pongaroa School, 1897–1947 (Wairarapa)
Porirua School, Seventy-fifth Anniversary, 1873–1948 (Wellington)
Port Chalmers District High School, 1856–1948 (Otago)
Rangitumau School Jubilee Celebrations, 1893–1946 (Wairarapa)
Ravensbourne School Jubilee, 1877–1927 (Dunedin)
Richmond School, 1875–1925 (Auckland)
Riwaka School Jubilee, 1848–1948 (Nelson)
Saint Alban's School District Jubilee, 1873–1933 (Christchurch)
Sawyer's Bay School, Seventieth Anniversary, 1861–1939 (Dunedin)
Souvenir of the Jubilee of the Main School, Timaru, 1874–1929 (Canterbury)
Union Street School, 1862–1929 (Palmerston North)
Waihou School Jubilee, 1880–1930 (Auckland)
Waikanae School, Jubilee Souvenir, 1896–1946 (Wellington)
Waianiwa Jubilee, Southland, 1863–1933 (Southland)
West Christchurch School Jubilee, 1874–1924 (Christchurch)
Whakaronga School, Stony Creek, Palmerston North, 1877–1937 (Manawatu)
Wylie's Crossing School, Taieri Plain, Otago, 1894–1944

appendix 2:
reminiscence sheet

As a prompter in interviews or in solicited reports, a *"reminiscence sheet"* was used with the interviewee, and an example is reproduced here. In all this work, the most important principle adopted was that attention should be given to names and practices that were replicated in many sources.

NEW ZEALAND CHILDREN'S PLAY AND GAMES

This questionnaire is part of an attempt to build a comprehensive record of the play and games of New Zealand children over a period of one hundred years. Please underline any of the following activities you have played and add the names of any others. On separate paper add details about activities on this list and others of your own, including information about: the rules or rhymes of the games; their season, site, and source; the age at which you played them; and the effects of school companions, climate, and environment. All material should be sent to B. Sutton-Smith, Education Department, Victoria University College, Wellington.

A. Imitative Play: trains, coaches, schools, houses, shops, dressing up, horses, dentists, etc.

B. Individual Conflict: (i) With play object: tops (whip, humming, peg), Knucklebones, Conkers, Stagknife, Tipcat, skipping (rhymes), marbles (names-games-moves-values), Egg Cap, £s.d., Hopscotch (diagram), Cap-on, Lazy Stick. (ii) Without material object: handstands, Leapfrog, Follow the Leader, Bull in the Ring, Fly the Garter, King of the Castle, Scrag, Sacks on the Mill, Bumpers, Cockfighting, Tip Tap Toe, Cabbages, Honeypots. (iii) Leader games: Colors, Queenie, Initials, Letters, Steps and Strides, Creepy, Statues, Film Stars, Giant Strides. (iv) He games, including all forms of Tag or Tig and sometimes counting-out rhymes (Eeny Meeny Miny Mo), also Bar the Door (King Seenie)—Red Rover, Sheep, etc.—Twos and Threes, Kick the Tin, Fill the Gap, Hide and Seek, Relievo, Puss in the Corner, Tom Tiddler's Ground, Ivory, Trades, Moonlight Starlight, Tip the Finger (This Is the Way the World Goes Round), French and English.

C. Team Games: (i) Make-believe: Cowboys and Indians, Witches and Fairies, Cops and Robbers, etc. (ii) Dramatic: Nuts and May, Oranges and Lemons, In and Out of Windows, Ring a Ring a Roses, Botany Bay, Diggley Bones, Wash the Dishes, Punchinello, Old Mother Gray, Round and Round the Village. (Please write out the words you used.) (iii) Formal: Variations on major sports, Cunning Joe, Longball, Prisoner's Base, Goosey, Shinty, Peg Ball, Chibby, Gag or No Gag, Punch King, Homp, Echo, Eggs in the Nest.

D. General Play with Objects: What playthings did you construct or invent, and what did you do with them? Shooting (shanghais, catapults, water pistols, peashooters, slings—how did you make these?), throwing and skipping stones, darts, hoops, kites, sleds, boats, stilts, trolley, whips, games with paper (Bangers, Water bombs), hands (Shadows), grass (Tinker Tailor), string (Cat's Cradle), peep shows, transfers, billycarts. What toys or animals or collections or hobbies did you play with most, and what did you do with them?

E. General Play Without Objects: fighting (was it arranged?), initiations (of a new boy), truancy (what did you do?), smoking (what?), play to and from school. Did you belong to a gang or set? What do you remember of its rules, secret language or code, activities? Play with sweets and food (cooking), climbing, balancing, burning (magnifying glass—gorse), burrowing (sand), daring, building huts and forts, nesting, sliding, swinging, scribbling (what/where?), stealing (what? where?), tracking, taboo play and language. Pranks on adults (which adult in district?), on children, in and out of school (Knick Knock). Skating, swimming, snowballing, gambling, constructive play (roads). Word play (Riddles—your favorites?—nicknames, rhymes—Bluebells Cockleshells, skipping), teasing rhymes (Giddy Giddy Gout), counting-out rhymes, obscene rhymes. Superstitions (Ghosts, crossed fingers, Black Cat, White Horse). Special occasions (April Fools' Day, Guy Fawkes, inspector's visit, holidays, picnics, parties). Tricks of all kinds.

F. Parlour Games: Which were the favourites of your childhood? Blindman's Buff, Hide the Thimble, Postman's Knock, Consequences, Forfeits, Mrs. McKenzie's Dead, Musical Chairs, Family Coach, Priest of the Parish, Simon Says, Poor Pussy, I Spy, Charades.

G. Old-timers and Others: Bingo, Jolly Miller, Draw a Pail of Water, Follow Me to London, Green Grass, Green Gravels, How Many Miles to Babylon, Jingo Ring, Merry Ma Tansa, Jack a Lingo, Jenny Jones, Poor Sally Is Aweeping, Saucy Jack, Three Dukes, Fire on the Mountains, Mother Mother the Pot Boils Over, Oak Ball, Pretty Little Girl of Mine, Thread the Needle, Pitch and Toss, Paper Chase, Chivvy Chase, Hot Cockles, This Is the Way the Wheel Goes Round, Space Ring, Wolf, Mingle the Bonnets, Horney, Tug of War, Chip Chop, Ducks and Drakes, Hares and Hounds, Hop the Hats, Hickety Bickety, Buck Buck, Namers and Guessers, Bedlams, Bells.

appendix 3:
place names cited in text with provinces

Amberley, Canterbury
Akaroa, Christchurch
Anderson's Bay, Dunedin
Ashburton, Canterbury
Auckland, Auckland
Balclutha, Southland
Bay of Plenty, Auckland
Blenheim, Marlborough
Brooklyn, Wellington
Carterton, Wairarapa
Catlins, Otago
Caversham, Christchurch
Charleston, Westland
Christchurch, Canterbury
Clyde Quay, Wellington
Colac Bay, Southland

Collingwood, Nelson
Cromwell, Otago
Dannevirke, Wairarapa
Denniston, Westland
Devonport, Auckland
Dunedin, Otago
Forbury, Dunedin
Gisborne, Auckland
Golden Bay, Nelson
Granity, Westland
Greendate, Dunedin
Greymouth, Westland
Hampden, Otago
Heriot, Christchurch
Hokowhitu, Palmerston North
Horoeka, Wairarapa

Horowhenua, Wellington
Hutt, Wellington
Invercargill, Southland
Island Bay, Wellington
Kaikohe, Auckland
Kaitangata, Otago
Kapuka, Southland
Kakaramea, Taranaki
Karamea, Nelson
Karori, Wellington
Kennington, Southland
Lawrence, Otago
Lower Moutere, Nelson
Manakau, Wairarapa
Mangatainoka, Wairarapa
Mangopeeki, Taranohi
Marton, Manawester
Masterton, Wairarapa
Mercer, Auckland
Millerton, Westland
Moeraki, Otaho
Motueka, Nelson
Moutere, Nelson
Murchison, Nelson
Nelson, Nelson
New Plymouth, Taranaki
Newtown, Wellington
Ngakawau, Westland
Ngaturi, Wairarapa
Nuhaka, Gisborne
Oamaru, Canterbury
Ohau, Wellington
Onehunga, Auckland
Ongarue, Auckland
Owaka, Otago
Paeroa, Auckland
Palmerston North, Maraweta
Palmerston South, Otago
Papakura, Auckland
Papanui, Auckland
Papatawa, Wairarapa
Petone, Wellington
Pigeon Bay, Canterbury
Poneke, Wellington City
Pongaroa, Wairarapa
Port Chalmers, Dunedin

Pukenhinau, Wairarapa
Purekireki, Otago
Queenstown, Otago
Rakaia, Christchurch
Rangariri, Auckland
Rangitikei, Manawaki
Rangitoto, Auckland
Ratapiko, Taranaki
Richmond, Nelson
Riwaka, Nelson
Rockville, Nelson
South Clutha, Southland
Stockton, Westland
Tahataki, Otago
Taieri, Otago
Taita, Hutt Valley, Wellington
Takaka, Nelson
Tapanui, Otago
Te Aroha, Auckland
Temuka, Auckland
Thomas, Nelson
Timaru, Canterbury
Tokomairiro, Otago
Tuakau, Auckland
Tua Marina, Marlborough
Tuapeka, Otago
Wadestown, Wellington
Waianiwa, Southland
Waihi, Auckland
Waikato, Auckland
Waikouaiti, Otago
Waimate, Canterbury
Waimea, Southland
Waione, Wairarapa
Waipu, Auckland
Wairau, Nelson
Waitara, Taranaki
Wakefield, Nelson
Wallacetown, Southland
Wanganui, Taranaki
Warkworth, Auckland
Westport, Westland
Whangaparoa, Wellington
Whakaronga, Manawata
Wellington, Wellington
Woodend, Southland

references and bibliography

Adams, J. J. (n.d.) School day reminiscences. Papanui, 1875–1883. Wellington: New Zealand Council of Educational Research.

Anderson, J. C. 1927. *Maori string figures*. Wellington: Board of Maori Ethnological Research.

———. 1949. *Old Christchurch in picture and story*. Christchurch: Simpson & Williams.

Ashburton. 1905. *Education Department File*. E.I.D., p. 7.

Auckland Herald. 1912. July, p. 24.

Auckland Star. 1930. Auckland Star Diamond Jubilee, May 7, 1930, p. 21.

Avedon, E., and Sutton-Smith, B., eds. 1971. *The study of games*. New York: Wiley.

Baird, D. 1942. History of physical education in New Zealand. Master's thesis, Victoria University, Wellington.

Bancroft, J. H. 1909. *Games for the playground, home, school and gymnasium*. New York: Macmillan.

Bannister, C. 1940. *Early history of Wairarapa*. Masterton: Times Age.

Barker, Lady. 1870. *Station life in New Zealand.* London: Macmillan.

———. 1875. *Station amusements in New Zealand.* London: William Hunt & Co.

Basketball Association. (n.d.) *Minutes of Wellington primary school girl's basketball association.* 1927–50.

Beaglehole, J. C. 1936. *New Zealand: A short history.* London: Allen & Unwin.

Beeby, C. E. 1936. *The intermediate schools of New Zealand: A survey.* Wellington: New Zealand Council of Educational Research.

Best, E. 1924. *The Maori.* Auckland: Whitcombe & Tombes.

———. 1928. Games and pastimes of the Maori. *Dom. Mus. Bulletin,* no. 8.

———. (n.d.) *Scrapbook No. 3.* Pilgrims afoot (*Evening Post,* April 5, 1912.); In drays to the races, and Once upon a time (*Evening Post,* November 5, 1912). Alexander Turnbull Library, Wellington.

Bett, H. 1929. *Origin and history of the games of children.* London: Methuen.

Board of Education, Great Britain. 1933. *Syllabus of physical training for schools.* London: H.M.S.O.

Bowman, H. O. 1948. *Port Chalmers: Gateway to Otago.* Dunedin: Otago Centennial Historical Publications.

Brereton, C. B. 1947. *No roll of drums.* Wellington: Reed.

Brewster, P. A. 1953. *American Nonsinging Games.* Norman. University of Oklahoma Press.

Bridges, C. E., and Bridges, O. E. 1941. *The physical training teacher's legal rights and responsibilities.* London: Foyle.

Brookes, E. S. 1892. *Frontier life: Taranaki, New Zealand.* Auckland: H. Brett.

Burns, C. D. 1932. *Leisure in the modern world.* London: Allen & Unwin.

Burns, C. S. 1914. *The handbook of British folklore.* London: Sidgewick & Jackson.

Butchers, A. G. 1929. *Young New Zealand: A history of the early contact of the Maori race and the European and of the establishment of a national system of education for both races.* Dunedin: Coulls, Somerville, Wilkie.

———. 1930. *Education in New Zealand; An historical survey of educational progress amongst the Europeans and the Maoris since 1878.* Dunedin: Coulls, Somerville, Wilkie.

Campbell, A. E. 1941. *Educating New Zealand.* Wellington: New Zealand Centennial Surveys.

Campbell, F. C. (n.d.) Some of my educational reminiscences, 1885. Typescript. Wellington: New Zealand Council of Educational Research.

Canterbury Times. 1900. December 16.

Cavallo, D. 1981. *Muscles, morals and team sports: Americans organize children's play, 1880–1920.* Philadelphia: University of Pennsylvania Press.

Chapman, F. R. 1898. The Maori game of Knuckle-bone. *Journal of Polynesian Society* 8:114.

Chibby. 1946 *Physical Education Society Bulletin* 2, No. 66.

Colec, W. C. (n.d.) *Reminiscences.* Greendale. Wellington: New Zealand Council of Educational Research.

Combs, F. L. 1939. *The harrowied toad.* London: Dent & Sons.

Cowan, J. C. 1948. *Down the years in the Maniototo.* Dunedin: Otago Centennial Historical Publications.

(Cricket). *Minutes of the Wellington Primary School Cricket Association.* 1929–50.

Curtis, H. S. 1909. The growth, present extent and prospects of the playground movement in America. *The Pedagogical Seminary* 16.

Daiken, L. 1949. *Children's games throughout the year.* London: Batsford.

Davin, D. 1947. *The gorse blooms pale.* London: Michael Joseph.

Douglas, N. 1916. *London street games.* London: Chatto & Windus.

Duff, O. 1941. *New Zealand now.* Wellington: Department of Internal Affairs.

Dulles, F. R. 1940. *America learns to play: A history of popular recreation 1607–1940.* New York/London: Appleton.

Eckenstein, L. 1906. *Comparative studies in nursery rhymes.* London: Duckworth.

Education Department Files (N.2), 1912, 38-1; 36-1A; E1 1912. E.I.D. Wellington: Education Department of New Zealand. These files deal with the abolition of the junior cadet system in 1912.

———. 1916. *Special reports on educational subjects, No. 12: The grading of teachers.* Wellington: Education Department.

———. 1920. *Syllabus for physical training for schools.* Wellington: Education Department. (Adopted largely from the 1909 and 1919 syllabuses of the Board of Education, London.)

———. 1928. *Examination and classification, grading, regulations and appeals.* No. 8:46. Wellington: Education Department.

———. 1929. *Physical exercises and games for infants.* Wellington: Education Department.

———. 1930. *Organization and management of public schools.* Wellington: Education Department.

Education Gazette. Wellington.

Elias, N. 1978. *The Civilizing Process: The History of Manners.* Oxford: Oxford University Press.

Evening Star News. Otago Jubilee Celebrations. 1848–1948. February 24, 1948, p. 19.

Ewing, J. L. 1960. *Origins of the primary school curriculum, 1840–1870.* Wellington: New Zealand Council of Educational Research.

Findlay, J. J. 1923. *The children of England.* London: Methuen.

Fletcher, T. A. 1939. *School football.* Wellington: Rugby Football Union.

Fox-Strangeways, A. H., and Karples, M. 1933. *Cecil Sharp.* London: Oxford University Press.

Fraser, A. B. (n.d.) *I remember 1848–1866.* Pamphlet. Dunedin: Early Settlers Association.

Fulton, R. 1922. *Medical practice in Otago and Southland in the early days.* Dunedin: Otago Daily Times.

Gomme, A. B. 1894. *Dictionary of British folklore:* Traditional games of England, Scotland and Ireland. London: Nutt; New York: Dover, 1964.

Gosse, E. 1907. *Father and son.* London: William Heinemann.

Gray, A. J. 1938. *An Ulster plantation: The story of the Kati Kati settlement.* Dunedin: Reed.

Hammond Band, J. L. 1947. *The bleak age.* London: Penguin.

Harcourt, N. 1940. *The day before yesterday: A short history of the Bay of Islands.* Dunedin: Reed.

Hart, E. M. 1934. The organized activities of Christchurch children outside the school. Master's thesis, Canterbury University College. (Headmaster's Association). *Minutes of Wellington Primary School Headmaster's Association.* 1937–50.

Heenan, Sir J. 1950. Mount Cook School. *Evening Post* (Wellington), June 10, 1950.

Henry, G. R. 1947. Egg cup. *New Zealand Physical Education Society Bulletin* 4.

Hole, C. 1940. *English folklore.* London: Batsford.

———. 1949. *English sports and pastimes.* London: Batsford.

Hunt, S. E., and Cain, E. 1951. *Games the world around.* New York: A. S. Barnes.

Hunter, M. 1929. The history of early Lyttleton from a social aspect. Master's thesis, Canterbury University College.

Ingram, W. 1948. *The World of sport.* Lower Hutt: Pennon Press.

Irvine-Smith, F. L. 1948. *The streets of my city.* Wellington: Reed.

Journal of Education. 1899–1940. (Later *National Education*) Wellington.

Katitata Nostalgia. 1969. *Otago Daily Times,* April 13, 21, 1969.

Katz, M. B. 1975. *Class, Bureaucracy and schools.* New York: Praeger.

Kempthorne, W. Oke. 1947. Kempthorne family history. Typescript. Otago: Early Settlers Association.

Kipling, R. 1968. *Stalky and Co.* New York: Dell.

Knapp, M., and Knapp, K. 1976. *One potato, two potato.* New York: Norton.

Knucklebones. 1947. *New Zealand Physical Education Society Bulletin* 11, No. 4.

Leckie, F. M. 1933. *The early history of Wellington College, New Zealand, from 1867–1883.* Auckland: Whitcombe & Tombs.

Lee, J. A. 1939. *Children of the poor.* London: T. Werner Laurie.

Lord, E. 1939. *Old Westland.* Auckland: Whitcombe & Tombs.

Lunn, A. 1913. *The Harrovians.* London: Methuen.

McIntosh, A. D. 1940. *Marlborough: A provincial history.* Blenheim: Marlborough Provincial Historical Committee.

McIntosh, P. C. 1964. *Sport in society.* London: Watts.

McKenzie, N. R. 1933. *The Gael fares forth.* Wellington: Whitcombe & Tombs.

Maclagan, R. C. 1901. *The games and diversions of Argyleshire.* London: Nutt.

MacMillan, P. G. 1929. What does the Kauka South School mean? Master's thesis, Otago University.

MacMorran, G. 1900. *Some schools and schoolmasters of early Wellington.* Wellington: S. & W. Mackay.

Marsden, F. H. 1932. Some notes on the folklore of Upper Calderdale. *Folklore* 43, No. 3:249.

Martens, R. 1978. *Joy and sadness in children's sports.* Champaign, Ill.: Human Kinetics.

Mason, B. S. 1937. *Primitive and pioneer sports for recreation today.* New York: A. S. Barnes.

Mayhew, W. R. 1949. *Tuapeka: The land and its people.* Dunedin: Otago Centennial Historical Publications.

Menke, F. G. 1944. *Encyclopedia of sports.* New York: A. S. Barnes.

Millar, D. P. 1972. *Once upon a village.* Wellington: New Zealand University Press.

Miller, H. 1950. *New Zealand.* London: Hutchinson's University Library.

Ministry of Education, Great Britain. 1945. Memorandum on the draft building regulations, no. 345. London: H.M.S.O.

———. 1948. *Out of school: Second report of Central Advisory Council.* London: H.M.S.O.

Mitford, M. R. 1947. *Our Village.* London: Harrap.

Montgomerie, N., and Montgomerie, W. 1946. *Scottish nursery rhymes taken from Robert Chambers.* London: Hogarth.

Morice, S. 1946. *The Book of Wiremu.* Hamilton: Paul's Book Arcade.

Morris, B. 1946. The leisure activities of some city children. Master's thesis, Victoria University College.

Muir, T. 1949. Buller mining district's community centres. *Education* 2, No. 2:27.

Mulgan, A. 1944. *From track to highway.* Wellington: Whitcombe & Tombs.

———. 1949. The past has another pattern. *New Zealand Listener,* December 30, p. 6.

Murdoch, J. A. 1943. *The high schools of New Zealand.* Wellington: New Zealand Council of Educational Research.

National Education. See *Journal of Education.*

Nevill, R. 1924. *Old English sporting books.* London: The Studio.

Newell, W. W. 1963. *Games and songs of American children.* New York: Dover (originally published 1883)

North, R. 1947. *Town and country games.* New York: Crowell.

Northall, G. F. 1892. *English folk rhymes of places, persons and customs.* London: Paul.

New Zealand Education Gazette. 1921–1950.

New Zealand Herald. 1913. November 13, p. 10.

Opie, I., and Opie, P. 1969. *Children's games in street and playground.* Oxford: Oxford University Press.

Opie, P. 1963. The tentacles of tradition. *The Advancement of Science* 20, No. 10.

Opie, P., and Opie, I. 1959. *The lore and language of school children.* Oxford: Oxford University Press.

Otago Evening Star. 1948. Early sports. February 24, 1948, p. 19.

Page, H. 1942. *Toys in wartime.* London: Allen & Unwin.

Parry, W. S. 1938. The new and old order of things. Address on the formation of the Physical Welfare Branch of Internal Affairs. Wellington: Department of Education.

Physical Education Syllabus. 1912. Wellington: Department of Education. Revised 1921.

Polack, J. S. 1840. *Manners and customs of New Zealanders. Vol. 11.* London: J. Madden & Hatchard & Son.

The Press. 1940. New Zealand Centennial, 1840–1940. March 19, 1940.

Price, F. R. 1929. An Educo-sociological survey of the X-district. Master's thesis, Canterbury University College.

Read, D. H. 1914. Moutray games sports and pastimes. In C. S. Burne, ed., *The handbook of British folklore.* London: Sidgwick & Jackson. P. 257.

Reed, A. H. 1929. *The story of Canterbury.* Wellington: Reed.

Reese, T. 1927. *New Zealand cricket 1841–1914.* Christchurch: Simpson & Williams.

Reeves, W. P. 1934. *The long white cloud: Ao Tea Roa.* London: Allen & Unwin.

Regulation IV. 1904. *Inspection and examination of schools.* Regulation under the Education Act. Wellington.

Regulations: Grading of Teachers. 1916. Regulation 8, Special Reports on Educational Subjects, no. 12. Wellington.

Regulations: Inspector's reports. 1919. Wellington: Department of Education.

Roberts, E. 1935. *New Zealand: Land of my choice.* London: Allen & Unwin.

Roundhouse, A. P. 1945. *Physical education: Scheme of 18 lessons for infants.* Otago: Otago Education Board.

Seffern, W. H. J. 1896. *Chronicles of the garden of New Zealand known as Taranaki.* New Plymouth: Taranaki Herald.

Sevens. 1948. *New Zealand Physical Education Society Bulletin* 4, no. 1:181.

Shanks, A. M. 1931. What is the significance of the Wharetoa School? Master's thesis, Otago University College.

Sharpe, C. J. 1907. *English folk song: Some conclusions.* London: Simpkin.

Sharpe, C. J., and Oppe, A. P. 1924. *The dance: An historical survey of dancing in Europe.* London: Halton & Truscott Smith.

Shaw, M. S., and Farrant, E. D. 1949. *The Taieri Plain.* Otago Centennial Historical Publication.

Silk, D. V. 1923. *History of Puhoi.* Dunedin: Tablet Printing and Publishing Co.

Simpson, H. M. 1940. *The women of New Zealand.* Wellington: Department of Internal Affairs.

Sinclair, H. I. 1927. Elementary rival schools of New Zealand. Master's thesis, Canterbury University College.

Singer, J., and Singer, D. 1978. *Partners in play.* New York: Harper.

Soljak, P. L. 1946. *New Zealand Pacific pioneer.* New York: Macmillan.

Soper, E. L. 1948. *The Otago of our mothers.* Dunedin: Otago Centennial Historical Publications.

Spence, L. 1947. *Myth and ritual in dance game and rhyme.* London: Watts.

(Sports Association). *Minutes of Wellington primary school sports Association.* 1949–1950.

Stallworthy, J. 1916. *Early northern Wairoa.* Dargaville: Wairoa Belland.

Stevenson, R. L. 1946. *Virginibus Puerisque* (1881). London: Penguin.

Stewart, W. D. 1934. *The Journal of George Hepburn on her voyage from Scotland to Otago in 1850.* Dunedin: Coulls, Somerville, Wilkie.

Story, E. M. 1926. *Our fathers have told us.* Pamphlet. Dunedin: Early Settlers Association.

Strutt, J. (revised by J. C. Cox). 1903. *The sports and pastimes of the people of England* (1801). London: Methuen.

Sutton-Smith, B. 1950. *Our street.* Wellington: Reed; Republished: Price-Milburn, 1975.

―――. 1951. The meeting of Maori and European cultures and its effects upon the organized games of Maori children. *Journal of Polynesian Society* 60:93–107.

―――. 1952. New Zealand variants of the game Buck. *Folklore* 63: 329–33.

―――. 1953*a*. The traditional games of New Zealand children. *Folklore* 12:411–23.

————. 1953*b*. The fate of English traditional games in New Zealand. *Western Folklore* 11:250–53.

————. 1953*c*. The game rhymes of New Zealand children. *Western Folklore* 12:14–24.

————. 1953*d*. Seasonal games. *Western Folklore* 12:186–93.

————. 1959. *The games of New Zealand children.* Berkeley: University of California Press.

————. 1959. A formal analysis of game meaning. *Western Folklore* 18:13–24.

————. 1961. *Smitty does a bunk.* Wellington: Price-Milburn. Republished 1976.

————. 1972. *The Folkgames of children.* Austin: University of Texas Press (This work includes *The games of New Zealand Children* [Berkeley: University of California Press]). Revised 1981.

————. 1975. *The cobbers.* Wellington: Price-Milburn.

————. ed. 1976. *Studies in play and games.* New York: Arno Press.

Sutton-Smith, B., and Rosenberg, B. G. 1961. Sixty years of historical change in the game preferences of American Children. *Journal of American Folklore* 74:17–46.

Sutton-Smith, B., and Sutton-Smith, S. 1974. *How to play with Children.* New York: Hawthorne.

Sutton-Smith, B. 1978. Die Dialektik des Spiels. Schorndorf: Hofmann.

Sumpter, D. J., and Lewis, J. J. 1949. *Faith and toil: The Story of Tokomairiro.* Dunedin: Otago Centennial Historical Publications.

Sutch, W. B. 1942. *The quest for security in New Zealand.* London: Penguin.

Sutcliffe, J. R. (n.d.) Reminiscences, Marton, 1903–9. Wellington: New Zealand Council of Educational Research.

Swan, A. C. 1947. *History of New Zealand rugby football, 1870–1945.* Wellington: Reed.

(Swimming Association). *Minutes of the Wellington Primary School Swimming Association.* 1941–1950.

Taranaki Chronicle. 1891. Taranaki Jubilee Issue.

Thompson, A. B. 1945. *Adult education in New Zealand.* Wellington: Council for Educational Research.

Thompson, F. 1945. *From Lark Rise to Candelford.* Oxford: Oxford University Press.

Thomson, J. M. 1905. *The bush boys of New Zealand: Or Dinkums and Mac.* London: Tamblyn.

Trease, G. 1948. *Tales out of school.* London: New Education Book Club.

Trevellyan, G. M. 1942. *English social history.* London: Longmans, Green.

Turner, E. S. 1948. *Boys will be boys.* London: Michael Joseph.

Tylor, E. B. 1888. Remarks on the geographical distribution of games. *Journal of the Anthropological Institute* 9:23.

Uttley, A. 1946. *Country things.* London: Faber.

———. 1948. *Carts and candlesticks.* London: Faber.

Waite, F. 1948. *Pioneering in South Otago.* Dunedin: Otago Centennial Historical Publications.

(Wakefield School). 1942. Centennial of Wakefield School. *Nelson Evening Mail,* September 30, 1942.

Watson, G. 1978. *Little athletics and childhood socialization.* Perth: Western Australia Community Recreation Council.

Weller, A. 1949. Our rugby: Alive and kicking. *Here and Now* October, p. 24.

Whistler, L. 1947. The English festivals. London: Heinmann.

Wilkinson, J. R. (n.d.) Early reminiscences from 1866. Christchurch. Wellington: New Zealand Council of Educational Research.

Wymer, N. 1949. *Sport in England.* London: Harrap.